# The Changing Constitution

Kevin Harrison and Tony Boyd

Edinburgh University Press

© Kevin Harrison and Tony Boyd, 2006

Edinburgh University Press Ltd
22 George Square, Edinburgh

Typeset in 11/13pt Monotype Baskerville by
Servis Filmsetting Ltd, Manchester, and
printed and bound in Great Britain by
Antony Rowe Ltd, Chippenham, Wilts

A CIP record for this book is available from the British Library

ISBN-10    0 7486 2223 3 (paperback)
ISBN-13    978 0 7486 2223 8 (paperback)

The right of Kevin Harrison and Tony Boyd to be identified as authors of this work has
been asserted in accordance with the Copyright, Designs and Patents Act 1988.

Published with the support of the Edinburgh University Scholarly Publishing
Initiatives Fund.

# Contents

# Boxes

# Tables

# Preface

Constitutional matters are often regarded as something of a side issue in British politics, the preoccupation of academics, far removed from the concerns of the average voter. Although since 1997 New Labour has embarked on a major, even revolutionary transformation of the constitution, remarkably little attention was given to this upheaval in its election campaigns of 2001 and 2005.

It is the contention of this book that in fact debate on the constitution is, should be and historically often has been the very stuff of British political life.

Sufficient time has now elapsed for some sort of assessment and appraisal of recent constitutional reforms to be possible. This we have attempted to do. Limitations of space have, however, imposed a certain selectivity: the monarchy is an obvious example of an element of the constitution that has not been awarded a chapter of its own. Nor have we been able to say much about constitutional change before 1997.

We wish to offer our heartfelt thanks for the tireless work of Angela Dale in reading the script and suggesting many emendations that have proved invaluable to the overall clarity of the text. Ruth Locket of St Bede's College, Manchester, also deserves grateful mention here for the loan of her highly interesting MA thesis on the West Lothian question. Needless to say, any errors and omissions are our responsibility.

# CHAPTER 1

# The Legislature: The House of Commons and the House of Lords

## Contents

### Overview

British parliamentary institutions are, or at least were, among the most admired of any modern democracy. The House of Commons and the House of Lords play important roles in representing many economic and social interests in Parliament; providing the members of the government; and attempting to make the executive accountable for their policies and decisions.

Parliament is, however, subject to growing criticism over its failure to make government properly accountable and there has been considerable pressure for reform: none more so than during the period of the present Labour government. Parliamentary reform has been to many critics piecemeal, incomplete and inadequate in modernising British democratic institutions. It is to these issues that we shall now turn.

### Key issues to be covered in this chapter

- What is meant by the term 'responsible government'?
- What is meant by the following terms: 'collective responsibility' and 'individual ministerial responsibility'? When do they apply?
- What are the 'prerogative powers' of government?
- Will the proposed reforms give the Lords greater democratic legitimacy and therefore the need for more political power?
- How effective are the means by which the House of Commons attempts to make the government accountable to the elected representatives of the people?

# Parliament

It is a commonplace that Britain has 'representative government'; representative, that is, in the sense that the ultimate political authority, Parliament, has its main chamber elected on a franchise which includes, to all intents and purposes, all adult citizens. Moreover, elections are held to appoint the people's representatives in other political authorities, such as local councils, the European Parliament, the Welsh Assembly and the Scottish Parliament.

These bodies are examples of 'indirect democracy', in which citizens choose persons to 'represent' them and make decisions on their behalf. Edmund Burke, the great eighteenth-century parliamentarian, made the classic distinction between a 'delegate' and a 'representative' which still holds true today.

Essentially, where delegates follow closely the mandate or instructions of those who elect them, representatives make up their own minds freely, bound only by their own judgement and conscience.

To this well-established system of indirect democracy has very recently been added a form of 'direct democracy', in which the people, through referendums, themselves make major political decisions. Referendums do not fit well with the principle of parliamentary sovereignty and the generally accepted Burkean notion of representation, but there has been relatively little debate on the constitutional implications of this development.

---

### Box 1.1 Edmund Burke's *Speech to the Electorate of Bristol* (1774)

Your representative owes you not his industry only, but his judgement; and he betrays you instead of serving you if he sacrifices it to your opinion . . . authoritative instructions arise from a fundamental mistake of the whole order and tenor of our constitution. Parliament is not a congress of ambassadors from different and hostile interests . . . [it] is a deliberative assembly of one nation, with one interest, that of the whole. . . . You choose a member indeed; but when you have chosen him, he is not a member of Bristol, but he is a member of Parliament.

In British constitutional theory Parliament is made up of three parts: the monarch, the House of Lords and the House of Commons. Only the last has some basis in democratic legitimacy by being directly elected by the sovereign people. Citizens of states with written constitutions consider this odd. They are often astonished that Britain, one of the world's leading democracies, still has strong elements of hereditary and political patronage in the composition of its Parliament. Indeed, despite the proposed reforms of the composition of the House of Lords, much of this undemocratic practice will remain. Nevertheless, pragmatism rather than political theory has always directed the development of the British constitution, and foreign observers would be hard-pressed to argue that in practical terms the British are less 'free' or 'democratic' than the citizens of most other Western democracies.

We will look first at a number of constitutional principles in relation to Parliament, and especially the House of Commons. In particular we are concerned with the degree to which the Commons is effective in making the government accountable to it as the representative body of the peoples of the UK. Then we will look at the House of Lords and concentrate on proposals for its reform, discussing some of the constitutional implications of this process.

## The House of Commons: parliamentary sovereignty and responsible government

It has been suggested earlier that the British constitution embodies a number of 'myths' – beliefs generally regarded as true or at least acted upon as if they were true. One of these myths is that of 'representative and responsible government'.

The British people have, in the House of Commons, an elected body to represent them to which the organs of government are responsible. This situation is underpinned by the doctrine of 'parliamentary sovereignty', the constitutional principle that the ultimate authority in Britain is Parliament (in strict constitutional terms, the 'Queen in Parliament'). In principle, at least, that has not changed since the eighteenth century. As Sir William Blackstone observed in his *Commentaries on the Laws of England* (1765):

> The power and jurisdiction of Parliament is so transcendent and absolute, that it cannot be confined, either for causes or persons,

**Box 1.2  The Right-wing approach to parliamentary sovereignty**

Right-Wingers see parliamentary sovereignty as emanating from the sovereignty of the monarch. Political and constitutional authority thus proceeds from the top down and is embodied in Britain's national heritage and history; authority that is enshrined in the age-old sovereignty of British political institutions. Parliament ensures the continued loyalty of the people to their state; elections to the House of Commons are a mechanism whereby the emotional and political tie between the British people and their state is reaffirmed.

**Box 1.3  The Left-Wing approach to parliamentary sovereignty**

A Left-Wing view, on the other hand, affirms that, whatever the historical origins of parliamentary sovereignty, the Commons had by the twentieth century become the representative organ of the **sovereign people**. In other words, the source of its authority was basically democratic. It is because they hold this view that veteran Left-Wingers, like ex-Labour MPs Michael Foot and Tony Benn, have been such jealous guardians of the rights and privileges of Parliament.

within any bounds. . . . What Parliament doth, no authority upon earth can undo.

There are two modern interpretations of this doctrine: what might be called a **'Right-Wing'**, or conservative, and a **'Left-Wing'**, or liberal/socialist, approach.

## Ministerial responsibility and the government's relationship with Parliament

The crucial constitutional concept of responsible government exists in the conventions of 'collective' and 'individual' ministerial responsibility.

### Collective government responsibility

The government as a whole is collectively responsible to Parliament, in the sense that it must inform, explain and seek to justify to Parliament its actions. In the strongest demonstration of this doctrine, if the Commons is sufficiently dissatisfied with the government it can remove that government from office by a simple majority vote. Individual ministers who find they cannot publicly support the collective decision of the government are expected to resign; after all, ministers are collectively responsible for all decisions and policies of the government. In practice, it is politics, not constitutional principle, that will determine whether a minister remains in government pursuing policies he/she dislikes, or even whether the minister will be sacked for covertly or overtly opposing government policy.

### Individual ministerial responsibility

There is a particular responsibility attaching to individual ministers to explain and justify their own actions and those of the departments for which they are responsible to Parliament, with the implication that a dissatisfied House of Commons can force them to resign. Again, it is politics and not constitutional principles that will determine the survival of a minister. Is the minister willing to fight to stay in office? Does he have the support of the **backbench MPs** of his own party? And, crucially, does the minister enjoy the backing of the Prime Minister, with all the authority that he commands? If any one of these factors is absent the minister will almost certainly fall.

### The principles in practice: government and ministerial dominance and the Commons

These principles seem fairly simple and straightforward; but they are very much the creations of the mid-nineteenth-century supposedly 'Golden Age' of parliamentary power vis-à-vis the executive. How far they are operative elements in the constitution nowadays, at least in the 'strong' sense of being able to force resignations, is debatable.

The principles, as we have stated, are based on convention and so are without legal sanction if ignored (although, if they were, they might rapidly involve illegalities in practice). Constitutional conventions are characteristically flexible and open to considerable adaptation over time in response to the political consequences of social and economic change.

Certainly by the late twentieth century, largely as a consequence of two world wars and the creation of an interventionist welfare state post-1945, the executive had become strikingly dominant over Parliament. This dominance was reinforced by strong party discipline, the power of government patronage and the dismal electoral consequences of perceived party disunity. Furthermore, the large parliamentary majorities usually enjoyed by governments since 1945 had made most of them virtually irremovable by votes in the Commons. Even the minority Callaghan government, which was finally brought down on a confidence motion in March 1979, lost by only one vote (310 to 311). Its survival in a **hung parliament** had been engineered by strict party discipline, deals with minority parties such as the Liberals, and promises of devolution to deliver the support of Welsh and Scottish nationalists.

Likewise, John Major's government (1992–7), whose majority dwindled to near vanishing point, hung on to power since there were at least eight other parties in the House besides the Labour Opposition which had to be united, along with the votes of dissident Tory MPs, to bring his government down. Moreover, according to some of his critics, Major extracted Unionist support in the Commons by adjusting his Northern Irish policy to their advantage.

By contrast, most of Margaret Thatcher's governments enjoyed such massive majorities at elections, and the Labour Opposition was so hopelessly divided, that the removal of the Conservatives by the Commons was never likely. In fact, backbench 'rebellions' were a regular feature of her administrations as rebels could indulge themselves, confident in the knowledge that their government would easily survive parliamentary votes. In this period it was the House of Lords which often provided effective opposition, inflicting several embarrassing defeats on the government: on school transport in rural areas, the pursuit of war criminals, the sale of council houses for the elderly, dental and eye charges, and local government reform.

Labour's landslide victories in 1997 and 2001, and the still strong majority after the 2005 election, together with Conservative divisions, put them in about as strong a position as the Conservatives had enjoyed during the 1980s and early 1990s (see Table 1.1). In fact, in

| Table 1.1 Parliamentary majorities since 1979 | |
| --- | --- |
| Year | Parliamentary majority attained by winning party |
| 1979 | 43 |
| 1983 | 144 |
| 1987 | 102 |
| 1992 | 21 |
| 1997 | 179 |
| 2001 | 167 |
| 2005 | 66 |

some ways Tony Blair was in an even stronger position as his party was more disciplined, centralised and managed, and less ideologically divided than the Conservatives under Mrs Thatcher. Backbench Labour revolts, or threats of revolts, over proposed changes to disability benefits and the Asylum Bill in the summer of 1999, the war in Iraq in 2003 and the proposed introduction of identity cards in 2004 do not undermine this point. Although Mr Blair has lost support among Labour backbenchers since 2001, especially in the wake of the Iraq War, a successful Commons challenge on a confidence motion still seems improbable. The present Labour leadership probably does not yet face the long-term deterioration in party control that occurred under the Major government, although some strains are beginning to show.

From the constitutional perspective, the 1990s would seem to be characterised by an 'arrogance of power' in which the executive, whether controlled by Conservative or by Labour, proceeded with only a token recognition of Parliament's authority or ability to hold it to account. This was strikingly exemplified by Lord Chief Justice Scott's report (1994) into allegations of wrongdoing under the Major government, concerning illegal sales of arms-manufacturing equipment to Iraq without the knowledge or approval of Parliament, which, it was alleged, had been systematically misled on this and related matters.

While stopping short of actually accusing government ministers of outright conspiracy, the Scott Report could hardly have been more critical. A Minister of State at the Foreign Office had repeatedly made inaccurate and untrue statements to MPs, and Foreign Secretary Howe's account to the enquiry was described as 'unconvincing'. Several other ministers were criticised but not one individual minister resigned, still less the government as a whole.

Paradoxically, far from the principle of collective responsibility empowering the House it did the opposite. The principle was used to protect individual ministers, and the government enlisted party discipline to achieve its own survival in Commons votes at the end of debates on this matter.

The position of government has, of course, been strengthened by the fact that something like a quarter of MPs presently hold at least junior ministerial office (the 'payroll vote'). They are, therefore, expected to support the government under the doctrine of collective responsibility. (The Labour governments of 1974–9 actually included, at times, nearly half their MPs in some government post.)

The Blair government would appear to be as dismissive of parliamentary authority as any of its predecessors; for example, it was sharply and publicly rebuked by the **Speaker of the House**, Betty Boothroyd, in early 1999 for making ministerial announcements to the media before informing Parliament. Moreover, while clearly committed to a wide range of constitutional reforms, its commitment has not so far extended to relations between executive and legislature. This is perhaps not surprising since governments are unlikely to introduce reforms that would diminish their own powers. What is surprising is the degree to which governments have introduced reforms that will actually make them more accountable; for example, the introduction of Departmental Select Committees under Margaret Thatcher, and devolved legislative bodies in Scotland and Wales under Tony Blair.

If collective responsibility seems to have faded somewhat from the constitution, individual responsibility seems to have lapsed almost completely, in the 'strong' sense of the phrase: that Parliament could require a minister's resignation for their own or even their department's failings. In fact, although twelve ministers resigned during John Major's period of office, no fewer than five departures were for sexual misbehaviour rather than ministerial errors and misjudgements.

Recent events would seem to confirm the unwillingness of ministers to resign for reasons of policy failure. Geoffrey Robinson and Peter Mandelson resigned as ministers in 1998 apparently because they were the targets of a sustained barrage of criticism in the media subsequent to revelations of their personal financial dealing, rather than because of attacks in the House of Commons. Along with Ron Davies, who resigned over aspects of his personal life, they had become a source of embarrassment to the government, rather than of incompetence. An exception was Estelle Morris, who resigned as Education Secretary in 2000 declaring that she felt inadequate to the post; she received many plaudits as a consequence of the unfamiliar admission of personal inadequacy by a minister.

## Table 1.2  Ministerial resignations since 1997

| Minister | Date of resignation | Reason for departure |
| --- | --- | --- |
| Ron Davies | October 1998 | Quit after 'moment of madness' on Clapham Common |
| Peter Mandelson, Geoffrey Robinson | December 1998 | Loan revelations: Mandelson borrowed from Robinson and did not declare transaction |
| Peter Mandelson | January 2001 | Resigned amid allegations that he was involved in a passport application: subsequently, seemed not to have done anything improper |

## Table 1.2  (continued)

| Minister | Date of resignation | Reason for departure |
| --- | --- | --- |
| Stephen Byers | May 2002 | Following months of pressure, resigned after his reputation had been seriously tarnished by a series of political misjudgements and amid suggestions of a seemingly misleading account of events |
| Estelle Morris | October 2002 | Left saying she did not feel up to the job, bruised by adverse comments in the media |
| Robin Cook | March 2003 | Left in protest on the eve of the Iraq War |
| Clare Short | May 2003 | After much hesitation, resigned over Iraq – after the war was over |
| Alan Milburn | July 2003 | Resigned to spend more time at home |
| David Blunkett | December 2004 | Collapse of initial support from party and ministerial colleagues, as evidence of a clear paper trail over his lover's nanny's visa application damaged his political credibility. |

This table appears in *British Government and Politics: A Comparative Guide* (Edinburgh University Press, 2006), a core text in this series written by Duncan Watts.

There are many examples of ministers not resigning over mishandling their departmental affairs. Indeed, Lord Carrington's resignation under this doctrine, along with two other ministers, over mistakes in the Foreign Office during the run-up to the outbreak of the **Falklands Crisis** (1982), stands out by its rarity. John Nott, however, did not resign as Defence Secretary, even though it was argued at the time that he had more culpability in the generation of the crisis, because his proposed defence cuts had signalled a lack of interest in the Falkland Islands by the British government. It would appear that there are political reasons, rather than strictly constitutional ones, which determine ministerial decisions whether to resign or not.

### Prerogative powers

It would be wrong, however, to assume that the constitutional relationship of the executive to Parliament is governed entirely by current political circumstances. There is one area of major importance known as the 'royal prerogative' where the government has a clearly defined independence from Parliament. 'Prerogative powers' are exercised by the government in the name of the Crown and are outside Parliament's remit. Historically they were the powers of the sovereign monarch and only gradually, by accident and change of political circumstance, have they shifted into the hands of the Prime Minister and departmental ministers.

---

**Box 1.4 'Prerogative powers' in the hands of the Prime Minister and departmental ministers**

- Declarations of war and the commitment of British troops
- Signing or ratifying international treaties
- Recognising foreign governments
- Assenting to European legislation
- Appointing peers, bishops of the Church of England, judges, ministers, ambassadors, the chairs of various public bodies
- Establishing **Royal Commissions**
- The issuing of many **'Orders in Council'**

(All are powers not conferred by statute.)

Whereas in most foreign constitutions many or most of such powers require parliamentary approval (for example in the USA, declarations of war and any foreign treaty require Senate approval), no such approval by the British Parliament is required. Moreover, such crucial power as the appointment of ministers is, in practice, in the hands of the Prime Minister, as is the date of the **dissolution of Parliament**. Only occasional Acts of Parliament relating to the impact of the EU on the British constitution, such as the Maastricht Treaty (1991), require the approval of Parliament, and that is only because the European Union insists upon it.

These prerogative powers greatly strengthen the position of the government in relation to Parliament. Nor are these powers purely formal: the ban on trade unions at GCHQ (a government intelligence unit) in the 1980s was made by an Order in Council and had important implications for civil rights; in 1999 the British military commitment in the continuing Iraq conflict proceeded without formal parliamentary approval or even much debate. (Admittedly, the government made strenuous, and ultimately successful, efforts to secure support for its Iraq policy through parliamentary votes in 2003, but there was a political rather than a constitutional imperative.)

Efforts to bring prerogative powers under parliamentary authority have had little success. In 1997 the Treasury Select Committee pressed unsuccessfully for membership of the Monetary Policy Committee of the Bank of England (which plays a key role in managing the UK economy) to be confirmed by the House of Commons. More recently, in the wake of the Iraq War, Peter Hennessy argued in a speech given at Portcullis House (November 2004) that there should be a War Powers Act to restrain the prerogative powers of the government by requiring a specific vote of the House of Commons to approve military action in advance of it being taken. In 1999 Labour MP Tony Benn's private member's bill, the 'Crown Prerogatives (Parliamentary Control) Bill', sought to bring these powers under Commons supervision; predictably, it failed. During 1999 the Public Administration Select Committee invested much effort in examining the accountability of public bodies, such as the many and varied Quangos (quasi-autonomous non-governmental organisations) that disburse some 40 per cent of public spending. The present government does not seem anxious for their sway in many important areas

of government to be reduced or to be made more accountable to
MPs.

## Agencies and ministerial responsibility

The creation of 'agencies', following the Ibbs Report (*The Next Steps*,
1988), with a wide measure of managerial autonomy in many areas of
departmental service delivery raised new issues, notably how far a
minister should accept responsibility for acts of an agency which,
although associated with his department, was not that minister's direct
responsibility.

The constitutional issue was highlighted by General John
Learmont's 1995 report into the circumstances surrounding a break-
out from Parkhurst prison. This led to the dismissal of the Director
General of the Prison Service, Derek Lewis. The Home Secretary,
Michael Howard, to whom Lewis was ultimately responsible,
defended the sacking by claiming a distinction between 'policy', for
which the minister was responsible, and 'operations', for which he was
not – a constitutional innovation dismissed outright by Learmont.

Constitutionally, the position would seem to be unresolved. At one
level Parliament seems to be making its own modest contribution to
constitutional change, in that Departmental Select Committees now
routinely question chief executives of the agencies on much the same
basis as they interrogate ministers. Governments in recent years have
attempted to reduce accountability to select committees by shifting
enquiries into the actions of their departments and agencies from
Parliament to enquiries chaired by government-appointed individuals with terms of reference also derived from the government – as in
Lord Hutton's enquiry into the circumstances surrounding the death
of Dr David Kelly, a government weapons scientist, in 2004.

## Departmental Select Committees and ministerial
## responsibility

Departmental Select Committees are the driving force in strengthening ministerial responsibility in the sense of informing, explaining and
justifying. These committees usually consist of eleven MPs, roughly
in proportion to party strengths in the Commons. They scrutinise the
work of a specific department or, as with the Public Accounts and the
Public Administration committees, the broad sweep of government

activity. Select committees meet weekly and subject ministers and, increasingly, civil servants, to close examination. For example, the Heritage Committee, chaired by Gerald Kaufman, closely and critically examined the management of the Royal Opera House in 1998 (and issued a lively report). The Home Affairs Select Committee questioned Sir Paul Condon, Commissioner of the Metropolitan Police, early in 1999 on the implications of the Macpherson Report into the racist murder of black teenager Stephen Lawrence in 1993.

Traditional mechanisms for making the executive accountable to the legislature, such as ministerial and Prime Minister's Question Time, have often degenerated into party political point scoring. Most questions, especially supplementary ones which cannot be easily prepared for by a minister, are probing and seek to make the government accountable; few are sycophantic and those that are invite ridicule from all sides of the House. Actually, a case could be made for saying that ministerial accountability in the 'weak' sense of making ministers justify their policies and actions is intensifying because of select committees, even if in the 'strong' sense of forcing ministers to resign it is in decline.

Not only do select committees report to Parliament but also their reports and even proceedings now receive wide media attention. It would seem that governments are becoming more unhappy over this: witness Foreign Secretary Robin Cook's reluctance in early 1999 to allow his officials to appear before the Foreign Affairs Select Committee to answer questions as part of its investigation into allegedly illegal British arms shipments to Sierra Leone.

This growing tendency for select committees to interrogate ministers and civil servants would seem to have produced a further development in the doctrine of ministerial responsibility. Until the 1980s, by convention, ministers only and not their officials were exposed to parliamentary scrutiny. In the early days of select committees the 'Osmotherly Rules' were applied, by which civil servants who were summoned to select committee hearings spoke only through ministers, a convention which now appears to have largely lapsed – a typical example of the incremental and almost imperceptible way in which the British constitution evolves.

The picture is further complicated by the growing significance of 'political advisors'. There is a blurring of constitutional distinctions between them, government ministers and an increasingly politicised civil service.

Partly as a result of these developments, a report in 1998 by the Lords' Select Committee on the Public Service advocated a new legal framework to establish the relative positions of ministers, civil servants and advisors, and especially to protect the political neutrality of civil servants. If such a framework were introduced, it would presumably restore the public accountability of ministers and civil servants to what it was before the creation of Departmental Select Committees in 1979. Such legislation does not at present seem likely.

Compared with reform of the Lords, reforms of the Commons have been modest indeed. In June 1997 the New Labour government set up the Select Committee on Modernisation which has produced change in some areas, the most significant being an additional chamber, 'Westminster Hall', in 1999. The chamber deals with uncontroversial matters such as bills, committee reports, private member's debates and adjournment motions, presumably leaving the chamber of the House freed for more contentious matters. However, it meets far less frequently than does the Commons proper, and attendance has been poor.

Some business rearrangements of the House have been made; a new parliamentary day, supposedly more 'family friendly', came into operation in 2003, involving earlier starting and finishing times together with abbreviated recesses. These changes have not proved universally popular; in late 2004 many backbenchers wanted them scrapped and forced a reviewing vote on them in 2005. The result of this was that on a free vote MPs decided by 292 to 225 that they wanted to reverse the earlier reforms, to take effect after the next general election.

Select committee arrangements have also been modified. Besides the fifteen Departmental Select Committees, there are now some that have a wider remit: Deregulation, Environmental Audit, European Scrutiny, Public Accounts, Public Administration, Science and Technology and Statutory Instruments. To some extent there has been an attempt to merge standing and select committee procedures, for example sending bills to select committees before the actual legislative process.

Other changes include 'rolling over' bills from one session to the next and alteration of Prime Minister's Question Time from two fifteen-minute sessions on Tuesdays and Thursdays to one thirty-minute session on Wednesdays. The timing of ministerial question times have also changed. While some of these innovations seem sensible enough, critics have argued that such measures as reducing opportunities to question the PM have damaged the power of the House to hold government to account. Perhaps to address this, Tony Blair began regular appearances before the Commons Liaison Committee (composed mostly of Select Committee chairs) in 2002.

It is difficult to appraise the value of these reforms outside the political context. Certainly some of the predicted benefits do not seem to have materialised; for example, the longer PM's Question Time was supposed to reduce its adversarial, partisan element, but clashes between Mr Blair and the **Opposition** leaders that have faced him since 1997 (William Hague, Iain Duncan Smith and Michael Howard) seem to have changed but little.

The effectiveness of select committees in making government accountable may be undermined by the way in which they are appointed: party whips, themselves subject to pressure from senior party figures, have considerable influence over which backbench MPs are appointed to which select committees. Potential troublemakers may not be recommended, while troublesome members on select committees may find themselves under party pressure to resign. Such pressure can, however, be effectively resisted: attempts by the Labour leadership to remove Gwynneth Dunwoody from the Transport Select Committee and Donald Anderson from Foreign Affairs were rejected by the House of Commons in 2001.

Robin Cook was a more vigorous advocate of change when he was Leader of the House than were his Labour predecessors Ann Taylor and Margaret Beckett, but with his resignation in 2003 the steam seems to have gone out of reform. The decree by his successor, Peter Hain, in 2004 that visitors to the House would no longer be dubbed 'Strangers' (as they had for centuries) was hardly earth-shaking.

The parliamentary election system is the major institution of accountability and perhaps only fundamental change here would produce radical results. No significant reform in this area has been introduced by the Labour government since 1997 – perhaps, a cynic might observe, just because such formal reform would make the most difference in increasing the accountability of the government to the elected representatives of the people.

Perhaps the most effective means of making the government accountable and checking its power rests with the informal areas of political power and influence: the media, the civil service, pressure groups, the factions within the ruling party, and the general economic and global political situation within which governments have to work.

## The House of Lords

If modifications to the Commons have proceeded quietly, incrementally, as a result of the impact of political realities, reform of the House of Lords has attracted intense publicity. Much thought, consultation, planning and major legislation is likely to be poured into the issue over the near future. The process, which has support at the very heart of the Labour government, has begun dramatically to change the constitution. It raises many issues – about the power of the Commons, the constitutional position of the sovereign, and the nature of British democracy – which will not be solved merely by alterations, however radical, in the composition of the Lords.

## The powers and composition of the House of Lords

The position of the Lords until the present reforms has been a curious constitutional anomaly. As Tony Benn and others have frequently pointed out, the legislature had three components in the British constitution: the monarch, the Lords, and the Commons. Only one of these could make a claim to democratic legitimacy.

Until the Life Peerages Act 1958, the Lords consisted only of hereditary peers, twenty-six bishops and two archbishops of the Church of England, eleven Law Lords, and Princes of the Blood Royal (who rarely spoke on non-party political issues under debate in the House). The development of 'life peers', whose titles and rights do not pass to their children, altered the composition of the Lords considerably over the following four decades. Nevertheless, even in 1999 only 503 of the 1165 members of the House of Lords were life peers (it is the only second chamber in any modern advanced democracy which was dominated by members who sit by hereditary right). Life peers remain in the Lords following the 1999 changes (see p. 27). They have made, and continue to make, a positive contribution in that they have widened the occupational and experience background of the Lords, and they participate far more than the hereditaries. On the other hand, they have tended to make the Lords even more geriatric, in that they are usually appointed towards the end of a distinguished career elsewhere.

While much of the traditional flummery of Parliament is concentrated in the House of Lords (like the State Opening of Parliament), the upper house is far from being simply what Bagehot called a 'dignified' or 'decorative' part of the constitution. Some government ministers such as the Lord Chancellor sit in the Lords by right of Cabinet membership. Others are there because of political appointment, in order to observe the constitutional convention that members of the government should sit in Parliament; for example, Margaret Thatcher recommended elevation of David Young, a businessman, as Lord Young, who then became Secretary of State for Trade and Industry in 1984.

The Lords also has a party structure (in early 1999 there were 476 peers who took the Conservative Whip and 175 Labour; by early 2005 Labour had slightly more peers than the Conservatives). Procedures in the Lords are generally similar to those of the Commons. Legislation, especially of constitutional significance, is sometimes introduced in the Lords, for example the 1985 Bill to abolish Metropolitan County Councils and the Greater London Council. Peers can put forward private member's bills, and the Lords has its own Question Time and select committees.

The House of Lords also has debates, which are often of a higher quality than those of the Commons because the members can draw on an extraordinarily wide range of talent and experience. For example, a debate on developments in the BBC early in 1999 included contributions from broadcaster Lord Melvyn Bragg, the former Chair of the BBC, Lord Hussey, film director Lord Puttnam and novelist Baroness James. The Lords also contains a wealth of political experience, including ex-Prime Ministers, ex-Foreign Secretaries and ex-Chancellors of the Exchequer. However, these debates are rarely given much prominence in the media or much public attention.

An exception was the public debate in March 2005 on that year's Prevention of Terrorism Bill, which received massive press attention. Participants included a remarkable array of important political, judicial, police and academic figures, such as Lord Brittan (former Tory Home Secretary under Mrs Thatcher), Lord Irvine (former Labour Lord Chancellor under Mr Blair), Lord Condon (former Metropolitan Police Commissioner), Lord Ahmed (Britain's leading Labour Muslim politician), Lord Morgan (Professor of History at the University College of Swansea) and several ex-Law Lords, such as Lord Lloyd, and Lord Donaldson, former Master of the Rolls, as well as Lord Onslow, Leader of the Tory hereditary peers.

Legislation can be amended in the Lords (the government often introduces its own amendments there during the Committee Stage). Although the Lords can, through the 1949 Parliament Act, only delay legislation for one year, it is far from powerless; such delay might well prove significant in the last year or so before a general election when in theory the Lords could in effect exercise a veto. Of more practical significance is the impact of the Lords on proposed legislation; for example, in 1989 proposed changes to the legal system were drastically modified after a torrent of criticism by distinguished legal figures such as Lords Gifford, Havers and Hailsham.

Moreover, the Lords arguably became more rather than less significant in the 1990s and after. Attendance rose sharply: a seat in the Lords is popular with former MPs. In many ways the Lords have an enviably powerful position vis-à-vis the executive in that they do not owe their position to popular election, with all the constraints that that implies. Patronage and party allegiance are far less effective instruments in the discipline of peers than of MPs in the Commons. Indeed, during the 1980s the Lords were in a sense the de facto 'Opposition' to the Thatcher government, which was articulately criticised and frequently defeated in the Lords in spite of the theoretical Conservative dominance of the House.

The Lords were equally lively throughout the 1990s and into the present century. The removal of the hereditary element in 1999 actually seemed to invigorate them politically. There were frequent collisions with the Blair government, for example over the banning of foxhunting and the proposal (dropped) to abolish the office of Lord Chancellor.

## Box 1.5  The ban on foxhunting

In this case, the Commons and the Lords were in outright conflict. This conflict had constitutional implications when in 2004, a month after the Commons had voted by a huge majority (356 to 166) for a total ban on hunting with dogs, the Lords voted 322 to 72 in favour of an amendment supporting the reinstatement of the government's original proposals to allow hunting to continue where it could be shown to be the least cruel method of pest control. This placed the government in the position of having to consider using the Parliament Act (1949) to push legislation through. The Parliament Act has only been used four times since 1949, three of those times since 1997, including the Hunting With Dogs Bill in November 2004 (which became an Act, coming into force in February 2005). In reality, the government would have preferred a compromise solution but as consensus could not be achieved Christopher Leslie, Constitutional Affairs Minister, said the will of the Commons must prevail.

In early 2005 the Lords dramatically challenged the government on its Prevention of Terrorism Bill. After thirty hours of debate and a series of rejections of government amendments, the Bill was drastically altered, notably by incorporating an element of judicial review of any decisions by the Home Secretary to imprison terrorist suspects without trial and, as the Conservatives and Liberal Democrats had demanded, a 'sunset clause in all but name' (a sunset clause provided an opportunity for MPs to review the Act within a year).

The proposed abolition of the office of Lord Chancellor was of even greater direct constitutional importance: the government sought a radical reform of the higher judiciary. The proposals were initially rejected by the Lords after a special select committee of peers failed to agree on any of them. Shortly afterwards the plan to abolish the office of Lord Chancellor was abandoned, even if his powers were to be substantially modified.

## Reform of the Lords

### Early attempts at reform

Reform of the Lords, or even its outright abolition, has been a regular demand of the political Left for decades, especially since the late nineteenth century, when the Lords defeated Liberal proposals on Irish Home Rule and other radical reforms. Lords reform was a standard item in Labour manifestos in the 1980s and 1990s, and even during the 1960s it appeared a serious possibility when the ideas of Richard Crossman, a Labour Cabinet Minister and political scientist, were embodied in a 1969 Bill. This envisaged phasing out the hereditary element and provided for the creation of a curious two-tier arrangement of voting and non-voting peers, with powers of legislative delay for six months. The proposal was attacked from the traditional Right for historical and traditional reasons and, interestingly, from the Left, most lucidly by Michael Foot, who argued that reform would actually strengthen the Lords at the expense of the Commons. Criticism that strengthening the powers of the House of Lords must parallel membership changes has frequently been applied to other proposals for reform: for example, those of Lord Home (a former Conservative Prime Minister) who in 1978 advocated a system of 430 peers, two-thirds elected on a proportional representation system, the rest nominated.

By 1978 the Labour Prime Minister, James Callaghan, had committed the party to outright abolition of the House of Lords if it was re-elected at the next general election. Labour's defeat in 1979 effectively halted Lords reform for two decades, as Margaret Thatcher and John Major had no interest in the matter. In fact, Mrs Thatcher seemed to favour a return to a remote past; in 1983 she resumed the practice of nominating hereditary peers, which had fallen into disuse since Edward Heath's premiership. John Major did not appoint any hereditaries.

Labour's shift to the Left in the early 1980s sharpened the Left's dislike of the Lords still further. Distaste reached its peak in 1988, when the Conservative government imported large numbers of 'backwoodsmen' (peers who rarely, if ever, attended) in order to prevent the defeat of their flagship **Poll Tax** Bill as it passed through the Lords.

The Lords' apparent failure to check the substantial erosion of civil liberties under the Thatcher governments made defence of its composition and powers even more difficult. Their failure was attributable less to an unwillingness to defend civil liberties than to their lack of power to resist a House of Commons dominated by a party with a large parliamentary majority.

The House of Commons hardly inspires confidence in its record on the defence of civil liberties in the face of executive power and popular opinion, with its frequent insistent but ill-thought-out demands for action on a range of controversial issues. Whether it be the Dangerous Dogs Act 1991 or the identity card proposals, the Commons acting with largely untrammelled powers can be a threat to civil liberties, not a defender of them.

### Lords reform as part of the Blairite agenda

Calls for Lords reform mounted from the Labour party during the mid-1990s. At the 1995 Labour Conference the New Labour Leader, Tony Blair, announced 'An end to the hereditary peers sitting in the House of Lords as a first step to a directly elected chamber'. Although, by 1996, this intention had been moderated to simply ending the voting rights of hereditary peers, the Labour victory of 1997 made it clear that some sort of reform was inevitable (reform of the House of Lords being in the party manifesto), although debate and controversy over reform continued well into the middle of the first decade of the twenty-first century.

In 1997 the case against the status quo was formidable and very widely accepted. There were broadly five lines of attack:

**1. The Lords was inherently undemocratic and inappropriate for the twenty-first century.** Although it undeniably performed some useful functions, these could be undertaken perfectly well by a reformed House. Some countries, for example Sweden and New Zealand, seemed to manage well enough without any second chamber at all. Besides, some of the supposed merits of the Lords, such as being part of the system of 'checks and balances' which protects the citizen against the unrestrained power of the Commons, were overstated. The House of Lords could hardly be defended by reference to its voting record on legislation that has civil rights implications. In any event the Lords' role here as the highest court in the land had been challenged by the growing number of cases that appeal to the European Court of Human Rights. In 1999, when the incorporation of the European Convention on Human Rights into UK law made the courts rather than the second chamber the prime defender of civil rights, the Lords lost more authority. Claims that the removal of the hereditary element would damage the monarchy were fallacious: there were several European monarchies, such as Spain, Belgium and the Netherlands, which did not have hereditary second chambers and where the monarchy seemed at least as secure as in Britain.

**2. Debates in the upper house contributed little to informing the public or the political class, although their deliberations on issues of concern had been highly praised by peers themselves.** Life peer Lord Winston, Professor of Fertility Studies at London University, said in a 1996 debate on alternative medicine, 'I'm much more impressed than I expected to be by the contribution some hereditary peers make'. However, during the same debate other hereditary peers offered anecdotes about their pets' illnesses and one advocated sleeping with one's feet in the air as beneficial to health! In any case many peers played little part in the proceedings: in 1999 there were 130 peers on leave of absence or without writ of summons; in other words, they didn't attend at all.

**3. Historically, the Conservative party had dominated the Lords, regardless of the outcome of general elections.** Even in 1997, while the Conservatives won only 34 per cent of the popular vote in the general election, they still held 66 per cent of the upper house. Nor was this dominance purely theoretical: during Labour's first parliamentary session, 1997–8, the Lords inflicted thirty-three defeats upon it. The Labour government has sought to change the party balance: new peers created after the 2005 election finally produced more Labour than Conservative peers in the Lords.

**4. Although the judicial function of the Law Lords is necessary, their presence in the Lords was an historical accident.** By convention they played no part in the non-judicial proceedings of the Lords. Law Lords could easily be 'hived off' to some form of supreme court, the powers and composition of which could be modelled on any one of many such final courts of appeal existing in Western democracies.

**5. Other parts of the constitution were changing dramatically, for instance the creation of Welsh and Scottish legislatures.** Some of the members of a reformed second chamber could be indirectly elected by these assemblies (thus strengthening the UK), while European integration would suggest that appropriate representation in the Lords would include members of the European Parliament.

By 1999, the case for reform seemed irrefutable. Even the Conservatives were by then prepared to accept change as inevitable. It is significant that Conservative opposition to the reform legislation introduced in January 1999 was based on criticism of the procedure adopted by the government, especially the plan (made without any clear notion of the ultimate objective) to abolish the voting rights of most of the hereditary peers. As the Conservative Leader in the Lords, Lord Strathclyde, said:

> There is a deep sense of disquiet and regret about what you have announced, not because we always want to be as we are or what we are. We do not. Are we not entitled to know in the long run where we are heading? We have seen no clear vision of the future for this House of Parliament, and to say it is modernisation is simply not enough.

The previous Conservative Leader in the Lords, Lord Cranbourne, even devised a scheme in confidential discussions with the Blair government in 1999 for an 'interim stage' with a transitional upper house composed of ninety-one hereditary peers. This was without his party leader's knowledge or approval. He was promptly sacked by Mr Hague. Nonetheless, the proposal was embodied in the government's **White Paper** on House of Lords Reform.

In January 1999 the Labour government revealed a two-stage plan for a radical reform of the Lords.

The first stage was the House of Lords Act 1999 which abolished the right of the hereditary peers to speak and vote in the Lords. In November 1999 a new session of Parliament was to meet, with a 'transitional' House of Lords of some 500 peers, with the hereditary peers reduced to ninety-two in strength, the rest being existing life peers and fifty-seven New Labour life peers. The remaining hereditary peers were intended to be a reward to the Conservatives for not obstructing the legislation required for these changes. Attempts were made to counter charges of 'cronyism' by the creation of an 'Independent Appointments Commission' to recommend new life peers to the Prime Minister. Once again, we can see here constitutional change being shaped by political compromise, rather than by adherence to theoretical constitutional models.

The second stage had already begun with the government producing a White Paper, *Modernising Parliament: Reforming the House of Lords* (1998), that stated:

> The Second Chamber must have a distinctive role and must neither usurp, nor threaten the supremacy of the First Chamber.

A Royal Commission was set up with broad terms of reference. A reformed House should take 'particular account of the present nature of the constitutional settlement, including the newly devolved institutions, the impact of the Human Rights Act and developing relations with the European Union'. Other suggestions favoured 'institutionalising' or abolishing the delaying powers of the House of Lords, creating a chamber of both nominated and elected representatives (with the possibility of including MEPs), and augmenting 'the representation in the Lords of other religious traditions'.

Lord Wakeham, a former Tory Cabinet Minister and Chair of the Press Complaints Commission, would, it was later announced, chair the Royal Commission. It reported in 2000. A joint committee of the Lords and Commons would then consider its recommendations, add its own reflections, and the Cabinet would consider these (though how far the Cabinet would modify any proposals is far from clear). The intention was that the proposals would be embodied in legislation to be outlined in the Queen's Speech in 2000 or 2001. Critics regard such a 'fast track' approach as inadvisable, since all major changes need very thorough examination. The critics appear to have been heeded as no further reforms of the House were in place by 2005.

Among the first proposals to be submitted were those of a Conservative party commission, headed by Lord Mackay of Clashfern, in April 1999. Rather surprisingly, these involved a mainly elected 'senate' whose members would serve for three parliaments and then resign. They would thus be democratically elected, but would not be 'responsible' in the sense of being liable to removal (or, for that matter, reinstatement) by the electorate after their term of office. This, it was argued, would prevent the Lords becoming a rival to the Commons, while avoiding the problems of patronage implied by a nominated chamber. Critics argued that the plan was simply a device to outflank Labour by presenting a more radically democratic arrangement than Labour envisaged.

Other critics seized the opportunity to advance schemes of their own. For example, Lord Richard (Labour Leader of the House of Lords until summer 1998) poured scorn on the plan for an interim chamber and urged an immediate, directly elected House with the object of curbing the executive's powers. No doubt there will be many other schemes devised by politicians and academics over the next few years.

Stage one of the Lords reform, the removal of most of the hereditary element, went ahead fairly smoothly; the ninety-one remaining hereditary peers were elected by their fellows, thus, curiously, constituting the only elected element within the chamber. (Each peer, the vast majority of whom received no votes at all, was allowed to present a case in seventy-five words for staying in the Lords; Baroness Strange, who was elected, said, 'I bring flowers every week to this House from my castle in Perthshire.') Following the 1997 changes the total number of remaining peers, hereditary, life and others, stood at 693. It has fluctuated around 700 ever since (see Table 1.3).

There was little further progress. Lord Wakeham's commission issued its report in January 2000. He attempted to answer three fundamental questions about the reform of the House of Lords:

1. What was the purpose of a second chamber?
2. What sort of people do you need to enable the second chamber to fulfil that purpose?
3. What is the best way of identifying people with the right characteristics for the upper chamber?

No dramatic changes were proposed for the functions of the Lords. As to composition, a complicated scheme was drawn up, the key feature being that the House be chiefly appointed rather than elected. These ideas were reflected in a government White Paper in November 2001 which suggested an elected element of only 20 per cent, with a further 20 per cent appointed by an independent Appointments

## Table 1.3 Membership of the House of Lords in March 2005

| Category of peer | Number |
| --- | --- |
| Life peers | 563 |
| Elected hereditaries | 90 |
| Law Lords | 28 |
| Archbishops/bishops | 25 |
| Total | 706 |

**NB** Membership of the chamber fluctuates. Of the total number of peers given, 125 were female.

Commission and 60 per cent by the major political parties. The Law Lords would remain, as would bishops of the Church of England (although only sixteen bishops of the original twenty-six would continue to sit in the Lords).

These proposals were attacked on all sides. A Commons select committee, the Joint Committee on Reform of the House of Lords, reported in 2002 in favour of a 60 per cent elected upper house, with outright abolition of the Law Lords and Lords Spiritual (Church of England bishops).

At this point the government established a joint committee of both houses to reassess reform proposals. The committee was agreed that the second chamber should have a number of features, namely: legitimacy, 'representativeness', independence, expertise and freedom from single-party domination. It was far less clear on the composition of the House; no fewer than seven alternatives were suggested, covering the whole spectrum from a fully elected to a fully appointed body. These proposals were debated by both houses in early 2003, resulting in a total impasse. In the absence of any consensus, the then Leader of the House of Commons, Robin Cook, advised that 'we all go home and sleep on it', advice that was clearly heeded as stage two of Lords reform was postponed until after the 2005 general election.

One simple, workable and in principle democratic idea for House of Lords reform came in 2003 from Billy Bragg, the radical songster. He proposed that seats in the upper house might be allocated in proportion to the votes cast in a general election from region-based party lists (so avoiding Prime Ministerial prerogative powers of appointment). In 2005 this would have created an upper house with around 270 Labour peers, 241 Conservatives and 180 Lib Dems: one might claim, however, that Mr Bragg's proposals would reinforce the role of political parties in parliament: but party membership is in decline and the accountability of party leaders to those members is reducing; both are characteristics associated with decaying political institutions: somewhat like the hereditary-based composition of the House of Lords.

The announcement of new life peers in 2005 finally removed the Conservative majority in the House of Lords, much to the anger of Tory Leader Michael Howard. It has taken just under one hundred years of radical attacks, Liberal and Labour, to achieve this. Perhaps the remaining reform of the House of Lords will take as long!

## Implications of reform

Any proposals for reform of the Lords raise objections, some of which were articulated in that White Paper. For example, a fully elected chamber would clearly be democratic, and thus enjoy a legitimacy it does not have at present, though it might in a nominated House of Lords lose the independence from party discipline, and lack the variety of backgrounds, experience and expertise that the Lords has now. Nomination also raises the question of who is to do the nominating and by what criteria. The formulation is an important matter, since the powers of the Prime Minister are massively enhanced by his present powers of patronage which currently include nominations to the peerage. Perhaps the biggest potential problem is a possible clash between a substantially democratically elected upper house and the Commons, which is especially likely if the second chamber were elected on some form of proportional representation. For this reason the White Paper recommended a part-nominated body.

The present proposals have been attacked from both Left and Right. Dennis Skinner, a Left-Wing Labour MP, complained that there will soon be more than enough elected 'assemblies' and the government should 'adopt the Third Way [a reference to the title given by Tony Blair to the direction of New Labour's policies] – get rid of it'. The former Conservative minister, Kenneth Clark, denounced the absence of any clear policy at all. Nevertheless, it is surely impossible for reform of the Lords to be evaded any longer. The government's strategy has the merit of permitting very full public debate and party consultation, though from the government's point of view long and detailed debate might not be entirely welcome, since it will inevitably spill over into other constitutional issues, not least the fundamental relationship of executive to legislature.

Indeed, one can discern advantages for the New Labour agenda in not reforming the House of Lords any further. Despite accusations of its being full of appointees favourable to the government (known not very affectionately as 'Tony's cronies'), the House of Lords in its present composition provides a useful whipping boy for Labour MPs when it rejects proposals passed by the Commons. To listen to many Labour MPs baying for the use of the Parliament Act to overturn the Lords' rejection of the Hunting With Dogs Bill in 2004, one might think that it was still overwhelmingly dominated by hereditary Tory peers and that stage one of reform had never taken place.

............................................................................

## ✓ What you should have learnt from reading this chapter

- The form of liberal democracy, which constitutes the British political system, is centred on the role of Parliament as the democratic sounding board of the British people and the means by which the government is both created by, and made accountable to, them.

- Parliament, while having an enviable history of ensuring political stability and freedom, is in need of massive reform. Two key issues need to be addressed: first, Parliament's power and effectiveness in making the executive accountable to the legislature needs to be strengthened; and second, the democratic legitimacy of the upper house needs to be improved as hereditary and appointed members of the legislature are now considered by most citizens inappropriate in a modern democratic society.

- One can discern the continuing decline of the Commons as an effective scrutiniser of legislative proposals under the present Labour government. Prime Minister Blair rarely attends the Commons, outside of Prime Minister's Question Time, and only very limited time for debate was allowed by the government on issues such as identity cards and house arrest for British citizens, which had far-reaching implications for civil liberties.

- Only the second issue, the reform of the House of Lords, is being exposed to radical reform at the moment, and such reform may not result in a more democratic or even representative and responsible government. Only partial reform has been achieved so far, which means that the Lords continues to have no democratic legitimacy and remains in a weak constitutional and political position to bring the government to account. Proposed further reforms may well occur in the wake of Labour's re-election in 2005, but one doubts whether they will involve increased powers to the upper house.

- Ultimately one can conclude that the present reforms of Parliament, especially those relating to the House of Lords, will be just the first step towards a much-needed, even more radical, reform of the whole system of representation and accountability in the Mother of Parliaments.

## Glossary of key terms

**Backbench MP** A member of Parliament who is neither a member of the government nor of the Shadow Cabinet. The front benches on either side of the chamber of the House of Commons are reserved for the leading political figures of the two major parties.

**Dissolution of Parliament** The procedure by which a general election takes place. The existing Parliament ceases to exist by order of the monarch, on the advice (always taken) of the Prime Minister.

**Falklands Crisis** A conflict which led to war between Britain and Argentina in 1982 when Argentina occupied the Falkland Islands (or 'Malvinas') which were a British colony. After a short spell of fighting, Britain successfully reoccupied the islands and defeated Argentina.

**Hung parliament** The colloquial term, popular among journalists, politicians and the public, for a House of Commons in which no one party has an overall majority of MPs in relation to other parties in the chamber.

**Opposition/'Official' Opposition** The 'opposition' in the House of Commons consists of all those parties that are not in the government. The second-largest party in the Commons constitutes the 'Official' Opposition, the Leader of which holds a Crown appointment and a salary above that received by an MP.

**Orders in Council** A device by which an executive order can be authorised, by using the royal prerogative. Technically, an 'order in council' is made by and with the advice of the Privy Council, a largely honorary body made up mainly of senior politicians of all parties that have held ministerial office.

**Poll tax**  Also known as the Community Charge. A highly unpopular local tax which came into effect in 1990, replacing the previous rates system. Its key principle was that every adult resident in a given local authority paid the same amount; it was abolished in 1993.

**Royal Commission**  A body technically appointed by the Crown on the advice of a minister to investigate and report on some particular area of government. Nowadays Royal Commissions are more or less obsolete, having been replaced by select committee enquiries or by the practice of appointing a high court judge to examine some issue of public importance.

**Sovereign people**  A term linked to the political principle that all political power in a nation ultimately resides in the people of that nation.

**Speaker of the House of Commons**  A sitting MP, elected by his/her fellow MPs to preside over the proceedings of the House of Commons. Historically, the Speaker had the perilous duty of representing the opinions of the Commons to the monarch and also to uphold its powers and privileges against royal power.

**Right-Wing/Left-Wing**  A convenient, if sometimes misleading, means of locating parties across the political spectrum. Historically, Labour has been seen as Left-Wing, the Conservatives Right-Wing, the Liberal Democrats Centrist, with communists and fascists positioned at the extreme Left and Right respectively.

**White Paper**  A government document outlining proposed legislation and inviting comment from interested individuals and organisations before it is introduced into Parliament as legislation.

## ？ Likely examination questions

To what extent is the government still collectively responsible to Parliament?

By what means and how successfully does the House of Commons attempt to control the executive?

'The constitutional convention of individual ministerial responsibility no longer applies.' Discuss.

It has been said of the House of Lords that: 'Its powers are limited, its impact on legislation modest and its contribution to public debate marginal.' Would you agree with this assessment of the role of the House of Lords within the constitution?

Examine the constitutional implications of reform of the second chamber.

'An institution in decline.' How accurately does this describe the position of Parliament within the modern British constitution?

## Suggested websites

www.parliament.uk   The UK Parliament

www.hansard-society.org.uk   Hansard Society for Parliamentary Government

www.parliament.uk/about_commons.cfm   House of Commons

www.parliament.uk/parliamentary_committees/select_committee_on_the_modernisation_of_the_house_of_commons.cfm   Modernisation Committee of the House of Commons

www.parliament.uk/about_lords/about_lords.cfm   House of Lords

www.archive.official-documents.co.uk/document/cm45/4534/contents.htm   Report of the Royal Commission on the Reform of the House of Lords (Wakeham Commission)

 ## Suggestions for further reading

Baldwin, M. (2002), 'Reforming the Second Chamber', *Politics Review*, 11: 3, 8–12.

Flinders, M. (2002), 'Shifting the Balance? Parliament, the Executive and the British Constitution', *Political Studies*, 50: 2, 23–42.

Johnson, N. (2002), 'The Missing Piece of the Constitutional Jigsaw', *Talking Politics*, 14: 2, 48–51.

Morgan, T. (1999), 'Teeth for the Commons Watchdog', *Politics Review*, 8: 4, 6–10.

Richard, I. and Welfare, D. (1999), *'Unfinished Business': Reforming the House of Lords*, London: Vintage.

Ryan, M. (2003), 'The House of Lords: Options for Reform', *Talking Politics*, 16: 1, 29–31.

Shell, D. (2000), 'Labour and the House of Lords: A Case Study in Constitutional Reform', *Parliamentary Affairs*, 53, 290–310.

Weir, S. and Beetham, D. (1999), *Political Power and Democratic Control in Britain*, London and New York: Routledge.

# The Executive

## Contents

## Overview

It is a feature of the unwritten British constitution that the executive is almost entirely founded on conventions. Except for isolated legislation neither the Prime Minister nor the Cabinet has a basis in law. They have been produced by conventions, customs and practices that have developed because of historical accidents or responses to particular crises and political developments. In fact, the executive can be described as a 'Cabinet system', made up of the Prime Minister, the Cabinet itself, non-Cabinet Ministers, and the senior reaches of the civil service. The relationship between them is based on slowly changing constitutional conventions and political circumstances, which can all change dramatically.

The many conventions governing the executive often appear to contradict each other; they are the sum total of political experience and demonstrate the essentially pragmatic nature of the British political system. Here we discuss some of the major constitutional principles associated with the executive, outlining their main features.

## Key issues to be covered in this chapter

- Why are conventions so important in the study of the Cabinet system in the British constitution?
- Would a constitutional conference create Prime Ministerial and Cabinet government in its present form?
- Is the term 'an elected monarch' really appropriate in describing the role of a British Prime Minister? Do the practical constraints on the office outweigh the freedom given by constitutional conventions?
- How might one reorganise the constitutional conventions surrounding Cabinet government?
- Are the present conventions adequate to meet the demands placed on modern government?
- Will the Freedom of Information Act contribute significantly to the enduring constitutional and political problems associated with making the executive accountable to the British electorate and the British Parliament?

## The nature of the executive

In the 1960s there arose a debate over the nature of the executive; the debate fell into two camps. One view was that a shift had taken place from Cabinet government to Prime Ministerial government. Academics such as R. H. S Crossman and John P. Mackintosh, who were also Labour politicians, the Conservative Lord Hailsham and the Labour Left-Winger Tony Benn all claimed that power was being concentrated in the hands of the Prime Minister, a trend that should be resisted and, if possible, reversed. This view is usually called the 'Crossman-Mackintosh thesis'. More recently, the 'presidential' interpretation of the PM's role has been reiterated by Peter Hennessy and Dennis Kavanagh. Presidential interpretations of PM power were challenged by, among others, Richard Rose, Anthony King and G.W. Jones, who all claimed this thesis was overstated, the Prime Minister being only as strong as the Cabinet he/she creates and is a member of.

It is not our intention here to assess the rival claims in this debate. One should not really talk about 'rules' or 'laws' of politics. The relative positions of the Prime Minister and the Cabinet depend upon many factors, of which the constitutional position is only one; also relevant are the political and economic circumstances of the time, the strength of the personalities in the Cabinet, the personal style of the Prime Minister, the length of time in office of leading government figures, and so on. Sometimes the Prime Minister will appear to be dominant. Sometimes the system will appear to be more collegiate. Even an apparently strong, 'presidential' Prime Minister such as Margaret Thatcher was removed with relative ease when she lost the confidence of her Cabinet and backbench colleagues.

## The Prime Minister

**The expansion of the executive during the twentieth century**
Constitutional conventions surrounding the office of Prime Minister were predominantly created in the eighteenth and nineteenth centuries. There was a tendency to underestimate the constitutional power of the PM in the past while overestimating it today. However, it is important to realise that the major developments strengthening

PM power over the last century have been mainly political rather than constitutional.

The current party system began to take its modern form after 1867 with the creation of a mass electorate by the Reform Act of that year. Party politics needed stronger party organisations both out in the country and in the Commons to mobilise votes. In Westminster, party discipline tended to increase and with it the controlling hand of the PM as the leader of the governing party.

Two world wars in the twentieth century required considerable enlargement of the powers and competence of government. The PM, as head of the executive, played a major role in organising government for **total war** (especially Lloyd George in World War One and Churchill in World War Two). Once the wars were won, most, but not all, wartime structures of power and control placed in the hands of the PM and government were dismantled; what remained further enhanced Prime Ministerial power.

The expansion of government activity in social and economic intervention after 1945 further enhanced the power of the Prime Minister. The growth of the welfare state, maintenance of full employment and stimulating economic growth all further empowered the executive to intervene in British society. The government's ability to intervene in many aspects of economic and social life grew greatly during the decades after the end of World War Two. With increasing government intervention the power of the PM as head of the executive also expanded.

Together with these developments more patronage became available to the PM. The expansion of the executive has produced more ministerial posts to be filled, so the number of MPs in government has proliferated. With control over these posts the capacity of the PM to reward MPs, and thereby strengthen his/her power, has grown. However, it is worth reiterating here that there have been no major constitutional innovations in Prime Ministerial power, only political ones.

## The constitutional position of the Prime Minister

It is difficult to differentiate between the constitutional and the political sources of Prime Ministerial power. This is only to be expected, as the office has evolved from political factors that became conventions.

Essentially, most of the constitutional bases of Prime Ministerial power derive from the royal prerogative – originally powers of the king or queen – exercised now on behalf of the monarch by the PM and Cabinet. This may seem strange in a modern democracy, but it is a good example of British constitutional development evolving from adaptation to political circumstances (chiefly, the steady reduction of the actual power of the monarch) creating the modern head of the executive.

**The constitutional sources of PM power**
The PM is the leader of the majority party in the House of Commons. In strict constitutional theory the monarch chooses the Prime Minister. In practice the monarch will choose the leader of the party commanding a majority over all the other parties in the House of Commons; or, on very rare occasions, the leader of the party which can command a majority in the Commons by some deal or coalition with other parties. Thus the concept of **monarchical sovereignty**, coming from the Crown, and popular sovereignty, deriving from the people, are fused in the creation of the Prime Minister. The electoral system usually produces a single-party government with a majority of the seats in the Commons, but based on a minority of the turnout. Not since 1935 has a government been elected with a majority of the voters backing it. The monarch has no significant choice in the matter of whom to call on to create a government. Only in replacing the sick Harold Macmillan in 1963 with Sir Alec Douglas Home or in the rather confused situation following the February 1974 general election did the possibility arise of the Queen becoming involved in the political choice of her government. As long as a Prime Minister can rely on the loyalty of Cabinet Ministers and of the majority of the party's backbenchers he/she will remain in power. MPs are usually loyal to their government: they are unwilling to bring down their party leader, however disgruntled they may feel. Prime Ministers are usually, therefore, very difficult to remove. It was, for example, the Cabinet and backbench MPs and not any vote in the Commons who forced Mrs Thatcher's resignation as Prime Minister in November 1990. This is a very rare example of a PM being forced out of office by their party.

Although **First Lord of the Treasury**, the Prime Minister does not in practice have the day-to-day burden of running a department.

Backed by the resources of the **Prime Minister's Office,** with its numerous civil servants and policy advisors, and armed with the constitutional remit of bearing responsibility for all the activities of the government, the PM is able to intervene in the internal affairs of all departments. In the case of an energetic and interventionist Prime Minister, such as Margaret Thatcher or Tony Blair, this can create the conditions for a considerable degree of personal control by the Prime Minister over government.

A Prime Minister is intimately involved in the creation of the Cabinet and non-Cabinet government posts and has the final say over the creation of the government. Ministers can be chosen, sacked, forced to resign or moved to other posts as the PM sees fit. In constitutional theory, appointments have to be approved by the monarch; in practice the PM has, constitutionally, a relatively free choice; the major constraints on his/her choice are political. The PM also decides the membership of Cabinet committees with, therefore, great influence on the outcome of their deliberations.

Cabinet meetings are chaired by the Prime Minister, who decides the agenda and, as there is usually no voting on issues discussed in the Cabinet, will 'sum up' the 'feeling' of the meeting. This summary will appear in the minutes, the official record of Cabinet decisions. Hence, the PM has considerable influence and, in effect, control over the outcome of Cabinet deliberations. The role of the Cabinet has apparently declined somewhat under Tony Blair; he calls fewer meetings and these tend to be far shorter than the two to three hours they lasted under previous PMs. As Prime Ministers also chair the most important Cabinet committees, they will have great influence over the decisions and therefore over what is likely to reach the Cabinet for approval. It would appear that this committee role is emerging as a constitutional provision.

Royal prerogative powers give the PM the constitutional right to choose the members of the government and thus exercise patronage. This is a huge source of power and influence – and discipline – among the members of the governing party in the Commons. Furthermore, most of the honours awarded by the monarch are on the recommendation of the Prime Minister: these include knighthoods, peerages, bishoprics of the Church of England, some academic posts, and so on. Other powers of PM patronage derive from the many posts that have to be filled on official boards, committees of enquiries and parliamentary committees.

The Prime Minister has the right to choose when to call a general election. In constitutional theory it is the monarch who dissolves Parliament and calls a general election. In practice this is done on the advice of the PM. A Prime Minister, therefore, can call an election at the most opportune time for victory: during an economic upturn or when opinion polls are favourable. The only legal constraint is that a general election must take place within five years of the previous one. Tony Blair, for example, called an election in 2001, a year before he was legally bound to do so, and the media seemed to take it for granted that the following election would take place well before 2006; months before it was announced, the date of 5 May 2005 became common wisdom among political pundits.

The development of an 'inner Cabinet' has strengthened the power of the Prime Minister. Prime Ministers often find the Cabinet too large for effective decision-making. There is actually little in the constitution which demands that decisions must be taken there. Prime Ministers often favour small, informal 'inner Cabinets' of close political allies and personal friends to reach important decisions. The outcome of such meetings may or may not be subsequently open to full Cabinet deliberation where political rivals might challenge them. These **'inner' or 'kitchen' Cabinets** have no constitutional status, but their political significance is such that they raise questions about the traditional view of the constitutional dominance of the Cabinet itself and the ways it can in actuality be bypassed by the Prime Minister.

The 2004 Butler Enquiry into the circumstances of the Iraq War threw the extent to which effective power can be shifted from the Cabinet into sharp relief. Key decisions were made in meetings between a small number of key ministers, officials and military officers, rather than by the Cabinet. These so-called **'sofa cabinets'** often included unelected advisors, such as Press Officer Alastair Campbell, Chief of Staff Jonathan Powell and Director of Government Relations, Baroness Morgan. Their meetings in Tony Blair's study ('the den') bypassed the Cabinet and were often un-minuted. Foreign Secretary Jack Straw and Defence Secretary Geoff Hoon often gave briefings to the Cabinet without the prior circulation of papers, thus making it, as

Butler stated, 'much more difficult to bring their political judgement and experience to bear on the major decisions for which the Cabinet as a whole must carry responsibility'. Butler went on to comment that 'government procedures [reduced] the scope for informed collective political judgement'.

Professor Peter Hennessy, in an interview with the *Mail on Sunday* in February 2005, was even more forthright; he said, 'This kind of thing used to go on in Eastern Europe or in medieval times, but not here, and certainly not on issues as important as peace and war. Not even a village cricket club would be allowed to conduct its business like this.'

## The constitutional checks on PM power

The Prime Minister does not, of course, have a free hand. In addition to the constitutional constraints of collective responsibility the Prime Minister is limited by practical and political circumstances that seriously reduce his power. Margaret Thatcher, for example, had little time for collective Cabinet decision-making and was eventually destroyed by her colleagues; whereas John Major had a much more collegiate attitude to the Cabinet – and a much weaker dominance over his colleagues than Mrs Thatcher had for most of her time in office – and was destroyed by the electorate.

Survive or fail, all Prime Ministers are constrained by the following conventions:

- Prime Ministers are subject to the convention of collective responsibility like all other ministers; once a decision is made, all the government, including the Prime Minister, has to defend it in public. A Prime Minister doesn't always get his/her own way. A PM may sometimes be overruled by the Cabinet and have to abide by the collective decision. Furthermore, the PM cannot chair all the Cabinet committees and control their deliberations and decisions. Indeed, committees may be a base from which powerful rivals might try to undermine or challenge the Prime Minister.
- It has become a convention that the Prime Minister should be a member of the House of Commons. The last Prime Minister who was a member of the House of Lords throughout his term in office was Lord Salisbury (1895–1902). The reduction in the power of

the House of Lords in 1911 further reduced the appropriateness and possibility of a peer becoming Prime Minister, and the strengthened convention took firm root in the 1920s when Lord Curzon was passed over for Prime Minister by the Conservative party in favour of Stanley Baldwin. It was confirmed by the choice of Churchill over Lord Halifax in 1940. The Renunciation of Peerages Act 1963 allowed Lord Home to replace Harold Macmillan as PM by giving up his peerage and becoming 'plain' Sir Alec Douglas-Home.

- The Cabinet is made up of senior members of the governing party, including powerful characters whom the Prime Minister may have defeated for the leadership; they will act as a check on the Prime Minister. If the Cabinet is one of the forums for political competition among the party elite, then this is a major source of constraint on the political power of the Prime Minister whatever the constitutional conventions may indicate. In the Blair governments, for instance, it is clear that the Prime Minister must take seriously into account the views of Gordon Brown, the **Chancellor of the Exchequer**, on all aspects of government including, it would appear, appointments to ministerial office.

- In the modern, party-dominated constitution the Prime Minister must maintain party support in the Commons, the Lords and the country at large. If the PM and the party leadership ignore the aspirations of ordinary party members the latter may refuse to co-operate at election time. The present Labour government is thought by many of its members to be too anxious to hold onto middle-class votes, too close to business and too neglectful of its traditional supporters. This potentially presents a political threat to the long-term future of Tony Blair as an effective party leader and Prime Minister.

- It does not automatically happen that a Prime Minister will get his/her policies carried out by the civil service. The traditional constitutional view of the relationship between ministers and civil servants has always been that ministers supposedly determine the policies for a department and the civil servants meekly and loyally carry them out: in reality, departmental civil servants tend to develop their own policies over the years, sometimes in conflict with those of the government. Indeed, senior civil servants can slow down or sabotage government policies they disapprove of and produce a practical brake on the constitutional dominance of the PM.

- Prime Ministers lack the burden of departmental responsibilities, but they do have a considerable workload. To the ordinary citizen and to foreign governments the Prime Minister embodies the British government. He/she is expected to have an overall managerial responsibility for the government and its policies. No aspect of government is too unimportant for the Prime Minister, though in practice no individual is capable of detailed involvement in the workings of all government departments, though Margaret Thatcher was and Tony Blair is noted for interventions and for overriding ministers in potentially sensitive areas; one example: during the Foot and Mouth Disease crisis of 2001 Mr Blair took 'personal control' over the government's response (although whether his control made any actual difference to government actions is questionable, however dramatic it appeared to be at the time).

Thus, the real political constraints on a Prime Minister's power are considerable, even if the constitutional conventions appear to give him/her almost untrammelled power within the political system.

## Cabinet government

### Conventions and the Cabinet

Of fundamental importance in the operation of Cabinet government is the fact that it is based on 'convention'. Although already briefly alluded to, this principle demands further exploration.

The development of modern party politics after 1867 encouraged the Cabinet to act as a single body. Whereas eighteenth-century Cabinet members would often speak against the policies of their own government, from the mid-nineteenth century onwards party discipline created modern doctrines of collective and ministerial responsibility, making the Cabinet, as Walter Bagehot discerned in *The English Constitution*, the crucial institution of government:

> A Cabinet is a combining committee – a *hyphen* which joins, a *buckle* which fastens the legislative part of the state to the executive. In its origin it belongs to the one, in its function it belongs to the other.

Despite the many changes since Bagehot's time, chiefly the expansion of the executive and the growth of PM power, the Cabinet remains the central institution of government, although its significance is subject to academic debate.

Cabinet government is based on convention not law; conventions evolve and are often revised by powerful politicians responding to major events in a manner which can only be described as revolutionary; most conventions have been subject to considerable alteration in recent years. The major conventions associated with Cabinet government will be outlined below.

- Members of the government, both Cabinet and non-Cabinet Ministers, are bound by the doctrines of collective and individual ministerial responsibility: these conventions are intended to ensure strong government and its accountability to Parliament, although, as we have observed, they have been significantly modified over the last three decades.

- Senior members of the government will be in the Commons, except for ministers in charge of those posts that have to be filled from the House of Lords. Most ministers holding posts such as Defence Secretary, Home Secretary and Chancellor of the Exchequer will be in the Commons, as convention dictates they must be accountable to MPs. However, Lord Carrington, Foreign Secretary (1979–82), remained in the Lords with Sir Ian Gilmour (holding the Cabinet post of **Lord Privy Seal**) as his spokesman in the House of Commons. Similarly, Lord Young of Graffham, Employment Secretary (1985–7) and Secretary for Trade and Industry (1987–9), demonstrated that Cabinet Ministers do not always have to be MPs. Lord Sainsbury was appointed as the Labour government's science minister in 1997 and in 2005 Andrew Adonis was elevated to the Lords so that he could hold the post of an education minister.

- The Cabinet should be chosen from the largest party of the House of Commons. The electoral system usually creates a single-party majority in the House of Commons. This convention ensures co-operation between the legislature and the executive. The government is able to dominate and, to a great degree, control Parliament by virtue of its majority. 'Hung parliaments' (where there is no overall parliamentary majority and a party holds the balance of power in the Commons) are rare: the 'Lib-Lab Pact' of 1976–8 was the last time this situation existed, and then only after the Labour government had lost its overall majority following by-election losses. Coalition governments, made up of two or more parties, are also rare, occurring only during times of national crises, such as world war or economic collapse. This convention removes any significant role for the monarch in the creation of governments.

- A government defeated on an issue of importance in the House of Commons should, according to convention, resign. This was a convention that declined after the early 1970s when both Conservative and Labour governments, struggling with weakening party discipline, were defeated on crucial issues and yet remained in office. Usually, a government need not worry about defeat: it appeals to party loyalty, backed by party discipline, to secure a parliamentary majority that brings victory. Governments are still expected to resign when defeated in a vote of 'no confidence' in the House of Commons, but such defeats are extraordinarily rare (only in 1924 and 1979 have minority governments, both Labour, been so defeated). Thus by the 1990s a convention had been established that governments resign only on defeat in a 'no confidence' motion. In practical political terms this means that a government with a working majority is unlikely to be forced to resign.

- However, a government defeated in a general election almost always resigns immediately: a defeat means that the party has lost its parliamentary majority and would not, therefore, get its legislative programme through the House. A government defeated in a general election could possibly try to carry on, or to form an alliance with another party, but if unable to muster a majority in the Commons it would be defeated in a vote of 'no confidence'. Nevertheless, this convention is still flexible in the face of political realities. Prime Minister Edward Heath, leading a Conservative party which had fewer MPs than Labour but had more votes, offered the Liberals Cabinet seats after the February 1974 election, which would have created a majority for a Conservative/Liberal Government. However, Liberal MPs and their party rejected this deal and the proposed coalition failed:

Heath resigned and the Labour party formed a minority government until it could call another election later in the same year.

## Conventions and the construction of the Cabinet

The Prime Minister knows that the Cabinet plays a key role in the constitution; hence, choices made about the construction of the Cabinet are very important, as they shape the 'character of the administration' and departmental policies. Convention and political considerations will influence these choices. Before finalising the government, the PM will consult with senior members of the parliamentary party.

The PM exercises what were once the powers of the monarch in the creation of the Cabinet. It is worth reiterating that no formal transfer of power from the monarch to the PM has occurred at any specific time; these prerogative powers have arrived in Prime Ministerial hands through historical circumstance and the creation of constitutional conventions over the last two and a half centuries. Even now, the PM and Cabinet are the Queen's ministers in Her Majesty's Government and, constitutionally, are still answerable to her for their appointment and their policies.

Yet it is the Prime Minister and only the Prime Minister who by convention has the final say in, and the ultimate responsibility for, the creation of the Cabinet, as can be observed in the following account of the conventions surrounding the construction of the Cabinet.

The choice of Cabinet members by the Prime Minister will be determined by both constitutional convention and prevailing political circumstances. Many factors are taken into consideration, among which are:

- Ministers must, by convention, be members of either the House of Commons or the House of Lords, or become so soon after being appointed, although no law requires them to be so. Prime Ministers can create by-elections in the Commons or peerages in the Lords for individuals they want in government who are not members of the legislature. Most Cabinet Ministers must be members of the House of Commons.
- Ministers will usually be members of the same political party. Only the rare coalition governments discard this rule. Prior to the

1997 general election there was speculation that the Liberal Leader, Paddy Ashdown, might be offered a Cabinet post, an offer which did not materialise: the sheer scale of the Labour victory removed the need for such a deal, and also the Liberal Democrats in the Commons and the country were reluctant to get too closely involved with the Labour government.

- Of course a potential minister must be sufficiently able or experienced to hold the post. This can usually be assessed on an individual's past ministerial career. However, the incoming Labour government of 1997 contained no one who had held Cabinet rank and very few who had experience of junior government posts in the previous Labour governments of 1974–9.
- The ministerial team should reflect the various elements that make up the party. On occasion, a potential rival – or rivals – may be brought into the Cabinet to be subject to some control and discipline by the Prime Minister and his fellow senior members of the party. This device has the added advantage to a Prime Minister of removing a potential faction leader from his/her supporters within the parliamentary party. Over time, as the PM becomes more assured in office, has won political victories and is able to bring more members of his/her own wing of the party into government, such a strategy of attempting to maintain an ideological balance within the Cabinet becomes less important.
- Finally, there are legal constraints on the choice of ministers. Modern governments have upwards of one hundred members, of whom ninety-five at most can come from the Commons under the legal limits established by the House of Commons Disqualification Act 1975. Some Cabinet posts have to be held by lawyers: Lord Chancellor, **Attorney General, Solicitor General** and their Scottish equivalents.

There are thus appreciable constraints on the breadth of choice open to the Prime Minister in the creation of the government.

The Prime Minister has a good deal of discretion under constitutional conventions in the choice of which ministries to include in the Cabinet. The PM can create new offices, merge or abolish existing ones and change the functions of ministries with little interference from either the constitution or the law. Much change does occur.

Almost all Cabinet posts today have changed in their powers and responsibilities compared to, say, fifteen years ago. In practice, however, the form of the Cabinet is largely decided by the demands of government. There will, for example, always be ministries of Defence, Education, Health and the Exchequer represented in the Cabinet. The political and social climate of the time will also influence the choice of ministries. Manifesto commitments of the governing party and the PM's need to reward senior colleagues with high-prestige posts will also influence the construction of the Cabinet. Prime Minister Blair's Cabinet in 2005, for example, included Gordon Brown, a potential rival for party leadership, as Chancellor of the

## Table 2.1  The composition of the Blair goverment following the 2005 election

| Office held | Person in charge |
| --- | --- |
| Prime Minister | Tony Blair MP |
| Deputy Prime Minister and First Secretary of State | John Prescott MP |
| Chancellor of the Exchequer | Gordon Brown MP |
| Secretary of State for Foreign and Commonwealth Affairs | Jack Straw MP |
| Secretary of State for Work and Pensions | David Blunkett MP |
| Secretary of State for Environment, Food and Rural Affairs | Margaret Beckett MP |
| Secretary of State for Transport, and Secretary of State for Scotland | Alistair Darling MP |
| Secretary of State for Defence | Dr John Reid MP |
| Lord Privy Seal and Leader of the House of Commons | Geoff Hoon MP |

## Table 2.1  (continued)

| Office held | Person in charge |
| --- | --- |
| Secretary of State for Health | Patricia Hewitt MP |
| Secretary of State for Culture, Media and Sport | Tessa Jowell MP |
| Parliamentary Secretary to the Treasury and Chief Whip | Hilary Armstrong MP |
| Secretary of State for the Home Department | Charles Clarke MP |
| Secretary of State for Northern Ireland, and Secretary of State for Wales | Peter Hain MP |
| Minister without Portfolio | Ian McCartney MP |
| Leader of the House of Lords and Lord President of the Council | Baroness Amos |
| Secretary of State for Constitutional Affairs and Lord Chancellor | Lord Falconer |
| Secretary of State for International Development | Hilary Benn MP |
| Secretary of State for Trade and Industry | Alan Johnson MP |
| Secretary of State for Education and Skills | Ruth Kelly MP |
| Chancellor of the Duchy of Lancaster (Minister for the Cabinet Office) | John Hutton MP |
| Chief Secretary to the Treasury | Des Browne MP |
| Minister of Communities and Local Government | David Miliband MP |

NB In addition to the twenty-three members of the Cabinet, three people also attend Cabinet meetings: Lord Grocott (Lords Chief Whip), Lord Goldsmith (Attorney General) and Douglas Alexander (Minister of State for Europe in the Foreign and Commonwealth Office).

Exchequer, and John Prescott, a representative of the Old Labour and trade union wing of the party, in the post of Deputy Prime Minister.

The size of the Cabinet is supposed to be another factor that a Prime Minister has to take into account when forming a government, but Anthony King believes that 'no PM since 1945 has probably spent more than half an hour, at most, thinking about the subject'. The Cabinet consists of the senior governing party members holding the major offices of State. Cabinet size is not determined by either law or convention and has greatly changed over the centuries. During the nineteenth century it had twelve to sixteen members; over the last one hundred years or so Cabinets have grown in size, a consequence of the expansion of government and the desire of full-time and professional politicians to achieve ministerial office and advance their careers.

No modern PM attempts to include all the government in the Cabinet. The size of the Cabinet has varied from sixteen to twenty-four members, with upwards of eighty to one hundred members holding non-Cabinet posts in the government. Nevertheless, there have been complaints that modern Cabinets are too large: it is thought that Cabinets of over twenty ministers undermine the con-stitutional and political role of the Cabinet in both co-ordinating gov-ernment at the very top of its organisational structure and acting as a constraint on Prime Ministerial power.

## The constitutional structure of Cabinet government

Cabinet government operates, as we have seen, within highly flexible constitutional conventions that work according to political circum-stances, the policy requirements of the governing party and the per-sonal style of the Prime Minister.

It is rather difficult to establish the details of how the system works. Cabinet structure and its support services are shrouded in secrecy: indeed, British governments seem to be obsessed by secrecy. Labour's Freedom of Information Act was designed to reduce this culture within British government, although it is unlikely to change significantly the culture of secrecy so deeply entrenched in the British political system.

Secrecy is, however, necessary for Cabinet discussions to take place in confidence and free of the hedging and trimming of their expressed judgements that would be likely to occur if ministers knew that every statement would appear in the next day's newspapers. Cabinet deliberations on policy are, as we have observed, somewhat less important today than was the case in the past and also in constitutional theory. Nevertheless, many highly controversial policy options on any issue have often to be considered and discussed in full Cabinet. Hence, policy-making has to take place in secret.

R. H. S. Crossman's *Diaries of a Cabinet Minister* appeared in the mid-1970s, in the face of government opposition and legal attempts to block publication. Since then, there has been a fashion for government ministers, especially Conservative ones from the Thatcher and Major governments, to 'set the record straight' in their published memoirs soon after leaving office. Ministers have also, during the 1980s and 1990s in particular, used the **Lobby system** of unattributed statements to 'leak' policy controversies to the press. Such tactics have encouraged decision-making to shift to other parts of the government and away from the Cabinet itself. Recent academic studies, such as those by Peter Hennessy, *The Prime Minister: the office and its holders since 1945*, have cast further light on the inner workings of the Cabinet, among which have been the diversity of the decision-making styles of different Prime Ministers and a surprising range of informal decision-making procedures.

There is enough known about the workings of Cabinet government to stimulate a lively debate as to how its constitutional framework operates. One can identify two approaches towards the Cabinet system: the 'traditional' and the 'revisionist'.

The traditional view of the Cabinet system accords very closely with the generally accepted assumptions about Cabinet conventions. The Cabinet, supporters of the traditional view assert, sits atop a highly complex government structure. Power rests with the Cabinet which, chaired by the Prime Minister, plays a key role in co-ordinating the government. All the most important members of the governing party and all the political heads of government departments sit in the Cabinet. It therefore acts as the political head of the civil service. Operating through a network of committees, the Cabinet ensures effective government for the United Kingdom.

Traditionalists believe that the most important political and governmental decisions are still made at Cabinet meetings, where detailed discussion takes place and a collective decision is reached. As a consequence, members of the Cabinet have a collective responsibility for their decisions, and individual ministers can seek support there to resist interest group or other pressures inimical to the interests of the government and its programme.

The traditionalist view reflects what many citizens believe is, or should be, the nature of Cabinet government.

That the traditionalist view reflected the reality of Cabinet government in an age of minimal government before the world wars and the post-1945 interventionist state is open to doubt. The revisionist argument propounds that the Cabinet system, whatever the reality was prior to the mid-twentieth century, is certainly not characterised today by the traditionalist model.

According to the revisionist view – which has become something of an orthodoxy among academic specialists on the Cabinet – the Cabinet cannot possibly have control over or efficiently manage government, and cannot therefore be the core of the Cabinet system. After all, the Cabinet meets for only two to three hours once or twice a week (once a week, for twenty-five to forty-five minutes, under Tony Blair). How can there be sufficient time for all issues to be properly discussed in such a body?

Even if there were adequate time to discuss policy in Cabinet meetings, revisionists argue, ministers in reality lack the expertise effectively to discuss every aspect of government. Ministers lack specialised knowledge of the remit of even their own department, let alone of other departments. Regular ministerial reshuffles mean that ministers rarely acquire deep knowledge of their own departments. Both John Major and Tony Blair have, in their respective governments, tended to keep Cabinet Ministers in office for much longer than the average of two years which was previously the case. However, under the present Labour administration there has been a notably much higher turnover of junior ministerial posts than under previous governments.

As a consequence of these factors and of the sheer burden of work that a minister has to shoulder, Cabinet deliberations are reduced to general discussions on policy and principle. Little serious decision-making takes place in the Cabinet; its prime function in the modern British political system, according to the revisionists, is to act as a forum for competition among leading members of the government and a means of managing the power relations between them.

Most decisions that reach Cabinet have already been made elsewhere in the system, such as committees, inner Cabinets, the Prime Minister's Office, and by civil servants or by policy advisors. The Cabinet gives the final 'stamp of approval' to these decisions and irons out their implications for the overall government programme and their influence on public opinion. It acts as a 'court of final appeal' within government on those issues and conflicts that cannot be settled elsewhere, particularly in departments and in Cabinet committees.

One might, however, question the effective scrutiny of policy by the Cabinet as a final decision-making body on top-level decisions. There has been an increasing trend by Prime Ministers in recent years to bypass the Cabinet on key decisions. This has been the case during both Conservative and Labour periods in office, but two examples from the Blair government illustrate the problem: both relate to the Iraq War. Firstly, it has been claimed by ex-Cabinet Minister Clare Short that prior to the invasion of Iraq in 2003 no Cabinet-level discussions or thorough analysis of the risks involved took place; neither was there discussion in full Cabinet of the military, political and diplomatic options available to the government. Secondly, the revelation in early 2005 that the Attorney General's advice on the legality of invading Iraq involved no Cabinet-level scrutiny of the legal documents related to this advice, just a question-and-answer session in Cabinet, reinforced the view among many that the Cabinet had been bypassed as a decision-making body on the most crucial decision a government can make: going to war.

## Ministers and officials in government departments and Cabinet committees

Two important areas of constitutional/political decision-making in the Cabinet system worthy of investigation are firstly, ministers and their relationship with their senior departmental officials, and secondly, Cabinet committees (sometimes identified as 'Cabinet sub-committees').

Every government department has a Cabinet-level minister and junior, non-Cabinet Ministers, who may, on invitation, attend Cabinet meetings. Constitutionally, ministers have ultimate responsibility for both policy and management of their departments under the convention of individual ministerial responsibility, while routine departmental management and policy advice to the minister is in the hands of senior professional civil servants, known as Permanent Secretaries.

The relationship between ministers and civil servants is governed by constitutional conventions, the most important of which supposedly determines that the minister decides policy and the civil service administers policy. This convention can be demonstrated when ministers and civil servants from the same department appear before the relevant Departmental Select Committee; only ministers are allowed to answer questions of policy, while civil servants must, when answering questions from select committee members, confine their replies to administrative matters only. In practice, however, senior civil servants have considerable influence over policy, especially in its details and implementation, but constitutional convention seeks to keep civil servants from involvement in political controversy. Even if the minister is weak, incompetent or lazy the work of the department still goes on; policy has to be carried out and the usually vast departmental resources efficiently administered. Under such circumstances the senior civil service will have greater influence on policy formation than under a powerful, competent and hardworking minister.

One of the most important conventions governing ministerial and civil service relations is that of civil service neutrality. This convention is designed to establish and protect senior civil servants from being sucked into political controversy. Senior levels in the civil service are made up of professional, full-time career officials who are not replaced when the party of government changes. They are expected loyally to carry out government policy; if they cannot, then they should ask to be transferred, resign or face the possibility of being fired. It will, therefore, be predominantly the same civil servants who served the Thatcher and Major governments who carry out the policies of the Blair administration. The professionalism of senior officials should safeguard that, whatever their personal political views, they will be as loyal to the present Labour government and as competent in carrying out its policies as they were to the previous Conservative administrations.

There has been some concern over the maintenance of this convention of neutrality. Both Left-Wing ministers, such as Tony Benn, and Right-Wing politicians, most notably Margaret Thatcher, have claimed to detect political bias in the civil service. Obviously, there is a difference over what that bias might be. Left-Wingers suggest that the overwhelmingly white, male, public school, Oxbridge, upper-middle-class nature of the senior civil service inevitably produces an in-built bias against socialism and radical policies. In other words, the senior civil service is distinctly conservative – or even Conservative – in its politics. Mrs Thatcher, and other Tory ministers, on the other hand, claimed that the senior civil service was moulded by the social-democratic ideologies of the post-war consensus and therefore resistant to her government's Neo-Liberal/New Right political agenda.

Recent Conservative governments, therefore, have brought in political advisors from the world of business or ideologically sympathetic 'think tanks' to offer ministers an alternative source of advice to that coming from the civil service. This has weakened the constitutional basis of minister–civil service relations. Government distrust damaged the morale of senior civil servants. When one considers the open hostility to public service from Mrs Thatcher and some of her ministers, combined with dramatic falls in real pay, huge cuts in the size of the civil service, and the contracting out of many civil service functions to agencies and the private sector, one might wonder that the civil service has not become more politicised. Although somewhat more sympathetic to public service than its predecessors, the Labour government has also introduced large numbers of highly paid advisors from outside the civil service. Clearly, the civil service has lost its major constitutional role of being the sole source of advice to government.

Cabinet committees are an exceedingly important arena of government activity: most government deliberation and decision-making work takes place in Cabinet committees. In the nineteenth century Cabinet committees existed in an unsystematised form. World wars and the post-1945 expansion of government created the present committee system, but until the 1970s ministers often denied their existence. In the 1980s the system became better understood by non-government politicians and the general public owing to a greater willingness on the part of ministers to identify committees and their functions, and became more important to the work of journalists and academics such as Peter Hennessy who specialise in the arcane world of central government. The committee structure is becoming 'conventional' – in both senses of the word.

## Box 2.1  Types of Cabinet committee

Cabinet committees are of two types: standing and ad hoc committees. Standing committees are named, permanent committees; they are responsible for a particular policy area that is of lasting concern for government: there are always such areas in a department. They include, for example, Public Expenditure Scrutiny, Northern Ireland, Economic Policy, Home Affairs and Social Policy committees. ad hoc committees, on the other hand, are concerned with particular policy issues, such as the implementation of manifesto pledges or dealing with a crisis. Such committees are identified by their given number, and when the policy has been implemented or the crisis dealt with the committee is disbanded. Some ad hoc committees exist so long, because the policy area has been a concern of government for many years, that they become effectively a form of standing committee while retaining their ad hoc status.

The Prime Minister creates both types of committee and chairs the most important ones. Departmental ministers usually sit on those committees directly relevant to their departments, although they may sit on or chair committees outside their departmental remit.

It is in Cabinet committees that most of the deliberative work of the government is carried out. Issues are considered in greater detail than is possible in Cabinet; in fact, many important decisions are made in Cabinet committees without reference to the full Cabinet, which only gets involved if there are major differences of opinion to be resolved or if the chair agrees to bring the issue under debate to the Cabinet. The Prime Minister is often a committee chair and always on the key committees on defence, foreign affairs and economic policy. Committees can call upon the participation of non-Cabinet Ministers, civil servants and outside experts in their work, thus improving the overall quality of government. Cabinet committees do, however, remain subordinate to the full Cabinet; their decisions are reported to the Cabinet, which retains the right to veto or revise any committee proposals it disagrees with or which comes into conflict with the overall strategy of the government. They can be regarded as a major contribution to the efficient work of the Cabinet system: so closely are the full Cabinet and Cabinet committees interwoven in their work that it is more correct to say that they both form part of a single system rather than being in competition with each other.

A number of criticisms have been made about the constitutional impact of committees. R. H. S. Crossman considered them as one of the symptoms of the 'Passing of Cabinet Government' which began when the new committee system was created in the 1940s. In his 1963 introduction to Bagehot's *The English Constitution* Crossman claimed that:

> The point of decision . . . was now permanently transferred either downwards to these powerful Cabinet Committees, or upwards to the Prime Minister himself.

The conventions connected with the creation and composition of committees have been a key element in strengthening Prime Ministerial power. Ministers tend to spend more time in the detailed work of Cabinet committees than in the strategic planning role of the Cabinet, a situation that undermines the collective decision-making culture of the Cabinet, compartmentalises government and clouds any real meaning associated with the doctrine of collective responsibility.

Whatever one's view of Cabinet committees, they are vitally important areas of government activity, with major roles in determining and deciding government policy and a considerable impact on the constitutional structure of Cabinet government.

The well-established paradigm of central government, in which decisions are collectively made by the Cabinet, itself answerable to Parliament, and implemented by a loyal and non-partisan civil service, fits neatly with constitutional theory as evolved in the nineteenth century. Recent studies, however, suggest that in the twenty-first century it bears no resemblance to reality. Notions of Prime Ministerial as opposed to Cabinet government are equally misplaced.

Power, it is clamed by most contemporary commentators on British government, resides within a **'core executive'**, which includes not only the PM and Cabinet but also senior civil servants, advisors and Cabinet committees. Moreover, power within the core executive hinges not simply on command but on dependency. Each actor within the system, including the Prime Minister, depends, to a greater or lesser extent, on others; this is illustrated, for example, by the complex, interdependent relationship between Tony Blair and

Gordon Brown, the Chancellor of the Exchequer. Even the most powerful Prime Ministers recognise the cost of alienating the most troublesome Cabinet member. This is especially true if that person is the Chancellor, the man who controls the government's purse strings, or a high-profile member of a faction of the party – witness Tony Blair's strenuous efforts to dissuade Clare Short from resigning from the Cabinet over Iraq during 2003–4. The extent of one actor's dependency varies with the issue, with political circumstances, with electoral and media reactions and with specific political developments. Power can wane as well as wax; for example, the position of John Prescott, Deputy PM, was generally considered more powerful during 1997–2001, when he was needed by Tony Blair as a link with 'Old Labour' and the unions, than he subsequently became after the 2001 election victory consolidated Tony Blair's position.

Certainly any analysis of the Blair governments would seem to confirm the claim that Cabinet government in is decline. According to the Hutton Report (2004) on events leading up to the Iraq War, key decisions on these matters were taken by a 'sofa cabinet' in the PM's study by an elite group of senior advisors that included Alastair Campbell, Jonathan Powell and Sally Morgan (who held the posts of Press Officer, Chief of Staff and Director of Government Relations respectively). According to Clare Short, in *An Honourable Deception?* (2004), in her experience Cabinet members were systematically excluded from crucial discussions. Beyond a number of high-profile advisors to ministers lies an extensive array of advisors, consultants, 'tsars' of various kinds, task force leaders and so on who influence the policy-making process. It should not be imagined that such advisors constitute a phenomenon confined to the Blair governments. Margaret Thatcher famously settled many issues in person-to-person discussions and constantly imported outside advisors from beyond Whitehall, such as Charles Powell, a foreign affairs advisor to the Prime Minister, and Bernard Ingham, the Downing Street Press Officer.

Not everyone is convinced of the 'core executive' approach to government. Who counts as being 'in' and who 'out'? Apparently this can vary enormously from issue to issue. The Falkland (1982), Kosovo (1999) and Iraq (2003) wars evidently involved narrow decision-making bodies – 'war cabinets' in the popular parlance – that included the military and intelligence chiefs, and senior party and press relations figures, but not, for obvious reasons, education or welfare ministers and advisors. One might ask how many members constitute this core executive: suggestions in answer may vary from the twenty or so members of the Cabinet to the 100 to 150 MPs who can make up a government. A concept of the core executive that is so elastic must surely be of dubious worth as an analytical tool.

Moreover, the 'traditional', institutional structures of government have a habit of reasserting themselves. Margaret Thatcher's forced resignation as PM in 1990 can be interpreted as the consequence of a revolt of alienated Cabinet Ministers. John Major's fundamental weakness in Parliament and the Conservative party effectively restored power to the Cabinet during his term as Prime Minister. Blair may very well discover that he faces a more assertive Cabinet in the backwash of the Iraq War – especially if the war inflicts damage on the party similar to the damage done to Blair's personal authority by Britain's involvement in the conflict. One might, however, claim that Tony Blair appeared to be overcoming the damage to himself and his party as a consequence of the Iraq War with the reassertion of 'traditional' domestic political issues during the run-up to the 2005 general election. Victory in May 2005 with a majority of sixty-six should have re-established Mr Blair's personal and political authority within the Cabinet, the parliamentary party, the Labour party in the country and among voters. Iraq and questions about his personal integrity did damage Mr Blair's political credibility, even though he had led Labour to an unprecedented third consecutive election victory; calls within the Labour party for his resignation grew if anything louder.

## Freedom of information

The late R. H. S. Crossman, academic, Labour politician and Cabinet Minister, once described official secrecy as 'the British disease'. Peter Hennessy, in *Whitehall*, agreed: 'Secrecy is the bonding material which holds the rambling structure of central government together.' It has been a commonplace among students of government in Britain that the British state is extremely secretive, that it should not be so and that the solution to this problem is a Freedom of Information Act.

The culture of secretiveness is partly the product of a system of government based largely on convention; for example, the conventions of ministerial responsibility and collective Cabinet responsibility. The principle of the royal prerogative (the powers once held by the Crown but now exercised by the government independent of parliamentary scrutiny or approval) reinforces this pervasive atmosphere of secrecy.

Legislation has strengthened the powers of the authorities to restrict public access to information; the Official Secrets Act 1989 declares that the release of information that is deemed harmful to the public interest is a criminal offence. It is no defence to claim that public disclosure is in fact in the public interest, or that the information is available abroad, still less that it is true. The prosecution need not prove that the information is potentially or actually harmful. The Act applies to journalists and editors as well as civil servants, and has created some 2,300 offences. Not surprisingly, critics argued that, far from liberalising access to information, the Act has had the opposite effect. A series of high-profile court cases relating to the disclosure of official secrets emphasised the impression of a repressive stance towards the release of information: for example, Peter Wright's *Spycatcher* revelations of the often illegal activities of the **intelligence services**; the prosecution of senior Ministry of Defence employees Sarah Tisdall and Clive Ponting for passing classified information to the press in the 1980s; and the prosecution of David Shayler during 2001–2 for his embarrassing revelations about the workings of the British Security Services.

In fairness to the government, it must be admitted that national security during the Cold War, during the IRA bombing campaigns and the more recent 'war on terror' is a genuine concern. Moreover, the Major governments did make modest efforts in the field of greater openness, such as the **Citizen's Charter** (1991), and the publication at the discretion of government of more information on the inner workings of government.

Nevertheless, private member's bills on freedom of information in 1992 and 1993 were quashed. Official reports, like the Scott Enquiry into arms for Iraq (1995), showed just how little progress had been made. The Labour government in 1974 originally promised a Freedom of Information Act, but with a small parliamentary majority and a maelstrom of economic and political crises to manage, nothing came of this intention. Campaigning organisations such as Charter 88 and the Campaign for Freedom of Information, and prominent politicians like Labour's Roy Hattersley, demanded a full-blown Freedom of Information Act. Labour Leader Neil Kinnock promised one in 1992 and in 1996 Tony Blair promised an act that would 'signal a new relationship which sees the public as legitimate shareholders in running the country'. In 1997 this became a manifesto commitment and was thought to symbolise the commitment of New Labour to reform and new ways of governing. Personal commitment by Mr Blair to greater freedom of information in government and a large Labour majority in the Commons generated early action on this issue. A bill was introduced in 1999 and enacted in 2000. Britain was finally to join the (over fifty) developed nations that have freedom of information legislation.

The Freedom of Information Act 2000 proved to be something of a damp squib, at least when compared with the preceding White Paper, entitled *Your Right to Know*, presented by David Clark, the **Chancellor of the Duchy of Lancaster**. It offers a relatively weak access to government information when compared to similar legislation in the USA, New Zealand or the Republic of Ireland.

However, and crucially, there were no fewer than twenty-three exemptions. For example, the intelligence services were not covered. Information that could cause harm to national security or law enforcement, the public, the environment or the safety of individuals would

---

**Box 2.2  Key points of the Freedom of Information Act 2000**

- Some 70,000 (later rising to 100,000) public authorities and publicly owned companies were covered
- An Information Commissioner and an Information Tribunal were set up to enforce it and by applying to them aggrieved members of the public could seek to exercise their 'right to know'
- Authorities which did not disclose information had to show that this was in the public interest; otherwise they could be fined and individuals might be imprisoned
- An answer to a request for information had to met, free of charge (except for minor printing, postage and packing costs), within twenty working days.

not be released. Ministers could withhold information that was not in the 'public interest' or prejudiced the conduct of public affairs. They could even refuse to say whether information asked for even existed. Most exemptions are subject to the test of 'public interest', although this term is left undefined. Refusal could also be made on the grounds of expense if the costs of gathering the information amounted to more than roughly three-and-a-half days' work for a government department (and slightly less for other public bodies).

Unsurprisingly, the Act was strongly criticised by papers such as *The Guardian* and *The Independent* and by pressure groups like Liberty and Charter 88. Critics pointed to the right of ministerial veto, included in the Act, as a cause for concern, as it could be used to block information that might be politically embarrassing. The Labour government has, in the view of critics, already a very poor record in complying with the existing non-statutory 'open government' code for civil servants and ministers.

Implementation of the Act in full began on the first day of 2005, under the guidance of Lord Falconer in his role as Constitutional Affairs Secretary. The Act makes it a criminal offence to destroy data after a valid request has been made for information. There were numerous reports towards the end of 2004, that as the implementation deadline approached, Whitehall echoed to the sounds of shredding machines as potentially controversial (but releasable) information was weeded out of government files and destroyed; the Information Commissioner, Richard Thomas, sought to calm agitated folk with assurances that the exercise was mainly in the interests of 'good record housekeeping' and the discarding of unwanted trivia.

Whether the impact of the Act will be as fundamental as the government suggests is open to question. Lord Falconer himself has few doubts. In an interview with *The Guardian* (18 October 2004) he said that the Act 'is going to make a significant difference in terms of openness of public authorities'. He claimed that exemptions were 'uncontentious' and that 'we are absolutely determined that the exemptions should only be used in the interest of good government'. He added, 'Whenever the government makes a major policy announcement or publishes a bill, accompanying that will be all the factual material, statutes, analyses and foreign comparisons which show how that policy assessment or bill came to be arrived at.'

Potentially the Freedom of Information Act could have a major impact on the nation's political life. Tony Blair has described the Freedom of Information Act as one of the lasting achievements of his government. It could indeed be a constitutional development of great importance, but only if the government wishes it so: the track record of recent governments does not inspire confidence. The public may take some time to take advantage of the Act to seek out information; requests may run to many thousands a year, though Mr Thomas stated that he did not expect more than 2,000 appeals during the first year of the Act's existence.

One development that might give one pause is the unprecedented disclosure of intelligence information concerning the alleged weapons of mass destruction in Iraq prior to the invasion in 2003. Here the government released information in order to persuade Parliament and public opinion of the rightness of its action. Critics perceived this as a deeply troubling development: secret information being disclosed if it suited the government's purpose and withheld if it did not. That is not what campaigners for a Freedom of Information Act were trying to achieve.

 **What you should have learnt from reading this chapter**

- The system of Cabinet government in Britain is built on conventions that are subject to considerable change and adaptation as political and personal circumstances allow or dictate.

- Unlike much of the rest of the constitution, the Cabinet system has been subject to little debate, either in the past or during the present period of constitutional innovation. It is interesting to note that evidently Cabinet government is the one area of the constitution that is not presently subject to major constitutional 'improvement' and 'reform' by Tony Blair's government. It seems unlikely that there will be moves to create extensive legal constraints on the Prime Minister's powers or to give Parliament a greater say in the choice of Cabinet Ministers.

- Such lack of reform exposes the concentration of power in the central core of government. Other areas of the British political system can be subject to constitutional reform, creating impressions of strengthening democracy, so long as real power remains where it has increasingly been during the twentieth century – in the hands of the Prime Minister.

- Similarly, it is highly questionable that the Freedom of Information Act will guarantee overcoming the fundamentally secretive nature of the British political system and offer significant contributions to making the executive more accountable to the members of the House of Commons, the Lords and the public.

## Glossary of key terms

**Attorney General/Solicitor General** These two legal posts are assigned to MPs who constitute the main legal advisors to the government. They are appointed by the Prime Minister, are members of the government and are always lawyers.

**Chancellor of the Duchy of Lancaster** A relic of medieval times, this Cabinet post has no specific departmental responsibilities and the holder is able to carry out such duties as the Prime Minister thinks fit.

**Chancellor of the Exchequer** The minister who heads the Treasury, the government department which is responsible for taxation, funding government spending and the overall direction of the economy.

**Citizen's Charter** John Major's 'big idea' in 1991, it was an attempt to improve public-sector services by establishing performance targets.

**Core executive** The network of individuals and institutions both around and including the Prime Minister and the Cabinet, which determines and co-ordinates government policy.

**First Lord of the Treasury** An historic title for the office of Prime Minister, who is still technically a Treasury minister. Ministerial responsibility for the Treasury rests, however, with the Chancellor of the Exchequer.

**'Inner' or 'kitchen' cabinets: related to 'sofa' cabinets** An informal policy group of politicians, public officials and advisors in whom the Prime Minister places a particular trust and who tend therefore to be particularly influential.

**Intelligence services** The semi-clandestine agencies that provide the government with secret information on internal and external threats. They include 'the Security Service' (MI5), the Secret Intelligence Service (MI6) and the Government Communications Headquarters (GCHQ). Other security organisations include the Defence Intelligence Staff, the Overseas Information Department and the Special Branch of the police force.

**Lobby system** A name given to selected correspondents of newspapers, broadcasters and press agencies who are given privileged information by the government.

**Lord Privy Seal** A relic of the Middle Ages, this official is a senior member of the Privy Council. The Privy Council consists of about 300 members, including Cabinet Ministers, judges and others with records of public service. The full Privy Council meets for ceremonial occasions (such as on the death of the monarch), though some of its committees have additional functions such as some responsibilities for awarding honours.

**Prime Minister's Office** An organisation of about 100 people who directly serve the Prime Minister and which enables him to dominate government.
**Monarchical sovereignty** A situation in which the exclusive right to exercise legitimate political power is vested in the monarch.
**Total war** A conflict situation in which the whole resources of society are directed towards the prosecution of a war (as in the First and Second World Wars).

## ? Likely examination questions

'The British constitution gives the Prime Minister an enormous range of powers, which are highly circumscribed by political realities.' What are the constitutional powers of the Prime Minister and what are the political limitations on those powers?

'There is a considerable difference between the way modern Cabinet government works in practice and the constitutional model of how it should work.' To what extent would you agree with this statement?

'The "keystone" of the British constitution.' Discuss the relative merits of giving this title to either the Prime Minister or the Cabinet.

Are modern Cabinets still the 'key decision-making body' of the British constitution?

'The key issues are thrashed out in full Cabinet.' Is this still the case in the modern British constitution?

Outline the main features of the Freedom of Information Act and assess whether or not it is likely to provide a valuable contribution to the development of a more accountable and open government for the United Kingdom.

##  Suggested websites

www.number-10.gov.uk     Downing Street

www.cabinet-office.gov.uk     The Cabinet Office

www.open.gov.uk     Open Government

www.cfoi.org.uk     Campaign for Freedom of Information

##  Suggestions for further reading

Benn, T. (1980), 'The Case for a Constitutional Premiership', *Parliamentary Affairs*, 33: Winter.

Buckley, S. (2004), 'A Student Guide to the Hutton Enquiry', *Talking Politics*, 17: 1, 22–6.

Crossman, R. H. S. (1963), 'Introduction', in Walter Bagehot, *The English Constitution,* London: Fontana.

Foley, M. (1993), *The Rise of the British Presidency*, Manchester: Manchester University Press.

Hennessy, P. (1990), *Whitehall*, London: Fontana.

Hennessy, P. (2000), *The Prime Minister: The Office and its Holders since 1945*, Harmondsworth: Allen Lane.

Hogg, Q., Lord Hailsham (1978), *The Dilemma of Democracy*, London: Collins.

James, S. (1998), *British Cabinet Government*, London: Routledge.

Jones, G. W. (1965), 'The Prime Minister's Power', *Parliamentary Affairs*, 18: Spring.

Kavanagh, D. (2002), 'Tony Blair as Prime Minister', *Politics Review*, 11: 1, 14–17.

King, A. (1985), 'Introduction: The Textbook Prime Ministership', in Anthony King (ed), *The British Prime Minister*, London: Macmillan.

Mackintosh, J. P. (1962), *The British Cabinet*, London: Methuen.

McNaughton, N. (2002), 'Prime Ministerial Government', *Talking Politics*, 15: 1, 12–14.

Rathbone, M. (2001), 'The Freedom of Information Act', *Talking Politics*, 13: 3, 165–70.

Rose, R. (1989), *Politics in England: Change and Persistence*, London: Macmillan.

Rush, M. (2000), 'Royal Commission on the House of Lords (the Wakeham Report) (Cm.4534, January 2000) A Summary', *Talking Politics*, 13: 1, 35–9.

Seldon, A. (ed.) (2001), *The Blair Effect: The Labour Government 1997–2001*, London: Little, Brown.

Smith, M. (1999), *The Core Executive in Britain*, London: Macmillan.

Thomas, G. (1998), *The Prime Minister and Cabinet Today*, Manchester: Manchester University Press.

Thomas, G. (2002), 'Prime Minister and Cabinet', *Politics Review*, 12: 4, 22–5.

# CHAPTER 3

# The Judiciary

## Contents

## Overview

The neglect of the judiciary in many politics syllabuses at pre-degree and undergraduate level encourages the widespread impression that it has no substantial constitutional role. This is most unlike the situation in the USA, where the Supreme Court has the fundamental task of interpreting the actions of the legislature and the executive in the light of America's written constitution, and ruling those actions invalid that do not conform with it. Britain has no such written constitution with its accompanying entrenched rights so it is usually assumed that here the judiciary has no comparable political and constitutional role. This assumption is nowadays inadequate.

In recent years, the judiciary has begun to play a quasi-constitutional role in that governmental decisions have increasingly been the subject of 'judicial review', and struck down if found unsatisfactory according to judicial criteria. This process is likely to develop further now that the European Convention on Human Rights (ECHR) has been incorporated into UK law, expanding the criteria for assessing both legislation and executive action on their compatibility with the constitution.

## Key issues to be covered in this chapter

- In what senses can the judiciary be said to be (a) subordinate to the legislature, and (b) independent of the executive?
- What is meant by the term 'judicial review' and how has its development impinged on the relationship of the judiciary with other branches of government?
- How might the incorporation of the European Convention on Human Rights into British law enhance the constitutional significance of judicial review?
- It is widely believed that the constitutional role of the judiciary will become more significant in the near future. Why is this and how desirable is it?
- What constitutional confusions arise from the various roles of Lord Chancellor, Attorney General and Home Secretary? How might these be resolved?

## The judiciary and the relationship between the citizen and the state

British courts and judges have a very important role – perhaps more important in some ways than under a written constitution – in establishing the proper legal basis for the relationship between citizens and the state. The absence of a written constitution and an **entrenched** Bill of Rights, combined with the convention-based nature of Britain's constitutional arrangements, give British judges a central role in determining, by their judgements, the boundaries and limits to this relationship. This judicial role is less important in a written constitutional system, such as that of the United States, which makes clear what rights citizens possess and what powers the state has over the citizen. Despite the lack of a written constitution, the UK has legislation, for example, on devolution, freedom of information and on human rights that in other countries constitutes part of a written constitution: a very important constitutional role for judges exists, therefore, in interpreting this legislation.

The judiciary is said to be subordinate to the legislature in that judges cannot override laws passed by Parliament (in strict legal terms, the 'Queen-in-Parliament') on the grounds that they are unconstitutional, unethical, unwise or for any other reason. This principle is underpinned by the constitutional doctrine of parliamentary sovereignty, effectively established by the **Bill of Rights** (1689). The Human Rights Act 1998, for example, gave judges powers to rule legislation as incompatible with the Act, but judges were not given the power to strike such legislation down.

The judiciary is not, however, subordinate to the government. Courts can and do exercise the right to interpret legislation and to adjudicate on the actions of ministers to determine whether or not they conform, in their policies and exercise of their powers, to the law. The courts can thus decide whether ministers have acted outside the powers granted by statute (ultra vires) and can quash their actions if that is the case. Some recent examples are: Tameside Education Authority vs. Secretary of State for Education (1976) over comprehensive education plans; Greater London Council vs. Bromley Borough Council (1982) over the GLC's 'Fares Fair' public transport subsidy; Michael Howard, Home Secretary in the 1990s, was regularly subject to embarrassing defeats in the courts over the rights of asylum seekers and his attempts to refuse them residence in the UK. The late Lord Denning, former Master of the Rolls, was fond of quoting Edward Coke, Lord Chancellor under James I, to government ministers: 'Be ye ever so high the law is above you.'

During the 1980s and 1990s there was a huge increase in the number of cases where the courts exercised their rights of **judicial review**, so that there are now over 3000 cases per year. There has also been an extension of the type of law reviewed, which now includes prerogative powers as well as statute. Most remarkably, the grounds for such review have been enlarged and now include illegality, procedural impropriety and irrationality. The last mentioned is the most interesting. In the GCHQ case in the 1980s, when the legality of the government's banning of trade unions in high-security government installations was challenged, a senior judge, Lord Diplock, ruled that a decision was 'irrational' if it was 'so unreasonable that no reasonable authority could come to it'. This ruling potentially could give the courts very wide powers of interpretation indeed, but so far few cases have been upheld on this basis.

**Pressure groups** have become inclined to go to the courts as part of their campaigning. They challenge the legality of ministerial actions in relation to their cause, by seeking a ruling that the relevant minister does not have the powers to act in a way that challenges or impedes economic interests, or political or social cause. Alternatively, such groups will attempt to get the minister to implement powers in Acts that he/she is choosing to resist for political reasons. Recourse to law as a supplement to the more usual forms of political pressure and lobbying entails the possibility of forcing a minister to take action.

Pressure groups may attempt to interpret the apparently straightforward ground of 'illegality' to get the courts to stretch the term to include the idea that, in the exercise of lawful authority by a minister, irrelevant considerations were involved, or relevant ones were excluded. 'Procedural impropriety' is often claimed by campaign groups in court to apply to cases where 'natural justice', including the right to a fair hearing, has been infringed by a minister or a public body. Courts have, it appears, gradually moved into legal and political territory, and even that of national security, all of which were once regarded as excluded from their jurisdiction.

## Judicial activism

The ever-expanding role of the judiciary has become known as 'judicial activism'. It has been fuelled by several factors including:

- The tendency of legislation since the 1980s to give ministers very extensive powers to exercise at their own discretion.
- The preoccupation governments have with accountability, which has resulted in a large rise in the number of mechanisms for the oversight of public services, such as the National Audit Office. Agencies known as **Ombudsmen** have been established to deal with grievances from the public, such as the Health Service Ombudsman and the Prisons Ombudsman. Benchmarks, setting out standards of service citizens can expect, have been established for public services, such as the 'Citizen's Charter'. Numerous inspectorates have been created, such as **Ofsted** in education, and regulatory bodies set up, like **Ofwat** for water companies, **Oftel** for telecommunications and **Ofgas** for the gas industry.
- European Union law now takes precedence over British law. Consequently, the courts have to determine whether British law is incompatible with European law. Following a decision of the European Court of Justice, in the 'Factortame Case' in 1990, superior British courts can even suspend the application of British law until the case in question has been resolved in the European Court. The subsequent decision by the European Court of Justice to quash sections of the Merchant Shipping Act 1988, which legislated for UK-registered fishing boats to be 75 per cent British-owned and 75 per cent crewed by British residents so as to prevent other EU fishing fleets from registering in Britain to get access to the UK's fishing quotas, is a classic demonstration of the principle of the precedence of EU law over British law (see Box 3.1 on the Europeanisation of the British judiciary).

It would be a mistake to exaggerate the impact of 'judicial review' as a means of redressing the grievances of citizens. The procedure is expensive, and will probably become even more inaccessible to the ordinary citizen when changes in the legal aid system intended to reduce its costs make claims for legal aid more difficult to obtain. Judges vary widely in their attitudes to judicial review and even when

## Box 3.1 The Europeanisation of the British judiciary

The European dimension has become progressively more important in court cases in the UK. For example, British judicial decision-making has been influenced by the principle of 'proportionality', by which an action can be challenged on the grounds that the legal powers granted to a minister or public body have been exercised excessively. While being a commonplace in continental law, the proportionality principle has so far had a limited use in the UK; it has been used here mostly by plaintiffs intending to support their claims of 'irrational' decision-making by government officials.

The 'europeanisation' of the judiciary is likely to develop substantially as a result of the incorporation into British law of the European Convention on Human Rights, with European case law being likely to have a growing influence on the decisions of British judges. Moreover, although not part of the European Union, the European Convention on Human Rights and its associated legal institution, the European Court of Human Rights, have been framed by the same European Roman legal tradition as the European Court of Justice. Besides, many British judges and lawyers now have experience of working within the European legal framework and this is likely to influence them in future decisions. As British and European legal integration grows, so will the number of British legal practitioners who have been influenced by involvement in European legal culture.

cases do get to the courts, rulings against the executive are rare because the minister has usually been correctly advised by departmental lawyers. The Law Lords upheld the Conservative government's right to prohibit trade unions at its GCHQ intelligence-gathering site in 1984 as being within its legal powers, as its law officers had originally advised.

## Judicial review and judicial independence

From a constitutional perspective, judicial review has frequently brought the judiciary into conflict with the executive and raises the question of the supposed independence of the judiciary.

This issue has become even more salient with the incorporation of the European Convention on Human Rights into British law as the

Human Rights Act, which took effect in 2000. Under the Act, basic rights and freedoms will be guaranteed and government decisions (including those of public bodies such as the police, the NHS and the courts, as well as central and local government) are open to legal challenge. These rights and freedoms include the right to life; freedom from torture, slavery, arbitrary arrest and detention; the right to a fair trial; freedom from retrospective penalties; the right to privacy and family life; freedom from discrimination; and rights to education, the peaceful enjoyment of property and free elections. Several are itemised in Table 3.1.

The fact is that most of these rights are not given absolute protection under the Convention; the state may interfere with them 'if necessary to protect a democratic society' and they must be 'proportionate' to the situation under review. Judicial review is likely to become more important as a consequence of the Human Rights Act. One could envisage a wide range of issues relating to the 'right to life'; for instance, health care of the disabled, or the use of force by the police and the prison service. The courts also have to adjudicate in cases where rights clash, for example, the right to privacy and the right to free expression.

There has been much disquiet over the impact of the European Convention on Human Rights and the Human Rights Act on the judicial process. In 2004 the Conservative Shadow Home Secretary, David Davis, stated that between 1975 and 1996 the Convention was considered in 316 cases, affecting the outcome of just sixteen, while between October 2000 (when the Act came into operation) and April 2002 it was considered in 431 cases and affected the outcome of 318. This figure has to be put into the context of over 200,000 court cases heard every year. Arguably, though, human rights claims have become more difficult to achieve in recent years because of the reduction in legal aid. Parliament's Joint Committee on Human Rights was pessimistic in its 2003 report on the impact of the ECHR: 'We have not found evidence of the rapid development of awareness of a culture of respect for human rights and its implications throughout society.'

Despite doubts, it cannot be denied that some court cases have had major implications: for example, in 2002 a young woman conceived by sperm from an anonymous donor won the right to know the identity of her father. This ruling was based on Article 8 of the Human

## Table 3.1  The European Convention on Human Rights: selected contents

| | |
|---|---|
| Article 2 | The right to life |
| Article 3 | Prohibition of torture |
| Article 4 | Prohibition of slavery and forced labour |
| Article 5 | Right to liberty and security |
| Article 6 | Right to a fair trial |
| Article 7 | No punishment without law |
| Article 8 | Respect for private and family life |
| Article 9 | Freedom of thought, conscience and religion |
| Article 10 | Freedom of expression |
| Article 11 | Freedom of assembly and association |
| Article 12 | Right to marry |
| Article 13 | Right to effective remedy |
| Article 14 | Prohibition of discrimination |
| Protocol 1 | Article 1 – Protection of property |
| | Article 2 – Right to education |
| | Article 3 – Right to free elections |
| Protocol 6 | Abolition of the death penalty |

Rights Act which guarantees respect for family and private life as well as the right to form a personal identity. Using the same Article, a couple who had adopted an 'unmanageable' boy successfully sought compensation from officials who had failed to inform them adequately of the child's behavioural problems. In a case involving the model Naomi Campbell in 2004, her right to privacy from press investigations into her fight against drug addiction was confirmed by a court ruling. Another judicial decision granted a gay couple equal rights as husband and wife in the inheritance of tenancy rights.

It appears that the scale of judicial review and the shifting relationship between the courts and the executive constitute a radical constitutional advance. To accommodate this magnified role of the judiciary in political issues, two proposals for change have been made: firstly, that a 'Human Rights Commission' should be created to drive forward appropriate cases and encourage a culture of human rights protection by government to the extent that recourse to the courts would be rare; and secondly, the relationship of the courts to the rest of the political and administrative system should be redefined in a further constitutional document (or even a full-blooded written constitution).

The present government has shown little interest in either proposal. This is regrettable as, even under the system before the ECHR, tension between the judicial and executive branches of government was considerable, to the point where in the 1990s the judiciary appeared almost as an unofficial opposition to the government. A series of well-publicised cases took place in which the courts held the government to be acting unlawfully, the Home Office being judged the main culprit. (The issues ranged widely, involving criminal injury compensation, rail privatisation and asylum seekers.) The Home Secretary at the time, Michael Howard, who was concerned with the above cases, had more interventions overturned by the judiciary than any previous holder of the office. In the James Bulger murder case in 1996 he attempted, for example, to overrule the trial judge's sentence, only to be overruled himself by the High Court.

The quasi-judicial position of the Home Secretary has led to considerable controversy. Jack Straw, when Labour Home Secretary (1997–2001), decided against releasing the notorious 'Moors Murderer', Myra Hindley, after she had served over thirty years in prison. The Hindley case raised a number of issues about the role of the Home Secretary and the powers of this office to influence sentencing. Firstly, issues of justice: Hindley had served twice the sentence of a 'life prisoner' for murder; Straw unilaterally extended her sentence to 'life meaning life'. Secondly, political factors clearly affected the decision of the Home Secretary as Straw, like his predecessors in the office, did not want to incur public and tabloid newspaper wrath by releasing 'Evil Myra'. Some advocates of Hindley's release argued, as a consequence, that her continued imprisonment was tantamount to a form of political incarceration and contrary to the ECHR. However, attempts to test Straw's decision in the courts never came to pass as Hindley died in prison in 2003.

A second politico-legal controversy involving Jack Straw and his powers as Home Secretary is the case involving attempts to extradite the Chilean ex-President, General Augusto Pinochet, to Spain to face charges of murder and torture (1998–2000). Here, the Home Secretary used his powers to confirm the decision of the Law Lords that Pinochet should be extradited. Nevertheless, he could have ignored the Lords' decision in such a case on the grounds of 'national interest', which clearly involve political calculations about the UK's relations with Chile, Spain, and the much-vaunted 'ethical foreign policy' of the Labour government.

Since 1997 tension between the judiciary and the executive has persisted. Jack Straw's successor as Home Secretary, David Blunkett (2001–4), followed on with a robust attitude to law enforcement. He collided repeatedly with the courts, whose 'leniency' he blamed for undermining his efforts to suppress crime, and to deport illegal immigrants. Paradoxically, the Joint Council for the Welfare of Immigrants asserted in 2004 that such cases had been treated not leniently, but in a more draconian fashion in recent years.

Conflict between the courts and the Home Secretary is likely to continue under Charles Clarke, Blunkett's successor. The decision by the Law Lords in December 2004 that the incarceration of foreign terrorist suspects without trial was illegal provoked Mr Clarke into proposing changes to the law that would effectively introduce house arrest for foreign and British terrorist suspects and their families and friends. One can expect many future clashes between the courts and the government over this law.

## The separation of powers

The separation of powers principle, which is a characteristic of the US constitution, by which the executive, legislature and judiciary have separate functions and separate personnel, simply does not apply in the UK, as far as the upper reaches of those institutions is concerned.

It is true that the judiciary is independent in the sense that judges are not elected (as they are in some American states) but appointed, and these appointments are not made on political criteria. Moreover, a citizen brought before the courts can be assured of a fair trial in the sense that the executive will not suborn judges. The judiciary, executive and legislature are closely interwoven. For example, key personnel – notably the Lord Chancellor, the Attorney General and the Solicitor General (and their equivalents in the Scottish legal system) – are members of the executive and legislature, as well as of the judiciary; and the executive directly appoints senior judges. There is considerable tension within the British constitution over the actual workings of the separation of: powers tension that can be illustrated by reference to a number of high-profile clashes between the Lord Chief Justice and the Home Secretary.

Lord Chief Justice Woolf placed great emphasis on the role of the judiciary in interpreting the civil rights implications entailed in pending legislation. He has also emphasised the right of judges to comment on the actions of government when reviewing particular civil rights cases and especially the right of judges, rather than the government, to specify the length of sentence appropriate for particular crimes. For example, the 2003 Criminal Justice Act laid down a 'tariff' of a fifteen-year minimum sentence for murder. Lord Woolf, however, issued a statement to the effect that this could be reduced to ten years if the accused pleaded guilty. Home Secretary, David Blunkett, publicly contradicted this, saying that Parliament had been very clear that those convicted of murder should receive minimum sentences ranging from fifteen years to the rest of a person's natural life. In 2004 plans by the government to stop judges reviewing the cases of failed asylum seekers were dropped after public condemnation by Lord Woolf. In one case an appeal by Mr Blunkett to keep in jail a Libyan accused of having links with **al-Qaeda** was rejected, Lord Woolf saying that the prisoner had been held on 'wholly unreliable evidence'. Guidelines issued by his lordship in 2003, apparently advising judges to jail fewer burglars, were greeted by Mr Blunkett with evident fury. Press reports alleged that the Home Secretary had described Lord Woolf as 'a confused old codger'.

This tension between a liberal-minded Lord Chief Justice and a hard-line Home Secretary is unlikely to be eased if the Lord Chief

Justice becomes the head of the judiciary, as proposed by the Labour government. Such friction suggests that the actual separation of powers between the judiciary and executive is less complete than is commonly believed.

It should be noted that tension is not confined to executive–judiciary relations. In November 2004 the Home Affairs Select Committee was highly critical of the Sentencing Guidelines Commission, which suggested a sentence for murder should be reduced if the accused confessed. For some, the uneasy relationship between legislature and judiciary can only become exacerbated, with judges anxious to keep sentencing firmly in their own hands, while MPs are anxious to appease public opinion (and the tabloid press) by defining sentences by legislation.

Writers following in the footsteps of the great nineteenth-century constitutional lawyer A. V. Dicey have frequently asserted that two fundamental principles underlie the relationship of the judiciary to the two other key elements of government. First is the principle that the judiciary is subordinate to the legislature (unlike the situation in the USA), but second it is also independent of the executive.

Theoretically, the Queen appoints the eleven Law Lords (the most senior judges), but in reality the Prime Minister in consultation with the Lord Chancellor chooses them. Other senior official judicial appointments, such as those of Lord Chief Justice, the Master of the Rolls, the President of the Family Division, and the Lords Justices of Appeal, are made in the same way; the lesser judges are appointed by the Lord Chancellor. Such is the Lord Chancellor's authority in these matters that, as the outspoken Judge Pickles once observed, he 'has powers of patronage undreamt of by Henry VIII except that he cannot chop people's heads off'.

## The Lord Chancellor

The Lord Chancellor is a member of the legislature, in that he presides over the proceedings of the House of Lords, where he often takes part in debates and speaks for the government. He is also a member of the Cabinet. This position is no mere formality. Lord Mackay (1987–97) was a significant figure in Margaret Thatcher's and John Major's governments, like the present government's first

Lord Chancellor, Lord Irvine (1997–2003): the latter chaired several Cabinet committees that were concerned with Scottish and Welsh devolution, and played a key part in steering legislation associated with House of Lords reform. The present Lord Chancellor, Lord Falconer, is generally regarded as being politically and personally close to Prime Minister Blair, as was Lord Irvine.

The multiplicity of roles may create a conflict of interest between the position of Lord Chancellor as head of the judiciary and his position in government. This was strikingly shown when Lord Mackay in 1992 put pressure on the President of the Employment Appeals Tribunal to speed up cases. Mr Justice Wood considered such exertion of influence as a threat to the basis of judicial proceedings, which should be in the interests of justice rather than of financial efficiency. Lord Chancellor Mackay was subsequently severely criticised in the House of Lords for interfering in the administration of justice. There was similar criticism of Lord Mackay's promotion of government plans to reform the legal aid scheme. Lord Chancellor Irvine's closeness to the Prime Minister led to media attacks on both him and Tony Blair on the grounds of Irvine's alleged extravagance in refurbishing the Lord Chancellor's quarters at Westminster.

In 2003–4 the government embarked on radical change in the office of Lord Chancellor, the appointment of judges and the creation of a supreme court. Their proposals were embodied in a huge Constitutional Reform Bill, with 111 clauses and 190 pages of schedules, to become law in 2005.

In 2003 Lord Falconer, the Lord Chancellor, became also Constitutional Affairs Secretary, leading a Department of Constitutional Affairs. In January 2004 a 'concordat' between him and Lord Woolf set out the basis of their working relationship, to be eventually enshrined in law. Under it the Constitutional Affairs Secretary was to give up the judicial functions exercised by the Lord Chancellor, such as the authority to sit as a judge and the responsibility of appointing new judges: he would keep his ministerial responsibilities and accountability to Parliament, while the Lord Chief Justice took over as head of the judiciary.

The plan clearly amounted to a de facto separation of the judiciary and the executive. Lord Woolf said the 'concordat' was 'universally endorsed by the judiciary as providing essential protection for the independence of the judiciary into the future'.

Not everyone agreed. The proposal to abolish the office of Lord Chancellor was rejected by the House of Lords in July 2004 by 240 to 208 votes. Lord Kingsland, Conservative Front Bench Spokesman, said, 'The government wish to expunge the office of Lord High Chancellor of Great Britain from our constitution. This office still has a vital role in protecting the rule of law.' Lord Lloyd of Berwick, a former Law Lord, warned 'the task of defining judicial independence in Cabinet is a task of such critical importance that it should be given to a senior judge or lawyer who is a member of the House of Lords and not a politician on his way up the greasy pole'.

Many of the criticisms of the proposals have been inspired by the fear that the Home Office, under a formidable Home Secretary such as David Blunkett or Charles Clarke, would exert undue control over the judicial process.

There has been less controversy over two other major features of the Bill: the setting up of a 'judicial commission' independent of the Lord Chancellor to appoint judges, and a supreme court to replace the Law Lords. While the first proposal has been generally accepted, a select committee of the Lords appointed to examine the issue was divided on abolition of the Law Lords. A supreme court, as proposed for the UK, would not have powers to declare legislation unconstitutional as does the US Supreme Court. However, it would visibly demonstrate its independence from the legislature in that its members would not sit as members of the House of Lords. Lord Falconer, in a Consultation Paper on the Constitutional Reform Bill in 2003, declared that his proposals would 'reflect and enhance the independence of the judiciary'. As to the position of the Lord Chancellor, Conservative peers favoured the office holder's remaining a senior lawyer with a seat in the Lords, though with no judicial functions; the government's view was that, as minister for the courts and the rule of law, he should be called simply 'Secretary of State for Constitutional Affairs'; he need not be a lawyer to sit in the Lords.

Plainly, from a constitutional point of view, these are major changes which have given rise to unease: firstly, the announcement of the abolition of the post of Lord Chancellor was made in 2003 prior to the enabling legislation, and secondly, there was no intention of placing these constitutional changes before the nation in a referendum. This led Lord Woolf, in a speech in 2003, to suggest that 'additional constitutional protection may be necessary'.

## The role of the Attorney General

The position of the Attorney General is even more open to criticism. He is an MP, and, as such, represents a constituency; he is also a government minister and is bound by the conventions of that office, such as collective responsibility. His role is complex: he gives confidential legal advice to the government, may bring (or take steps to halt) criminal proceedings, and bring civil actions in the public interest. In this capacity he is supposed to act quite independently of the government; on the other hand he may represent the government in civil actions, where he clearly acts as a member of the executive.

This confusion of roles has led to a series of controversies when the Attorney General was widely perceived as acting in a political capacity rather than a judicial one. For example, in 1987 the then Attorney General, Sir Patrick Mayhew, sought to suppress the publication of Peter Wright's book, *Spycatcher*, about his experiences in MI5 in the early 1980s; he also refused to prosecute MI5 and RUC officers for conspiracy to pervert the course of justice in the 'Stalker Affair'. Here a senior police officer, John Stalker, Deputy Chief Constable of the Greater Manchester Police, was investigating claims of the existence of an RUC and army 'shoot to kill' policy in their struggle with republican terrorism in Northern Ireland. He was mysteriously removed from the investigation, amid allegations made about his supposed association with known criminals at social events. It is widely believed this disparagement was a consequence of his discovery of evidence incriminating the security forces. Sir Patrick told Parliament that, in spite of evidence, the public interest and 'particular considerations of national security' meant there would be no prosecutions of implicated members of the army, RUC or the intelligence services. (Sir Patrick Mayhew, significantly enough, became Northern Ireland Secretary in the early 1990s.)

The most severe criticism of an Attorney General was made by the report into a tangled affair involving allegations of government complicity in illegal arms sales to Iraq during the 1980s. The legal system, it was claimed, had been misused by the government so as to expose three directors of Matrix Churchill, a Coventry-based machine tools company, to the danger of unjust conviction for their company's part in the sales. The report by Lord Chief Justice Richard Scott in 1996 severely criticised the Attorney General, Sir Nicholas Lyell, at the time of the affair for a 'fundamental misconception of the law' in his advice to ministers. Although the 'Scott Report', as it came to be known, did not explicitly say so, it is hard to avoid the conclusion that the confusion of the political and legal roles of the Attorney General played a part.

The tension between the role of legal advisor to the government and membership of that self-same government was vividly apparent immediately before the attack on Iraq in 2003. Consulted as to the legality of the proposed invasion, the Attorney General, Lord Goldsmith, adjudged it to be 'lawful' (the grounds for this decision were never made clear to the public). It was a judgement of critical importance, since the entire moral, legal and political case of the government depended on it. Subsequently there were calls for the resignation of the Attorney General on the grounds that his decision was presumably based on intelligence reports later exposed as inaccurate.

Revelations that Lord Goldsmith's advice (presented on a single sheet of A4 paper) was delivered after he had attended a private meeting with two of Mr Blair's senior confidants, Lord Falconer and Downing Street aide Baroness Morgan, prompted speculation that they had 'pressurised' Lord Goldsmith to change his mind and legally approve the war after he had initially warned that attacking Iraq could be against international law.

●●●●●●●●●●●●●●●●●●●●●●●●●●●●●●●●●●●●●●●●●●●●●●●●●●●●●●●●●●●●●●●●●

## ✓ What you should have learnt from reading this chapter

- Developments relating to the judiciary raise the question of whether or not Britain is evolving towards something like the American model, with its formal separation of powers, its Bill of Rights, its Supreme Court, and a political process and culture in which the judicial system plays a crucial part. In the USA the judicial system has actually played a key role in bringing about social and political reforms, via court judgements, on issues that legislators have been unwilling to tackle, for example, civil rights and abortion.

- On the one hand, we are witnessing intensifying 'judicial activism', incorporation of the ECHR, fast-fading parliamentary sovereignty, the intensifying influence of European legal attitudes, and proposals for a Judicial Appointments Commission. On the other hand, there are crucial differences from a written constitution, which would delineate the role of the judiciary and which would form the basis of the Commission's decisions. On balance the evidence suggests that we have not yet reached the situation existing in the USA.

- Assessing some of the benefits, the question arises as to whether we should emulate America. A powerful argument against accepting that model is that through the transference of as much power to the judiciary as has already occurred, authority has significantly moved from a democratically elected, representative Parliament to a self-perpetuating legal elite, of conservative (and Conservative) outlook, drawn from a narrow social spectrum. (Of the seven Law Lords who adjudicated in the case of General Pinochet in 1999, for example, all were white, male, over sixty and educated at Oxford or Cambridge, and all but one were public school educated.)

- In any event, it might well be argued, the development of constitutionally independent judicial bodies with a role analogous to the American Supreme Court would require a written constitution for them to be viable. A more immediately realistic goal might be the restructuring of the complex arrangements involving the Home Secretary, Attorney General and Lord Chancellor, with a reallocation of their functions. So, for example, the Lord Chancellor's extensive fiefdom would be scaled down, with the Home Secretary concentrating on a 'Minister of the Interior' function, and the Attorney General becoming, in effect, 'Minister of Justice'. Such rationalisation would make practical sense and be more attuned to emerging constitutional and political realities.

## Glossary of key terms

**Al-Qaeda** An extremist Islamic terrorist organisation, led by Osama bin-Laden, to which many atrocities have been attributed, most notably the attacks on the United States on 11 September 2001.
**Bill of Rights (1689)** A statement of the rights of Parliament, accepted by the monarch, which limited the monarch's prerogative powers.
**Entrenched/entrenchment** Institutions or rights embodied in a constitution are 'entrenched' if a special procedure is in place for their removal or alteration. The Human Rights Act, for example, is not entrenched, in that it can be altered or abolished by a simple passage of legislation by the usual parliamentary procedures.

**Judicial Review** The mechanism by which the courts oversee public officials and institutions in the carrying out of their duties. Crucially, courts can nullify the actions of ministers and other public officials if the judges deem them illegal.

**Ofgas/Ofwat/Ofsted/Oftel** Regulatory bodies by which the government controls and monitors the prices, service and standards of various public services – Ofgas and gas supplies, Ofwat and water, Ofsted and educational provision, Oftel and telecommunications.

**Ombudsman** A term of Scandinavian origin; adopted originally to define the Parliamentary Commissioner for Administration who investigates complaints of maladministration in public bodies, it now has a wider application, such as, for example, the Northern Ireland Police Ombudsman.

**Pressure groups** Organisations that try to influence legislation, government decisions or public policy without themselves becoming the government. Broadly speaking they fall into two types: economic pressure groups that seek to protect the income and other working conditions of their members, and 'cause' groups that endeavour to change policy on issues which their members believe to be important.

## ? Likely examination questions

'The judges are increasingly playing a constitutional role.' How true and how desirable is this?

To what extent have judges been involved in making decisions on the constitution in recent years? How well equipped are they to carry out this role?

'The fusion of the legislative, executive and judicial functions of government, which characterise the upper reaches of the political system, is no longer tolerable.' Discuss.

'We may not have a 'Supreme Court' on the American model yet, but we are on our way towards it.' Do you agree?

## Suggested websites

www.dca.gov.uk/consult/supremecourt/index.htm   The Supreme Court Issue

www.courtservice.gov.uk   Court Service

www.lcd.gov.uk/judicial/judgesfr.htm   The Judges

## Suggestions for further reading

Foster, L. (2000), 'The Encroachment of the Law on Politics', *Parliamentary Affairs*, 53: 2, 328–46.

Griffith, J. A. G. (1997), *The Politics of the Judiciary*, London: Fontana.

Woodhouse, D. (2002), 'The Law and Politics in the shadow of the Human Rights Act', *Parliamentary Affairs*, 55: 2, 254–70.

CHAPTER 4

# The Debate over a Written Constitution and a Bill of Rights for the UK

## Contents

### Overview

It is important not to confuse the issue of a written constitution with that of a Bill of Rights. So, for example, it is possible, but rare, for a country to have a written constitution without a Bill of Rights. Conversely, it is possible, but even rarer, to have a Bill of Rights without a written constitution.

We will look first at the recent history and the growing demands for the introduction of a written constitution and a Bill of Rights for the UK. Then we will look at the debates over, first, the introduction of a written constitution and, second, the introduction of a Bill of Rights.

### Key issues to be covered in this chapter

- Would the introduction of a written constitution for the United Kingdom provide Britain with better government than at present? If so, in what ways would there be an improvement?
- Why did the first signatory to the European Convention on Human Rights, Britain, have to wait almost fifty years before it was incorporated into domestic law?
- Is the incorporation of the European Convention on Human Rights likely to strengthen the protection of human rights in Britain?
- Have the recent proposals for constitutional reform brought the introduction of a written constitution for the UK closer?
- Is constitutional reform in the form of a written constitution and the introduction of a Bill of Rights really needed?

## The rise of the issue over a written constitution and a Bill of Rights for Britain

Debate over a written constitution and a Bill of Rights began appearing on the political agenda during the 1970s. Until then the British constitution was largely uncriticised. As Anthony Lester in 1985 summarised:

> Only a few decades ago . . . Britain's constitutional arrangements were still generally regarded by the British as a glorious example, to be envied by less fortunate nations, of a flexible and adaptable method of governing a modern democracy with the consent of the governed and with freedom under the law. In the world of the 1950s, even a perceptive and critical student of government and law could have been forgiven for giving our constitution . . . a clean bill of health.

Things began to change during the 1970s: unemployment and inflation rose; devolution became a major issue in Scotland and Wales; Northern Ireland erupted in violence. In 1973 Britain joined the EEC, raising some constitutional issues. The electoral system produced unclear and, to some, 'unfair' results in February and October 1974.

Concern grew about the deleterious impact of powerful pressure groups, particularly trade unions, on the ability of British governments to govern. Trade union power contributed to the fall of the Conservative government in February 1974 and had great influence on the subsequent Labour administration. The fall of the Labour government in 1979 was perceived by many as the consequence of irresponsible trade union power. The unwritten British constitution, without a Bill of Rights, was judged by many, especially Conservatives, as impotent in the face of growing political instability; the aura of constitutional and political decay and decline extended to the condition of individual liberty, apparently also being undermined by inadequately restrained trade union power.

Demand for a written constitution, with or without a Bill of Rights, abated during the early 1980s as Margaret Thatcher's governments demonstrated both the will and the ability to govern in the face of economic crises, trade union resistance, terrorism, social disorder and fears of government 'overload'. Labour administrations under Tony Blair have refused to allow trade unions to return to the political influence they once were able to exert.

From the mid-1980s a series of strong Conservative governments stimulated the reappearance of constitutional change on the political agenda, this time coming mainly from Liberal and Labour thinkers. Strong Labour governments after 1997 have kept the issue of constitutional reform on the boil by both their constitutional innovations and their unwillingness to change some important aspects of the constitution.

The power of the Prime Minister was ineffectively constrained by over-flexible constitutional conventions. An ideologically committed Prime Minister, such as Mrs Thatcher, could use large parliamentary majorities based on a minority of the popular vote to push through radical economic and social reforms. Even Mrs Thatcher's downfall in November 1990 did not end concern over growing Prime Ministerial power. Labour's Tony Blair, after a number of years of relatively weak Prime Ministerial power under Mrs Thatcher's successor, John Major, reasserted the power of the Prime Minister over the government and Parliament. Blair's performance as Prime Minister has ensured that widespread concern over the '**elected dictatorship**' at the heart of the British executive has not gone away.

Conservative suspicion of Labour-controlled councils during the 1980s produced policies that reduced local authority autonomy at the same time as central government tightened its financial and political controls. Demands for devolution grew in Scotland and Wales, where support for the Tories declined, while the Conservative national government continued to centralise in London control over the regions and nations of the UK. Labour's devolution programme successfully created legislatures in Scotland and Wales in the late 1990s, while failing, though not for the want of trying, to re-establish a provincial government in Northern Ireland. Opinion in Scotland and Wales remains divided over whether their respective legislatures have been successes or expensive and largely ineffectual sops to nationalist opinion in those countries. Elected regional assemblies for England now appear to be unlikely after the rejection of the one proposed for the North East in 2004 – chosen as the most likely English region to favour one.

Conservative decline in Scotland and Wales during the 1980s and early 1990s raised the possibility that the UK's governing party could have no MPs in the non-English parts of the Union (this did not actually occur until the Conservative defeat in the 1997 general election). While not strictly a constitutional matter, this political marginalisation of a party claiming British national status and its reduction to little more than a Home Counties rump stimulated questions of its right to bring about constitutional changes in Wales and Scotland should it form a government.

Opposition parties at Westminster were unable to halt or modify Conservative radical economic, political and social programmes during the 1980s and 1990s. The House of Lords appeared to many citizens as a more effective opposition to Conservative policies than Labour and the Liberal Democrats in the Commons. The Labour government has also faced opposition from the Lords to many of its more controversial policies, even after the partial reform of its composition during Labour's first term: further reform of the Lords is long overdue, although the nature of that reform remains controversial.

The continued, if contained, violence in Northern Ireland from the late 1960s until the late 1990s was stimulated in part by bitter controversy within and between the nationalist and loyalist communities in the Province over the correct form of its constitutional status. Conservative and Labour governments strove to find proposals for a constitutional compromise that would meet the aspirations of all citizens in Northern Ireland. Continuing crises in the Province over the progress of the 'peace process' should leave no one in any doubt as to the crucial importance of constitutional issues in this corner of the UK.

A series of lost cases at the European Court of Human Rights indicated a problem arising from the lack of effective domestic legal safeguards of human rights. Until 2000 the UK did not offer its citizens an opportunity to challenge their government over abuses to their human rights in domestic courts. The incorporation of the European Convention of Human Rights into British law (see p. 71) in that year appeared to remove this potential for embarrassment in at least one international forum.

There were rows over the relationship between the UK and the EU, especially within the Conservative party. Membership of 'Europe' was controversial before Britain joined the EEC in 1973. Controversy has been a permanent feature of British political attitudes towards the

European Union: the Single European Act 1986, the creation of a single market (1992), the role of EU legislation, proposed British membership of the Euro (to be decided by a referendum), and the ratification of the European constitution (also to be decided by a referendum, albeit now unlikely to take place) have all stimulated constitutional controversy.

The election of the Labour party in 1997 with a huge majority, and its re-election in 2001 and 2005 alongside a stronger Liberal Democratic presence in the Commons, encouraged those who favoured constitutional change in Britain. The decline of the Conservatives, the party most resistant to constitutional change, has helped Labour's programme of constitutional reform, though this programme is often criticised as a mess of ill-considered proposals; they are thought to be so politically contradictory and such a source of possible conflict that a written constitution may ultimately be required to 'tidy up' the arrangements.

## Written constitution

### The debate over the introduction of a written constitution for the UK

A written constitution is a rather alien concept to the British. While one existed for a while in the 1650s, and many were produced for countries that left the empire in the 1950s and 1960s, the 'flexible', adaptable, unwritten constitution was considered a nearly perfect human institution; in fact, until the economic and political crises of the 1970s the issue of a written constitution for Britain was one that appeared, if at all, only as a short paragraph in politics textbooks.

From then on, constitutional debate included calls for wholesale reform, such as the introduction of a written constitution and a Bill of Rights. Lord Scarman, a leading judge, called for a written constitution and a Bill of Rights in his 1974 Hamlyn Lecture. Two years later the senior Conservative politician Quintin Hogg, Lord Hailsham, in his Dimbleby Lecture pronounced the British constitution 'wearing out' and also advocated a written constitution:

> by that I mean one which limits the powers of Parliament and provides a means of enforcing those limitations by both political and legal means.

The Liberal party stayed committed to a written constitution; although constitutional reform was off the post-1979 Conservative government's policy agenda, pressure for constitutional reform remained. The tricentenary of the **Glorious Revolution of 1688** was marked by the creation of Charter 88, a pressure group committed to wide-ranging constitutional reform (including a written constitution and a Bill of Rights).

The post-1997 Labour government has shown no interest in the introduction of a written constitution. Such a move has been explicitly rejected: for instance, in 2003 when the Lord Chief Justice, Lord Woolf, expressed the need for a written constitution the idea was promptly rejected by aides to Lord Falconer, who was Minister for Constitutional Affairs. Lord Falconer said, 'If we had a written constitution it would be open to judges' interpretation and lead to a clash between judges and politicians.' Lord Woolf had originally believed that 'our unwritten constitution, supported by **checks and balances**, provided all the protection which the judiciary, and therefore the citizen, required to uphold the proper administration of justice'. He now argued that government plans to abolish the position of Lord Chancellor and create a 'supreme court' were disturbing. These expressions of unease by a senior judge suggest that additional constitutional protections of rights may be necessary.

Constitutional reform remains an issue among academics, constitutional reform campaigners and Liberal Democrats – though not voters or most politicians. The issue of a written constitution was given little attention at the last party conferences before the 2005 election, with the predictable exception of the Liberal Democrats.

## Box 4.1  What might a written constitution include?

Should a written constitution ever come to pass for the UK one might suggest that a number of features would be likely to be included, such as the following:

- A statement of the fundamental constitutional principles, ideals and democratic basis of the constitution, and a commitment to human rights and the rule of law.

- A definition of the powers and structures of the different parts of government and their relationship to each other, such as:

    (a) the electoral system; when elections should be called; constituency boundaries;
    (b) the composition of Parliament, such as the number of MPs;
    (c) the powers of Parliament and the respective functions and roles of the Lords and Commons;
    (d) the powers, creation and status of the Prime Minister, Cabinet and civil service.

- How these provisions might be entrenched in the constitution and the procedures for constitutional reform, when required. Entrenchment involves setting up constitutional and legal provisions that would make it difficult for a government to change the constitution without due process being followed. Entrenching the constitution would challenge the concept of parliamentary sovereignty, as currently understood in Britain.
- The respective rights and duties of the state and the citizen. These usually appear in constitutions as entrenched rights, but a written constitution might also include statements of the duties of the citizen to both society and the state.
- The appointment and removal of the head of state, and his/her powers. Few supporters of a written constitution advocate the creation of a republic and the replacement of the monarch with a president. Nevertheless, under the present constitutional arrangements, the monarch's powers are unclear. The danger is always that the 'apolitical' head of state, whether monarch or president, could become embroiled in party politics, although Queen Elizabeth has avoided this. Prince Charles, should he ever become king, might be less successful, given his known controversial views on issues ranging from architecture to education to alternative medicine.
- The powers of the Scottish, Welsh and the English regional legislatures and their relationship with central government should be made clear in a written constitution.

The written constitution would become Britain's 'supreme law': all other legislation would have to conform to its provisions. In addition, some sort of 'supreme court' would have to be created to interpret constitutional provisions and resolve or manage disputes arising from them.

**Arguments for a written constitution**

The lack of interest in constitutional reform among the public and the political and chattering classes does not necessarily rule out the need for it. A written constitution would meet a number of fundamental constitutional concerns that have arisen in recent decades for the following reasons:

- Despite previous flexibility, great political, social, economic and cultural change during the twentieth century has demonstrated the inability of the constitution to adapt. The constitution is largely the product of a nineteenth-century pre-democratic or semi-democratic age, now out of step with a modern mass demo-cracy. A modern society requires a modern constitution and the present one belongs to another age. Essentially, modernisation of government is required and that involves modernisation of the constitutional framework if it is not to become merely part of the heritage industry.

- The archaic nature of the constitution is a factor, and to consti-tutional reformers the main factor, in explaining modern Britain's political and economic decline in world affairs, a decline that has had a damaging impact on British society. Take one element: the electoral system creates huge changes in party rep-resentation in the House of Commons on minor shifts in elec-toral support. There have been, therefore, regular changes in the government which have created inconsistency in government policy; the repeated nationalisation and de-nationalisation of the steel industry from the late 1940s to the mid-1980s may have contributed to Britain's demise as a major steel producer. Furthermore, the system produces governing parties that are over-represented at Westminster. They are able to impose radical programmes with little reference to public opinion, parliamen-tary opposition or the damage they do to the social and economic fabric of the country. This, it is argued, was the case in the Thatcher, Major and, possibly, Blair governments of the 1980s and 1990s and beyond.

- The unwritten constitution provides insufficient and ineffective 'checks and balances' on power. The rise of party politics over the last century or so has weakened Parliament's ability to ensure the executive accountability that supposedly existed in the mid-nineteenth century's parliamentary 'Golden Age'. The rise of 'party government' has concentrated power in the hands of the Prime Minister, with so few constitutional constraints on it that, as Prime Minister H. H. Asquith (PM from 1908 to 1916) said, the Prime Ministership is 'whatever the office holder wants it to be'. A strong PM will increase his/her power by stretching the constitutional provisions of his office; a weak PM will merely inherit expanded constitutional powers. Hence, the growing threat to civil liberties, alternative centres of power and, ultimately, the rule of law posed by the present unwritten constitution.

- The doctrine of parliamentary sovereignty has, to reformers, become less relevant in recent years. It has undergone considerable change since Britain joined the EEC. Principles of European supremacy over domestic law and restrictions on state sovereignty enshrined in the Treaty of Rome, the Single European Act, and the Maastricht and Amsterdam treaties have been accepted by British governments. Indeed, the Treaty of Rome acts as the written constitution of the European Union with consequences for the UK. If Britain adopted a domestic written constitution it would cease to be the 'odd one out' in the EU. A written constitution would also accommodate the proper constitutional relationship of the UK with the EU now that Britain is, in all probability, a permanent member of the European Union.

- Plans for a European Union constitution now seem doomed. If the European constitution were to have been ratified in Britain's referendum on the issue in 2006 (a referendum now abandoned) a paradoxical situation would have existed with Britain having an unwritten constitution within an overarching European written constitution.

- Labour's constitutional experiments are such that it can be argued there will eventually have to be a written constitution. Changes to the European parliamentary election system, the lack of Westminster electoral reform, devolved Scottish and Welsh legislatures, House of Lords reform, Northern Ireland's 'peace process' and the incorporation of the European Convention on Human Rights into British law all have major constitutional implications. These developments have been piecemeal, confused and often ill-considered. All sorts of conflicts are likely to arise. A constitutional convention leading to the creation of a written constitution may ultimately be the only solution to these problems.

### Arguments against a written constitution

Opponents of a written constitution have one major advantage: the status quo. Although there is some disquiet over electoral reform and the '**democratic deficit**' in England as a consequence of devolved legislatures in Scotland and Wales, the present constitutional arrangements have high levels of familiarity and legitimacy among the electorate. In an essentially conservative country a written constitution is seen as being, in the words of Philip Norton, 'unnecessary, undesirable and unfeasible'.

* A written constitution is deemed unnecessary because the present constitution works. Yes, there are defects – all constitutions, written or unwritten, have them – but they are not as serious as the supporters of change would claim. British democracy is relatively healthy. Governments do not always get their own way. The House of Commons is more powerful vis-à-vis the executive than in the 1960s and 1970s. The House of Lords does carry out useful reforming and checking functions. Compared with earlier generations, today's MPs, generally better educated and more professional, are far less likely to be '**lobby-fodder**' than their predecessors. Britain's changing society is probably better served by its 'flexible', unwritten constitution than by a 'rigid', written one.

* Its very adaptability is the present constitution's great strength. Look, so the argument goes, at the major changes in Britain's constitutional arrangements that have occurred during the twentieth century and look at the present reforms. All these reforms have been 'tailored' to meet particular issues, rather than attempting a dramatic and disruptive introduction of a 'written constitution' corresponding to some constitutional 'blueprint'.

* The introduction of a written constitution would be undesirable when governments need maximum manoeuvrability to adapt to events. An entrenched, written constitution would be difficult to reform and mistakes would take years to remove or rectify. The

investment in time and energy required to create a written constitution and pass the necessary legislation would disrupt government business.

- Even should these obstacles be overcome, the introduction of a written constitution would remain undesirable in that it would give non-elected judges an undue influence on political and constitutional issues, which are best left to politicians. After all, if politicians cannot protect the life, liberty and property of the citizen then judges would not be able to do so.

- The undesirability of a written constitution can be assessed on its disruptive impact on an ancient nation. Centuries of steady, sometimes violent but always pragmatic, political and constitutional development would be swept aside and replaced by a written constitution determined by the concerns of the present.

- The fact that constitutional change in the form of a written constitution is not a significant issue makes it an unfeasible option for reform. A new constitution usually follows a major political upheaval. Britain has not been defeated in a foreign war (and so has avoided the need to reform domestic political structures). It has not suffered domestic political upset such as a civil war. Neither has Britain recently withdrawn from an empire, as had the USA in the late eighteenth century, so requiring a new constitutional framework for post-colonial political activity. So none of the usual political conditions for a written constitution exist. Politicians are unlikely to devote time to this issue: there are no votes or political advantage to be gained from campaigning for the introduction of a written constitution or, for that matter, resisting piecemeal, limited reforms of parts of the constitution.

- Finding sufficient time for senior politicians to be involved in a constitutional convention would be a problem. Actually, the former Labour MP Tony Benn in May 1991 single-handedly produced a 'Commonwealth of Britain' Bill, in effect a written constitution, though it was soon defeated in the Commons. If a constitutional convention were successful in agreeing a basic outline and structure – a process that could take years in a modern, complex society – the required legislation would clog up the work of Parliament; other important legislation would have to be postponed, disrupting government business.

Such wholesale reform is not likely in the foreseeable future. However, the introduction of a Bill of Rights for the UK is another matter: it does not, in itself, involve the same degree of disruption as the introduction of a written constitution.

## The Bill of Rights

### The debate over the introduction of a Bill of Rights for the UK

*Rights and Bills of Rights*
A Bill of Rights should not be confused with the Bill of Rights 1689. The seventeenth-century Bill of Rights was passed after the overthrow of King James II (1688): it established many important elements of the British constitution, including the supremacy of Parliament; the reduction of the arbitrary nature of the royal prerogative; the tax-raising role of Parliament; principles of free speech, parliamentary privilege for MPs, and the redress of grievances; and finally, the forbidding of 'cruel and unusual' punishments.

A modern Bill of Rights is a codified set of rights enforceable in the courts. In Britain the debate has been won by the pro-Bill of Rights campaigners. The Human Rights Act 1998 made the European Convention on Human Rights enforceable in British courts from January 2000. It has been a long campaign.

Many modern Western democracies have citizens' rights enshrined in their written constitutions, incorporating such basic political and social rights as freedom of speech, freedom of religion and conscience, the right to a fair trial, the right to free assembly, and property rights. The most famous Bill of Rights makes up the first ten amendments of the United States constitution (1791) (see Table 4.1), guaranteeing many rights that would appear in any modern Bill of Rights:

> Congress shall make no law respecting an establishment of religion, or prohibiting the exercise thereof; or abridging the freedom of speech or of the Press; or the right of the people to peaceably assemble, and to petition the Government for a redress of grievances. (Amendment 1)

## Table 4.1 The American Bill of Rights

**The ten amendments to the Constitution ratified by the end of 1791**

| | |
|---|---|
| Amendment 1 | Freedom of religion, speech, press, and assembly; the right to petition the government |
| Amendment 2 | The right to bear arms and maintain state militias (National Guard) |
| Amendment 3 | Troops may not be quartered in homes in peacetime |
| Amendment 4 | There can be no unreasonable searches or seizures |
| Amendment 5 | Grand jury indictment is required to prosecute a person for a serious crime. There can be no 'double jeopardy' – a person cannot be tried twice for the same offence. It is prohibited to force a person to testify against himself or herself. There can be no loss of life, liberty or property without due process. |
| Amendment 6 | The right to speedy, public, impartial trial with defence counsel, and the right to cross-examine witnesses |
| Amendment 7 | Jury trials in civil suits where the value exceeds 20 dollars |
| Amendment 8 | No excessive bail or fines; no cruel or unusual punishments |
| Amendment 9 | Unlisted rights are not necessarily denied |
| Amendment 10 | Powers not delegated to the United States or denied to states are reserved for the states or for the people |

Some rights would certainly not be included in any British Bill of Rights:

A well regulated Militia, being necessary to the security of a free State, the right of the People to keep and bear Arms, shall not be infringed. (Amendment 2)

Any American can go to court to enforce these rights. The Supreme Court exists to ensure that citizens are protected. Indeed, the USA is not unusual in having a Bill of Rights written into its constitution: France, Germany, Ireland, Australia and Canada all have entrenched, codified documents with human rights written into their constitutions.

Such codified rights, given special constitutional status and enforceable in the courts, are usually described as 'positive rights'. They express what political and social rights a citizen can expect to be upheld in his/her dealings with the state, private organisations and fellow citizens.

Britain did not have any Bill of Rights in this sense until very recently. Indeed, the British political tradition tends to be wary of codified, **positive rights**. Here, there is a concept of **negative rights**, which means that a citizen is entitled to do whatever he or she wants as long as it is not illegal. So, for example, British citizens enjoy freedom of speech, freedom of the press and a right to 'peaceably assemble' (as do Americans). What Britons do not have is a right to slander or libel other people, foment racial hatred, or riot (neither do Americans).

The English liberal tradition, which has influenced American political culture, treats rights, positive or negative, as inherent: they are the citizen's birthright, given by God or nature, and it is the duty of the state to protect them. Even if rights are abused by the state it cannot remove them, as they were not the state's to give in the first place. Thomas Jefferson was speaking as a traditional eighteenth-century English liberal when in 1776 he wrote in the Declaration of Independence:

> We hold these truths to be self-evident, that all men are created equal, that they are endowed by their Creator with certain unalienable Rights, that among these are Life, Liberty and the pursuit of Happiness. That to secure these rights, Governments are instituted among Men, deriving their just powers from the consent of the governed.

In Britain all laws are created in a similar manner and are of equal validity as far as the constitution is concerned. There are no powers of judicial review like those that exist in the United States, whereby a law can be tested against a Bill of Rights and be struck down if it contravenes that 'higher' constitutional law.

The negative rights principle meshes with the 'rule of law' principle. The powers of government ministers, the civil service and local government officers all derive from Acts of Parliament. As a consequence these officials must act within the law. Their powers can be tested in the courts; their decisions struck down if contrary to law. Many cases have been brought to court over the last thirty years; many ministers have been found by the courts to be in breach of the law – so many that opponents of a Bill of Rights believe that citizens are already well-protected against ministerial abuse of power or, more accurately, mistaken use of assumed power.

The conservative tradition in British politics accounts innate rights a political myth. Edmund Burke, for example, argued that only societies could create rights for their people. Thus the only rights that exist to individuals are those created by the rule of law, whether those rights be positive or negative rights.

### Demands for the introduction of a Bill of Rights

There has been since the early 1970s growing concern that human rights were not adequately protected in Britain, or were actually under threat during the crises of recent years.

In 1974 Lord Scarman called in his Hamlyn Lecture for a Bill of Rights and a supreme court. Sir Keith Joseph, a leading Conservative politician, told the Society of Conservative Lawyers in 1976 that the party might introduce a Bill of Rights when next in government to 'define the fundamental rights of the subject to life, liberty and property'. Such a move would do something 'to stem the tide, to change the atmosphere of British politics in a way favourable to liberty'. Conservative politicians and thinkers were very sympathetic to a Bill of Rights during the Labour governments of the 1970s. Lord Hailsham, in his 1976 Dimbleby Lecture, did not regard a Bill of Rights as a panacea for Britain's problems, but thought it might be 'a modest, but desirable addition to the armament of liberty against populist or bureaucratic intrusion and oppression'. George Hutchinson, writing in *The Times* in August 1976, argued that a Bill of Rights would be useful to check the 'excesses of doctrinaire' administrations 'in an era of Labour government'.

By the early 1980s the Conservatives were in government and there was little desire to introduce a Bill of Rights: it never appeared in the

Conservative party's election manifesto. Advocates of constitutional reform and political opponents of the Conservatives made much of this, but accusations of hypocrisy were rejected by the Tories. Firstly, support for a Bill of Rights was always a minority issue in the party. Even Lord Hailsham had only slight interest in constitutional reform, despite his Dimbleby Lecture and book, *Dilemma of Democracy* (1978). More importantly, Mrs Thatcher was not interested in constitutional reform. She believed in political solutions to what might be thought to be essentially constitutional issues and the defence of individual rights and liberties. A major threat to human rights in Britain came, in her view, from the extreme Left: a Bill of Rights as such would not survive a Labour government dominated by extreme socialists.

By the late 1980s and early 1990s there was a wealth of evidence that civil liberties and human rights were under some degree of threat in Britain, often from government itself. The experience of industrial disputes, such as the miners' strike (1984–5), Security Service surveillance of anti-nuclear weapons protestors and environmental campaigners, the infringement of the rights of asylum seekers, and the government's loss of many cases in the European Court of Human Rights all strengthened demands for a Bill of Rights.

Real change became possible with Labour Leader John Smith's lecture 'A Citizen's Democracy' (March 1993), in which he called for the introduction of a Bill of Rights:

> The quickest and simplest way of achieving democratic and legal recognition of a substantial package of human rights would be by incorporating into British law the European Convention of Human Rights.

More ammunition was provided for the advocates of a Bill of Rights in 1995 by the United Nations Human Rights Committee, which administers the International Covenant on Civil and Political Rights. In a report of that year the UNHRC criticised the United Kingdom as a Covenant member failing to live up to the required human rights standards.

Labour's 1997 general election manifesto included a commitment to incorporate the European Convention on Human Rights into British law. A White Paper and the Human Rights Bill followed and became law in 1998, coming into force in October 2000 (although slightly earlier in Scotland and Wales as a consequence of decisions taken by the devolved governments of those countries).

The Convention removes from the political debate what should be included in a Bill of Rights. It identifies, among other things, a right to life and personal liberty (Articles 2 and 5); a fair trial (Article 6); privacy (Article 8); freedom of expression and freedom of information (Article 10); and freedom of assembly (Article 11). The Convention is monitored by the European Commission on Human Rights and has a legal instrument, the European Court of Human Rights. Britain was the first state to ratify the Convention in 1951. Although the European Court of Justice has increasingly interpreted the Treaty of Rome and other EU laws in the light of human rights outlined in the Convention, it is the Convention (which exists outside the European Union and is signed by almost all European states, whether in the EU or not) which is the main instrument of human rights protection in Britain. Since 1966 individual British citizens have been able to go directly to the European Court of Human Rights; however, the great expense involved means that, in practice, most cases brought before the Court are supported by pressure groups wanting to make legal points.

The European Court of Human Rights received many applications from British citizens claiming infringement of their human rights, not because human rights are more abused in Britain than in other European societies, or that the British state was a systematic abuser of human rights, but because there was no domestic legal remedy for citizens who felt their rights under the Convention had been infringed. Over the years Britain has lost cases on internment and interrogation methods in Northern Ireland, corporal punishment in state schools, the racist and sexist nature of immigration controls, the maintenance of union 'closed shop' deals with employers, and so on.

The incorporation of the European Convention on Human Rights into domestic law marked the end of nearly three decades of debate about the introduction of a Bill of Rights into Britain. Charter 88's Andrew Pudephatt welcomed the imminent incorporation in an article in *The Guardian* in October 1997:

> For the first time in our history, ordinary people will be able to challenge abuses of their rights through the British courts. This bill tips the balance of power from politicians to the people.

The main features of the arguments for and against the introduction of a Bill of Rights are discussed below.

## Arguments for a Bill of Rights

The introduction of a Bill of Rights was reckoned by many to be a vital and long-overdue contribution to the protection of civil rights in Britain. With the incorporation of the European Convention on Human Rights into British law as the Human Rights Act many of these concerns have been addressed, or can and will be addressed, improving the overall human rights situation in the UK.

- Many people feared that there existed great and growing dangers to the legal system, the rule of law, parliamentary sovereignty and individual liberty from a number of sources within the British political system. Firstly, the executive-dominated House of Commons, for example, ensures that a government can pass any law it likes, even a law that could undermine basic civil rights. James Fawcett, then President of the European Commission on Human Rights, called for a Bill of Rights for Britain in 1975, declaring that the British executive had more power than in any European country outside the Soviet Union. In particular, the resulting balance between state power and individual freedom in Britain was not a fair one: the citizen was involved in a very unequal struggle with the state. Secondly, tribunals and other forms of control and adjudication that exist outside the formal legal system with its high standards of evidence and legal expertise threatened civil liberties and basic principles of justice. Finally, the grafting of European-style legal systems, especially that of the European Union, onto the British system, undermined the accountability of law-makers to Parliament. A Bill of Rights appeared vital, therefore, as a legal bulwark of the freedom and rights of the citizen vis-à-vis the state.
- Britain would be associated with a strong and growing movement for the protection of human rights if it introduced a Bill of Rights into domestic law, helping to strengthen those elements in British political culture that underpin support for civil rights. All too often the lack of what Charter 88 calls a 'reforming rights culture' in Britain has resulted in an erosion of the rights of accused criminals, asylum seekers, and unpopular minorities.

- In addition, a greater awareness of and support for human rights and civil liberties at home would encourage the development of a stronger body of citizens who were concerned about human rights abuse abroad. This would help human rights groups in Britain influence government more effectively against, for example, arms sales to oppressive regimes in the developing world.

- A Bill of Rights should accompany the creation of devolved legislatures within the UK. Despite the growth of coalition politics in the legislatures of Scotland and Wales, there is the need to protect minority rights under devolved governments. The devolution experiment in Northern Ireland between 1921 and 1972 was hardly a model for human rights protection; had there been a Bill of Rights in Northern Ireland during the Stormont era, it is argued, minority and majority rights would have been assured and decades of conflict could have been avoided.

- Recourse to the European Court of Human Rights is slow and expensive, taking five years on average to get a case heard there: if 'justice delayed is justice denied' this is clearly a problem. The incorporation of the European Convention on Human Rights should reduce delays to justice: there is a limit of six months to take action on any perceived infringement. Action in domestic courts is expensive but, one hopes, somewhat less so than in the Court of Human Rights. The Human Rights Act 1998, which came into force in 2000, still allows an aggrieved citizen to go to the European Court of Human Rights.

- The absence of adequate domestic legal measures to protect human rights has meant that Britain was regularly embarrassed by decisions of the European Court of Human Rights. Indeed, Britain had one of the worst records under the Convention. Having judges make decisions on human rights issues would no more 'politicise' them than at present; as long as strong safeguards for judicial independence were maintained, this should not be a problem for the courts. The Human Rights Act does not assume that judges have the right to strike down legislation that appears incompatible with the Convention, even though they could declare it so in the hope that government would then change the law in line with the decision.

- A Bill of Rights reinforces the means by which citizens can seek redress of grievances. Individuals can write to their MP, organise a political campaign, contact the Ombudsman (via their MP) on issues of maladministration, and test the powers of government bodies in the courts. A Bill of Rights would enable people to test 'principles' of rights against legislation and support the search for justice rather than accept the mere interpretation of the letter of the law.

- The incorporation of the Convention on Human Rights into British law in the form of the Human Rights Act 1998 does not challenge the supremacy of Parliament: it is not a special law. Section 19 of the Human Rights Act states that legislation has to include a declaration of compatibility with the Act. Although the Act denies courts the power to strike down legislation, courts are allowed only to declare incompatibility with the Act and to invite Parliament to take remedial action. The Human Rights Act has been passed by the usual legislative process and, one assumes, could be amended or repealed by any future Parliament, though substantially to alter the domestic version of the Convention, let alone abolish it, would be a clear warning that civil liberties were under threat.

## Arguments against a Bill of Rights

Despite persuasive support in favour, there were strong arguments against the incorporation of a Bill of Rights into British law. It remains to be seen if such warnings will be proved correct by the operation of the Human Rights Act. Opponents of the Act raised many objections to the incorporation of the ECHR into British law.

- The institution of a Bill of Rights would conflict with the British tradition of citizenship rights being effectively protected by law, certainly as well-protected as in any other country. Many nations have Bills of Rights that look very good in a constitution but fail to offer adequate protection: for example, the Bill of Rights did not protect Black Americans from slavery until the 1860s, or ensure their full civil rights until the 1960s, or reduce their high levels of social deprivation in the present day.
- A Bill of Rights, its critics aver, would 'fossilise' a set of rights belonging to a particular time and would become steadily out of step with political, moral and social developments. New rights

would be difficult to add or defunct ones to remove, and they would become out of date and warp social development. One example of this problem can be seen in Amendment 2 of the US Bill of Rights (1791). Gun ownership is the major cause of violent death in American society, but attempts, backed by the majority of Americans, to introduce tighter gun-control laws run up against the 'constitutional' right to bear arms, which was appropriate in eighteenth-century America but seems dangerously archaic in a modern society; this 'right' has so far proved impossible to remove.

- Socialist critics claim that most discussion over a Bill of Rights tends to concentrate on political rights. They are couched in fine words and fine ideals, but mean little if citizens lack economic and social rights, such as the right to work and access to health and education. Without some sort of broader package of economic and social rights, the traditional Bill of Rights becomes marginal to most people.

- 'A Bill of Rights is incompatible with democratic principles' is a view with which the socialists and conservatives often agree. Some of the supporters of a Bill of Rights argue that there is an unholy alliance between the political Left and Right against them. The Right do not want a situation where the power of the police and the nature of immigration legislation are challenged in the courts. The Left do not want a Bill of Rights that might protect private schools from abolition, or forbid the possibility of nationalisation of industries without compensation. A Bill of Rights would become a source of political controversy as groups and individuals became aware of its ineffectiveness or its protection of 'undesirable' rights.

- There is a problem in entrenching a Bill of Rights in the British constitution as presently constituted because no sitting Parliament can bind its successors. Society expects that it is the job of politics and politicians to protect human rights. An entrenched Human Rights Act would not necessarily guarantee the safeguarding of the citizen: if Parliament is too weak to defend human rights, then a legal document is not able to do so. Lord Lloyd, a Law Lord, said in a speech to the House during the passage of the Human Rights Bill in 1997:

The fact of the matter is . . . that the law cannot be a substitute for politics. The political decisions must be taken by politicians. In a society like ours that means by people who are removable. . . . If what we fear is political tyranny, then we must seek to control that by political means.

- Essentially, the danger is that the introduction of a Bill of Rights would be an ineffectual alternative to what is really needed to protect human rights in this country: a reformed House of Commons with greater powers to keep the executive in check.
- The judges constitute a major problem in the opinion of many critics: they are too Establishment-orientated, are drawn from a very narrow social circle, and are too conservative – and Conservative – to be trusted to enforce a Bill of Rights. British judges are trained to analyse and interpret the meaning of the letter of the law and not to interpret what the moral and political framework of the law is intended to achieve. Lord McClusky, a Law Lord, questioned the role of judges in Bill of Rights issues in his 1986 Reith Lectures:

  Why should it be supposed that elderly lawyers with cautious and backward-looking habits of thought are qualified to overrule the judgements of democratically elected legislators? . . . I do not profess to understand it.

- Bills of Rights, usually being statements of general principles, would bring judges into political controversy and would contribute to the dangerous weakening of the authority of the law. The creation of an elaborate and expensive machinery of courts would be needed to enforce a Bill of Rights, which would further weaken the authority of the courts and legal system. Nevertheless, the Human Rights Act now in force does not involve setting up special courts to enforce it.

Critics of the Human Rights Act have not gone away. The Conservatives, always sceptical about anything that appears to have originated from outside the UK, remain committed to reviewing the Act and even possibly repealing it when on return to government.

## Citizens' rights in recent years

The incorporation of the European Convention on Human Rights into British law through the Human Rights Act has certainly had an impact on British life, but grave doubts exist as to its effectiveness in protecting the liberty of the citizen from abuse by the state.

Post-**9/11** anti-terrorism legislation has raised particularly grave concerns about the treatment of terrorist suspects by the government. In 2004 the Joint Committee on Human Rights (composed of MPs and peers) expressed deep concern over the Terrorism Act 2000 (under which thirteen **al-Qaeda** suspects were arrested and indefinitely detained in August of that year; jury-less trials in certain cases were allowed under the Act, as was the right of the state to remove UK citizenship from some individuals). The Terrorism Act has been used by the police to arrest and strip search protesters at an arms fair in London in September 2003 on the grounds of 'reasonable suspicion'; similarly, anti-Iraq War protestors at American bases in Britain have been subject to police action under the Act. The Committee warned that there was 'discrimination [against Muslims] inherent in the Anti-Terrorism, Crime and Security Act 2001 which allowed the indefinite detention of foreign nationals without trial and which involved the government derogating [opting out] from its international human rights obligations'. As they observed: 'Long-term derogations from human rights obligations have a corrosive effect on the culture of respect for human rights.' These concerns were highlighted by the release, without explanation, of one of the detainees in September 2004. The former Labour Foreign Secretary Robin Cook pointed out that during 2003 there were 30,000 raids under the Prevention of Terrorism Act, from which fewer than 100 individuals were charged with offences relating to terrorism.

The government seems anxious to acquire yet more powers. Its Civil Contingencies Act 2004 gave the government extensive new powers in an 'emergency' (defined as 'an event or situation which threatens severe damage to human welfare, the environment or the security of the UK or part of it'). The Act, which conferred on ministers authority to do almost anything once an emergency has been declared is, according to *The Guardian* (January 2004), 'potentially the greatest threat to civil liberty that any Parliament is ever likely to consider'. The radical journal *Statewatch* (January 2004) went further: 'the powers available to the government and state agencies would be truly draconian . . . This is Britain's **Patriot Act**. At a stroke democracy could be replaced by totalitarianism.'

While disquiet over anti-terrorist legislation exists among civil liberties groups and among British Muslims, ministers have been at pains to stress that the nature of the terrorist threat from Islamist organisations is both real, growing and likely to be around for many years to come. Home Secretary Charles Clarke in 2004 claimed that many terrorist plots directed against British targets had been thwarted in recent years; he believed that one should be in no doubt that in the post-9/11 world the lives of thousands are at risk from Islamist terrorism. Government spokespeople see civil liberties campaigners as failing to acknowledge the enormity of the terrorist threat and the need for the government to take strong and appropriate measures to defeat it, even after the July 2005 bombs in London.

A barrage of legislation enacted or proposed relating to crime, social disorder, fraud and illegal immigration has aroused justifiable fears. Between 1997 and 2005 there have been over 600 pieces of legislation relating to police powers. In 2004 the Information Commissioner, Richard Thomas, warned of the danger of 'sleepwalking' towards a surveillance society like the former communist East Germany through such measures as the National Identity Register, the Child Data Register (with extensive data kept on children from birth to 18) and the Treasury's Citizen Information Project. In 2004 the Home Affairs Select Committee expressed fears of a 'function creep' whereby data obtained for one purpose could be used for quite another.

The government has expressed full support for local authorities that vigorously implement **Anti-Social Behaviour Orders (ASBOs)**. In 2004 Police Minister Hazel Blears commended a Greater Manchester Police scheme to 'text' known criminals, 'visit' them in the early hours and send letters to inform them that the police are 'on to them'. ASBOs, their defenders argue, are far less of a constraint on the civil liberties of delinquents than those subject to an ASBO have on the civil liberties of ordinary, decent people affected by their anti-social behaviour.

Notwithstanding this commendation from the government, ASBOs have been severely criticised by such groups as Liberty, the Children's Society, the National Consortium for Sheltered Housing and by the Home Affairs Select Committee. Launched in April 1999, over 4,000 ASBOs had been issued by April 2005. Magistrates have proved quick to grant applications; of nearly 1,300 made by local authorities during the years 2000–4 only thirteen were rejected. ASBO legislation has been further strengthened, and extra funds granted by the Serious Crimes and Police Act 2005. One feature of ASBOs that has caused particular concern is the 'naming and shaming' orders which now accompany them, particularly in the case of children. Certainly some cases have been odd or disturbing; a child with Tourette's Syndrome was banned from swearing in public; a woman was banned from wearing a bikini in her garden or answering the door in her underwear; and another woman was forbidden to hit her brother with rhubarb.

The extent of the 'culture shift' in the direction of universal police powers was emphasised by a consultation document issued in August 2004 and intended as the basis for future legislation. Included was the extension of the right to arrest persons suspected of committing an offence, however trivial (and not just those liable to jail sentences). Fingerprints could be made at any location, covert DNA samples and fingerprints could be taken, and suspects X-rayed without their consent, search warrants could be issued to permit the search of any premises occupied or controlled by a suspect and further powers could be given to community support officers (CSOs). Civil rights groups have expressed unease. Shami Chakrabarti, Director of Liberty, said, 'When you create a broad, unnecessary power there is a danger of arbitrary and racially discriminating abuse.'

Perhaps the most vivid illustration of the perceived change in climate on civil rights has been the government's drive to create a compulsory identity card system for all citizens. Though plans have undergone much modification in the face of pressure group, media and parliamentary protest, current thinking (in early 2005) is that ID cards will become compulsory by around 2009. The government has explained the importance it attaches to this scheme. Home Secretary David Blunkett defended the introduction of identity cards; they were, he claimed, at 'the heart of our work to ensure the UK can meet the challenges of a changing world'.

The Identity Card Bill, put before Parliament in early 2004, provides for a 'biometric' card, with details of fingerprints and irises, and imposes on a plethora of offences heavy fines and even prison. For example, failing to obey an order to register, or giving false information, or not informing the authorities of a change of address all involve penalties. Cards will be linked to a massive computerised database, regularly updated. Citizens who withhold accurate information could be charged with committing a serious offence. ID cards will provide a considerable amount of personal detail, ranging from hospital appointments to benefit claims and tax details, to job records and property purchases. As the Bill currently stands, the Home Secretary will be able to disclose this data to various authorities including the police, Inland Revenue and Customs and Excise. It will also be available to the intelligence services.

The government has argued that ID cards are essential in its campaigns against crime, terrorism and social security fraud; an argument that would be strengthened if the proposed European constitution, which *inter alia* would have opened up Britain's national frontiers, were to be ratified (however unlikely this appears in mid-2005). Critics are not convinced and fear a grave undermining of civil liberties. A spokesperson for No2ID, a civil rights pressure group, has observed, 'Whatever the government says it will use the ID cards for . . . it will end up using them for so much more.' It is still not clear how a national ID card will tackle crime, terrorism and social security fraud. Criminals will presumably create false cards; so will terrorists, or else they will use their own cards when acting as suicide bombers. The projected costs of implementing the complex system will significantly outweigh the savings from reducing social security fraud. Legislation on ID cards was, however important it was supposed to be to the government's fight against crime, fraud and terrorism, one of the casualties of the dissolution of Parliament and the general election in 2005. After the Labour victory, Home Secretary Charles Clarke soon declared that the introduction of an Identity Card Bill would be a priority for the government in the new Parliament.

Suspicion about the government's motives in introducing new national security powers is well-founded. The Protection from Harassment Act 1997, ostensibly to protect citizens from stalkers, has, for instance, been deployed against political protesters. In 2004 the government announced plans to extend the Act 'to make it an offence to protest outside homes in such a way that causes harassment, alarm or distress'; what constitutes 'harassment', 'alarm' or 'distress' were to be defined by the police.

Such developments have led critics to protest that the incorporation of the European Convention on Human Rights into British law has signally failed to protect citizens' rights in practice. The Human Rights Act 1998 is not entrenched; it can be repealed, or amended by the ordinary legislative process. Besides, the only absolute rights it grants are the rights not to be tortured and not to be enslaved. Other rights are substantially qualified. Restrictions can be imposed as '. . . necessary in a democratic society, in the interests of public safety . . . [f]or the prevention of disorder or crime, for the protection of health or morals, for the protection of the rights of others'. A criticism much promoted by the tabloid press is that the Act chiefly benefits greedy lawyers keen to exploit the poor definitions of the rights, such as the 'right to respect private and family life'. A stream of claims under the Act has followed. Serial killer Dennis Nilson, for example, argued that his right to freedom of expression under the Act entitled him to watch hardcore pornography in jail; elsewhere an aggressive beggar banned from the centre of Nottingham won legal aid to argue that her right to freedom of movement had been breached.

In August 2004, following much-publicised cases involving gypsies, asylum seekers and prisoners, the Conservative Shadow Home Secretary announced that a future Conservative government would set up a commission to review the operation of the Human Rights Act, to consider 'all options, including reform, replacement or repeal of the Act'.

The Act has its defenders too, notably the legal profession. Edward Nally, President of the Law Society, has said, 'There have been far fewer claims under the Act than most commentators expected when it was introduced. But there is a greater awareness among public authorities of the need to respect basic principles of human rights.' Similarly, *The Economist* in November 2004 claimed that the Human Rights Act was neither as radical nor as weak as critics and supporters have asserted:

> The Human Rights Act has neither enabled more cases to be brought, nor made them much easier to win, since judges are still obliged to weigh individual rights against the common good.

For some people, at least, the Act has made a major difference. In 2004 a Mr Leslie Burke, a sufferer from a degenerative brain condition, went to court to challenge professional guidelines on sustaining life by artificial feeding and hydration, fearing that his wish to go on living until he died naturally could be overridden. He argued the guidelines would breach his right to life under the Act and he won his case.

The existence of the ECHR has also influenced the content of legislation during its passing through Parliament. In early 2005 the Joint Committee on Human Rights expressed grave concern that some provisions of the Mental Capacity Bill did not conform to the ECHR, notably concerning the provision of food and water to seriously ill patients; the definition of such provision as 'medical treatment' potentially violated their right to life, and their right to freedom from degrading treatment. At the time of writing (early 2005) it seemed likely that these concerns would be addressed in amendments in the House of Lords.

A potential further development relating to human rights legislation is the 'Charter of Fundamental Rights' which is part of the European constitution; signed in October 2004, it is not likely to be fully ratified before 2007. The rights in this document include rights of social security, housing assistance, health care and environmental protection. The rights would not be enshrined in British law, but would be interpreted and enforced by the European Court of Justice. In some ways this Charter might become de facto part of English and Scottish law.

. . . . . . . . . . . . . . . . . . . . . . . . . . . . . . . . . . . . . . . . . . . . . . . . . . . . . . . . . . . . . . .

### ✅ What you should have learnt from reading this chapter

- The debate over a written constitution for Britain has not gone away. The eventuality of a written constitution may still be remote, for the reasons mentioned above, but it might become necessary as the Labour government's constitutional reforms develop.

- The Bill of Rights, however, is now a reality. Since January 2000 citizens and other residents of the UK who feel their fundamental human rights have been infringed or abused are able to take legal action in British courts. Only time will tell whether the supporters or the opponents of a Bill of Rights will be proved correct.

### 🔎 Glossary of key terms

**Anti-Social Behaviour Orders (ASBOs)** A legal procedure to reduce public disorder, such as vandalism, begging, threatening behaviour and other neighbourhood disturbances. Most are granted by magistrates at the request of local authorities if a magistrate is satisfied on a balance of probabilities that the accused's behaviour is 'likely to cause alarm, harassment or distress'. An ASBO is granted as a civil power, but a breach of the order is treated as an offence punishable by up to five years in prison.

**Checks and balances**  Mechanisms that prevent any single branch of government (legislature, executive or judiciary) from dominating the others.

**Democratic deficit**  A term used to describe political institutions that appear in the eyes of critics to lack a full degree of democratic legitimacy as a consequence of inadequate election procedures, insufficient popular support or some other apparent failing of the democratic process.

**Elected dictatorship**  A phrase, first attributed to Conservative politician Quintin Hogg (Lord Hailsham), which implies that once elected the leader of the majority party in the Commons (the Prime Minister) can do more or less what he wants without any effective constraint.

**Glorious Revolution (1688)**  The political upheaval that overthrew King James II and replaced him by William III. It established the King's dependence on Parliament, and so may be regarded as the beginning of a constitutional monarchy in Britain.

**'Lobby fodder'**  A colloquial and pejorative term for MPs who constantly vote in parliamentary divisions as their party requires; the term implies that they make little or no use of their critical faculties in their voting decisions.

**Negative rights**  A term used to describe those civil and political rights that citizens have unless ruled out by law. Until the Human Rights Act 1998, which is a statement of positive rights, negative rights were the dominant manifestation of rights existing in the United Kingdom.

**9/11**  A short-hand term for the terrorist attacks on the United States on 11 September 2001, which killed some 3,000 people and had a profound effect on American domestic politics and foreign policy.

**Patriot Act 2001**  A package of anti-terrorist measures passed by the US government in the wake of 9/11. The Act intensified government secrecy and strengthened the executive, especially the powers of the Central Intelligence Agency (CIA) and the Federal Bureau of Investigation (FBI). Critics regard it as a grave violation of the principles of freedom enshrined in the United States constitution.

**Positive rights**  Political and civil rights that are clearly set down in a legal document (such as a Bill of Rights) and therefore have the protection and the force of law. Such positive rights are likely to include freedom of speech, conscience, religion and assembly, as well as a right to a fair trial. The European Convention on Human Rights is an example of a document enshrining positive rights.

**Soviet Union (the Union of Soviet Socialist Republics – USSR)**  The title of the state, ruled on strict Marxist-Leninist principles, which succeeded the Russian empire after the Bolshevik Revolution in 1917. The Soviet Union was created in 1922 and dissolved in 1991.

## ? Likely examination questions

Outline and assess the major features of what would, or should, be included in: (a) a written constitution, and (b) a Bill of Rights for the United Kingdom.

'A Bill of Rights for Britain is neither desirable nor feasible.' To what extent would you agree with this statement?

Assess the arguments for and against the proposition that British government and the British political system would be improved by the adoption of a written constitution.

Analyse the advantages and disadvantages of the incorporation of the European Convention on Human Rights into British law.

To what extent has the United Kingdom in recent years moved nearer to having a written constitution?

##  Suggested websites

www.liberty-human-rights.org.uk    Liberty

www.charter88.org.uk    Charter 88

www.echr.coe.int    European Court of Human Rights

##  Suggestions for further reading

Benn, T. and Hood, A. (1993), *Common Sense: A New Constitution for Britain*, London: Hutchinson.

Bogdanor, V. (1997), *Power and the People*, London: Gollancz.

Freeman, M. (1997), 'Why Rights Matter', *Politics Review*, 7: 1, 31–3.

Hogg, Q., Lord Hailsham (1976), The Dimbleby Lecture, 'Elective Dictatorship', *The Listener*, BBC: 21 October.

Hogg, Q., Lord Hailsham (1978), *The Dilemma of Democracy*, London: Collins.

Johnson, N. (1980), *In Search of a Constitution*, London: Methuen.

Lester, A. (1985), 'The Constitution: Decline and Renewal', in Jowell, J. and Oliver, D. (eds), *The Changing Constitution*, Oxford: Clarendon Press.

Marr, A. (1995), *Ruling Britannia: The Failure and Future of British Democracy*, London: Michael Joseph.

Mount, F. (1992), *The British Constitution Now: Recovery of Decline?* London: Heineman.

Norton, P. (1992), *The Constitution: The Conservative Way Forward*, London: Conservative Political Centre.

Peele, G. (2001), 'The Human Rights Act', *Talking Politics*, 14: 1, 22–3.

Ryan, M. (2004), 'A Supreme Court for the United Kingdom', *Talking Politics*, 17: 1, 18–20.

Zander, M. (1997), *A Bill of Rights?* London: Sweet and Maxwell.

Zander, M. (1998), 'UK Rights Come Home', *Politics Review*, 7: 4, 18–22.

# CHAPTER 5

# Devolution: Northern Ireland, Scotland, Wales and the English Regions

## Contents

## Overview

Historically, the United Kingdom has been a unitary state, with authority concentrated at the centre. It is true there are local institutions with considerable functions such as local councils but their powers are very strictly subordinate to Westminster. Centralisation of power reached its zenith under the Thatcher governments when the metropolitan county councils and the Greater London Council were abolished (1986). The remaining local authorities were brought under tighter central control (the semi-autonomous government in Northern Ireland had already been 'suspended' in 1972).

This centralisation of power is now being dramatically reversed with the emergence of new institutions in Northern Ireland, Wales, Scotland, Greater London and the English regions. Some commentators have even spoken about Britain's reinvention as a 'federal state'. While it is true that this process is described as 'devolution', implying the delegation of strictly specified powers to bodies ultimately subordinate to central government, such is the scale and rapidity of change that it is apparent that the British constitution is undergoing a fundamental restructuring: with great potential for future political conflict.

## Key issues to be covered in this chapter

- Why was it reasonable, until 1999, to describe the UK as a 'unitary state'?
- How and how far is the process of devolution for Wales and Scotland restructuring the relationships between the constituent parts of the United Kingdom?
- In what ways do governmental structures proposed by the 'Good Friday Agreement' in Northern Ireland involve a unique constitutional experiment?
- How has constitutional change for (a) Northern Ireland, (b) Scotland, and (c) Wales been brought about?
- Is the UK likely to become a federal state?

## Background to devolution

The United Kingdom is a unitary state and not a federal state; but it is also a multi-national state, comprising several distinct nations: England, Scotland, Wales and Northern Ireland. A strong sense of British national identity, shared political and social values, unites most people in the UK. British political parties, for example, fight similar political campaigns in all parts of the UK (with the exception of Northern Ireland, where Labour, the Liberal Democrats and the Conservatives do not, for historical reasons, contest seats). There is, one must make clear, little conclusive evidence that devolved parliaments and assemblies have, in themselves, weakened this sense of Britishness among the peoples of the UK.

Nevertheless, the different devolution plans that have been devised do reflect distinct elements of the national and regional cultures that exist within the UK. In the English regions, for example, there are strong identities and loyalties to counties, cities, towns and villages, as well as to identifiable regions; but there is little desire by the English for regional identity to be expressed in regional assemblies or for national identity to be reflected in an English Parliament. Scottish devolution is clearly an expression of national identity, while also being a means by which nationalist demands for full independence can be defused. Devolution in Wales is an expression of national cultural identity, rather than a move towards independence. Northern Ireland, by contrast, was until the late 1990s the only part of the United Kingdom where a devolved Parliament existed for a significant period (between 1921 and 1972); devolution in the province has always been a factor in seeking a solution to Northern Ireland's constitutional and political problems.

There is no uniform model of devolution applied to all parts of the UK. Each nation has been dealt with separately, with a distinct 'solution' being proposed for each and, where possible, introduced. It is to these different devolutions that we will now turn.

## Devolution and Northern Ireland

### Historical background to the Northern Irish constitutional position

In one region of the UK there has been for the last thirty years – arguably for the last eighty years – a permanent constitutional crisis. There are many dimensions to the Northern Ireland problem but the focal point is the constitutional status of the UK state in the Province.

From the beginnings of the Northern Ireland state in the 1920s a significant section of the population has never accepted the **legitimacy** of its institutions. This minority, mainly Catholic-Nationalist-Irish in their national identity, has felt itself oppressed by both the Stormont government and the British state. A substantial minority of these (Irish Republicans) has never recognised the authority of the British state in Northern Ireland. Some have been prepared to take their rejection as far as armed uprising, aiming at fundamentally reordering the entire constitutional status of Northern Ireland. Armed elements of the majority Loyalist-Protestant-Unionist population have been willing likewise to use violence to defend the position of 'Ulster' as a constituent part of the UK.

The peculiar constitutional status of Northern Ireland within the UK emerged from the upheavals throughout Ireland immediately after World War One. These stemmed from many decades of campaigning, sometimes violent, for and against 'Home Rule', that is a Parliament separate from Westminster for the whole of Ireland, which at that time was part of the UK.

In 1921 the conflict was temporarily ended by a 'Treaty' between the British government and the Irish rebels. Under it Ireland was divided into a 'Free State' in the South, which had only limited links with the UK (for example, the King remained its Head of State), and the six counties of Northern Ireland, which received their own devolved Parliament at Stormont Castle in Belfast.

These six counties eventually became, in effect, a 'state within a state' of the UK; they had their own Parliament, Prime Minister and Cabinet, based on the 'Westminster model', with their own laws, judiciary, police, and educational and social policies. However, Stormont remained a devolved administration, subject to the Westminster Parliament for its powers and even its existence.

This arrangement continued until the mid-1960s, when the situation was transformed with the emergence within the Nationalist community of the civil rights movement. Crucially, the civil rights movement concentrated on a radical improvement in the political rights and social conditions of Catholics, rather than the old Nationalist goal of Irish unification. Furthermore, it sought to achieve these goals by operating within the existing constitutional framework, albeit with the ultimate intention of transforming Northern Ireland from within.

The extremely negative response of the Unionist Establishment led to serious **sectarian** conflict, which reached such a pitch in 1969 that the British government sent over army units to restore law and order. Unfortunately, a combination of political mishandling, army and police brutality and opportunism by Nationalist extremists reduced the Province to virtual civil war. In 1972 the Northern Ireland constitution was suspended, Stormont abolished and 'Direct Rule' from Westminster imposed. Northern Ireland's laws were now made in London, although the Province's parliamentary representation in Westminster was expanded. A Secretary of State for Northern Ireland, with a seat in the Cabinet, acted almost as a colonial governor of that part of the UK.

Northern Irish Unionist politicians at this point found themselves in a strikingly new political and constitutional situation. Before 1972 they had been the ruling political power in a Protestant-dominated Province: now they were a tiny minority of MPs in a British Parliament concerned with many other matters than Northern Ireland. In addition, although Labour and Conservative governments remained committed to the re-creation of some form of devolved Parliament for Northern Ireland, this was to be on the basis only of some form of 'power sharing' by Unionists and Nationalists, and not, as under Stormont, a Unionist-dominated statelet with minimal external accountability and control.

### Constitutional solutions
Early in the conflict British governments recognised that the problem was partly a constitutional one. Improvements to the security position, social measures such as more jobs and better housing, and the elimination of electoral abuses such as gerrymandering, were important,

but a permanent solution would require substantial modifications to the constitutional 'status quo'.

Innumerable solutions were proposed and several attempted; for example, a 'power-sharing executive' in 1974, a constitutional convention in 1976, and an assembly in 1982 were all tried. Nothing succeeded. Many people came to the conclusion that the problem was beyond solution. However, the 'solutions' tried did lead to some interesting constitutional innovations, such as proportional representation (used for the 1982 elections to the Northern Ireland Assembly) and referendums (used to confirm that the Northern Ireland people wished to remain in the UK). These innovations were subsequently to feature in the 1998 Good Friday Agreement.

Perhaps the most remarkable constitutional development was the Anglo-Irish Agreement of 1985 (sometimes referred to as the 'Hillsborough Agreement'). Perceived by the British government as a device to induce the Irish government to take an even tougher line with terrorists operating from its territory, the Agreement included formal recognition by the Republic of the rights of the Unionist majority in Northern Ireland to block moves towards unification. Most importantly, there was provision for the Irish government to have a consultative role in the affairs of the Province by means of a joint authority set up by the Agreement. This component of the Agreement sought to convince Nationalists in Northern Ireland that their interests would be protected by the Irish Republic, being the state most closely identified with Irish national identity. Although it ultimately failed, it was to lead to major developments in the 1990s.

By late 1994 the main paramilitary groups had agreed to a ceasefire. In February 1995 the British and Irish governments issued quite radical proposals, apparently to form the nucleus of constitutional discussions, entitled *Frameworks for the Future*. These were essentially two documents, *A Framework for Accountable Government in Northern Ireland*, concerning devolution based on power sharing, and a *Framework for Agreement*, outlining how the British and Irish governments envisaged the relations between the two states should develop. The key proposal here was for a North/South institution endowed with executive, harmonising and consultative powers that would encourage the development of a political consensus favouring peace in the island of Ireland.

The first stage was an election to a 'Forum', a procedure of extra-ordinary complexity, in May 1996. The Forum had 110 members with five members for each of the eighteen Westminster constituencies, plus elections on a list system for the whole of Northern Ireland, with two seats for the top ten parties. Representatives of the Forum would take part in discussions about the future of the Province. In reality the Forum proved unconstructive: if anything it deepened the political divide.

Labour's election victory in May 1997 reinvigorated the search for a solution, with particular energy being shown by Mo Mowlam (the then Northern Ireland Secretary of State) and Tony Blair, who sought as much inclusiveness of the various political groupings in talks as possible. Seemingly endless wrangling continued, with all manner of strategies, compromises and manoeuvres, until Good Friday 1998 when the seemingly impossible was arrived at – an Agreement approved by Britain, Ireland and (almost) all the political forces in Northern Ireland, which superseded the 1985 constitutional arrangements.

## Box 5.1  The key provisions of the Good Friday Agreement

The key provisions of the Good Friday Agreement were in the form of three 'strands':

### Strand 1

(a) an elected Northern Ireland Assembly of 108 members, elected on a PR system (STV)

(b) an Executive of twelve members, headed by a First Minister and Deputy Minister, with parties represented in proportion to their support in the Assembly. The parties would register, or 'designate', themselves as either 'Unionist' or 'Nationalist'. The Assembly would have full legislative and executive authority over the existing six Northern Ireland government departments, with the possibility of others in future

(c) decision-making in key areas would be on a cross-community basis by either 'parallel consent', in other words a majority of three members present in each of the 'designated identities' (Unionist or Nationalist), or a weighted majority (60 per cent) of members present and voting including at least 40 per cent of each of the Nationalist or Unionist designations. What constituted 'key areas' would be decided in advance of the vote

(d) a committee system for the Assembly, membership being based roughly on party strengths, would be set up. The Assembly would have the right to remove ministers (who would be appointed by their parties), voting on a cross-community basis

(e) the Secretary of State for Northern Ireland would have responsibility for any matters not devolved to the Assembly and would represent Northern Ireland in the British Cabinet.

**Strand 2**
There would be a North/South Ministerial Council 'to bring together those with executive responsibilities in Northern Ireland and the Irish government.' Various topics for its attention were suggested, such as animal welfare, tourism, inland fisheries and teacher qualifications.

**Strand 3**
This concerned relationships between Britain and Ireland, and the various constituent nations of the British Isles:

(a) there would be a British–Irish Inter-governmental Conference, with regular meetings of representatives of the two governments. It would monitor the workings of the Agreement

(b) a British–Irish Council would be set up with representatives of the British government, devolved institutions in Scotland, Wales and Northern Ireland, plus the Isle of Man and Channel Islands and, if appropriate, other parts of the UK. It would have regular meetings in various formats and proceed by consensus.

## Northern Ireland's constitutional revolution

Whatever the future (and at the time of writing it is too early to say), the Agreement is a remarkable one. The most important new features are: a power-sharing executive which would be, in effect, a permanent coalition; formal mechanisms by which the Irish Republic can exercise a measure of authority in Northern Ireland; and the British–Irish Council (the 'Council of the Isles'), which might ultimately lead to a redefinition of the relationship between the nations that comprise the British Isles.

The actual adoption of the new arrangements had to be legitimised. The appropriate legislation in the Dublin and Westminster Parliaments was passed, all the participating groups signed the Agreement, and in 1999 separate referendums were held both north and south of the border, at which the proposals were resoundingly endorsed (Northern Ireland: 71.12 per cent 'Yes' vote on a turnout of 80.98 per cent; Irish Republic: 94.39 per cent 'Yes' on a turnout of 55.59 per cent).

The implication must surely be that if reform on this scale can take place in one part of the UK, more modest proposals for the rest of Britain are no longer unthinkable. Whether the Northern Ireland Agreement is workable is another matter. There is no close parallel in British political experience and the Agreement's success depends on a remarkable degree of consensus in a society where consensus has been strikingly absent.

The Good Friday Agreement since 1998 has not given grounds for optimism. There were grave difficulties in establishing a multi-party executive focusing on the issue of decommissioning Provisional Irish Republican Army (PIRA) weapons. With great difficulty the Ulster Unionist Leader, David Trimble, persuaded his party to accept a decommissioning process under the supervision of the Canadian General John de Chastelain, in November 1999, but slow progress here threatened Trimble's position in his party and thus his role as First Minister. To forestall the executive's collapse, the Secretary of State for Northern Ireland, Peter Mandelson, suspended the Good Friday Agreement structures in January 2000. Complicated negotiations then followed and by June 2000 the institutions were reinstated.

In 2001 Peter Mandelson was replaced by John Reid, who in 2002 was replaced by Paul Murphy and he in turn by Peter Hain in 2005 as Secretary of State for Wales and Northern Ireland. Within Northern Ireland, however, relations between Catholic/Nationalists and Protestant/Unionists deteriorated. Although there was nothing on the scale of earlier years, low-level violence continued. Since the Good Friday Agreement was signed until May 2005, more than 2,000 people had suffered 'punishment beatings' by **paramilitaries**. By 2003 de facto religious segregation of Belfast was almost total. The moderate Social Democratic and Labour Party (SDLP) and Ulster Unionist Party (UUP) lost ground to the more extreme Sinn Fein and Democratic Unionist Party (DUP) (which had not signed the Good Friday Agreement). A Sinn Fein spy scandal at Stormont in autumn 2002 led to Trimble and the Unionists withdrawing from the executive; yet again the devolved institutions were suspended and direct rule from Westminster was restored.

Election results in Northern Ireland confirmed the trend towards political polarisation, making the prospect of a revival of devolved institutions even less likely. In the elections to the European Parliament in 2004 the Democratic Unionist Party confirmed its lead over the Ulster Unionist Party among Protestant voters with a 32 per cent share of the vote, and Sinn Fein similarly overtook the SDLP to be the largest party among Catholic voters in Northern Ireland with 26 per cent of the turnout.

A review of the Good Friday Agreement in June 2004 started badly with the Democratic Unionist Party MEP Jim Alister warning Tony Blair that his party would not work with Sinn Fein 'terrorists'. Efforts to resolve the crisis at a summit of Tony Blair and his Irish counterpart Bertie Aherne, together with Sinn Fein and DUP leaders, came to nothing. By mid-2005 the Good Friday Agreement institutions remained suspended. Whether they will ever be restored is still uncertain.

The crisis deepened with the theft of £26 million from the Northern Bank in Belfast, publicly attributed by the head of the Northern Ireland Police Service to the Provisional IRA; the denunciation of Sinn Fein leaders Gerry Adams and Martin McGuinness as still-active IRA Army Council members by the Irish Justice Minister Michael McDowell; and the murder of Robert McCartney, allegedly by IRA activists, alleged intimidation of witnesses and the astonishing subsequent offer of the IRA to shoot the murderers. In the wake of these events the Westminster parliamentary allowance of £500,000 paid to the four Sinn Fein MPs (who have never taken their seats) was withdrawn.

Sinn Fein's anomalous position with regard to the police was emphasised by the fact that, although Gerry Adams urged witnesses of McCartney's murder to go to the authorities, he himself has given information on this and other crimes, not to the police directly, but to the Northern Ireland Police Ombudsman.

Critics of the Good Friday Agreement have complained that there are fundamental flaws within it, the most serious being the 'institutionalisation of sectarianism' in that parties have to formally declare themselves as Unionist or Nationalist. Moreover, the Westminster model of government and opposition is replaced by a sort of enforced coalition of major parties. This, it is argued, could only work in a context of general political consensus, a consensus which does not exist. It is difficult to see where matters will go from here. Key political figures within and outside Northern Ireland have made a huge personal and political commitment to the Good Friday Agreement, in some cases to the peril of their lives. The referendums of 1999 which confirmed widespread support for the Agreement throughout the island of Ireland have made it difficult to change.

The general election results of 2005 did not augur well for the Good Friday Agreement. The moderate UUP, which had supported the Agreement, suffered severely at the polls: it retained only one MP in Westminster (even John Trimble, the party leader, lost his seat), while the DUP won nine seats on 39 per cent of the Northern Ireland poll. Republican Sinn Fein, with five seats, gained substantially at the expense of the moderate nationalist SDLP, with three MPs, to become the second-largest party in the province (Sinn Fein will continue to boycott Westminster because they refuse to swear an oath of allegiance to the Queen). This polarisation of opinion implies that the Good Friday Agreement and the entire 'peace process' is in great difficulty.

Optimists suggest that, having reached bottom, there is nowhere else to go but up: the more extreme parties have won – the electorate cannot go further to the Right or Left. In this circumstance Sinn Fein and the DUP will out of necessity develop some sort of unenthusiastic co-existence leading to limited but growing co-operation. There will be some kind of cosmetic 'renegotiation' of the Good Friday Agreement, as the DUP demands, and paramilitary weapons will simply 'rust in peace', while life in Northern Ireland slowly normalises. This may be the best that can be hoped for, although the announcement by the IRA in September 2005 that substantial amounts of its weapons had been destroyed raised hopes that one should not be overpessimistic about Northern Ireland's future.

## Devolution and Scotland

### Historical background to Scottish devolution

The constitutional relationship of Scotland to the rest of the United Kingdom has had a rather complex history. English attempts to conquer Scotland in the late Middle Ages ultimately failed and

Scotland remained independent of England until 1603 when, on the death of the childless Elizabeth I, James VI of Scotland succeeded to the English throne as James I. Scottish and English destinies were further entwined by the civil wars of the mid-seventeenth century. In 1707 the Scottish Parliament was persuaded to amalgamate with the Westminster Parliament in the 'Act of Union'. That this was scarcely a marriage of equal partners was illustrated when, after the unsuccessful Jacobite rebellions of 1715 and 1745, Scotland was in effect placed under English military rule. The integration of Scotland into the 'United Kingdom' was consolidated over the next two centuries by the industrial revolution, migration of Scots to England and Ireland (and by the Irish into Scotland), by the development of the British Empire and two world wars.

Integration was, however, far from complete. Despite losing or, one might say, sharing its sovereignty within the UK state, Scotland retained many distinct attributes of nationhood. It maintained its own legal system, local government, educational arrangements, its own paper currency, and a strong sense of national identity and distinctiveness from its larger southern neighbour. Although the body that legislated for Scotland was the Westminster Parliament, and the key decision-making remained with the British Cabinet, much administration was, in the 1960s, devolved to a 'Scottish Office' that dealt with education, agriculture, policing, prisons, economic development, and so on.

The Scottish Office was headed by a Cabinet-level minister, the Secretary of State for Scotland. There were other concessions to Scotland's special status; for example, at the committee stage, legislation applicable only to Scotland went to the Scottish Grand Committee of the House of Commons, and in the Commons itself Scotland had far more MPs than its population size would warrant.

Until the 1970s there was, outside the political fringe, little challenge to these arrangements. By October 1974, however, the Scottish Nationalist Party (SNP), claiming new-found North Sea oil to be 'Scottish', and arguing that its revenues should be spent in Scotland, won eleven seats in the Commons on 30.4 per cent of the popular vote. In the same election the Liberal Party, which had also done well in Britain as a whole, was firmly committed to Scottish devolution. As the then Labour government had a knife-edge majority (which by 1976 had slipped to a minority) it was reluctantly forced to take Scottish devolution seriously. In return for the support of Welsh and Scottish nationalist MPs a Bill was presented in 1978 by which Scotland was to have its own elected Assembly, with an executive drawn from it, responsible for such matters as had previously been within the remit of the Secretary of State and his fellow Scottish Office ministers. To take effect the Bill would depend on a referendum in which 40 per cent of the Scottish electorate (and not simply those voting) would have to express their approval. In the event only 32.9 per cent did so and the project collapsed.

The incoming Conservative government in 1979 had no sympathy with Scottish devolution. Nonetheless, events during the Thatcher governments had a profound effect on Scotland. Economic policies aimed at reducing inflation hit employment in Scottish regions and cities dependent on heavy engineering, steel, shipbuilding and coal mining. The introduction of the poll tax in Scotland, a year ahead of its introduction in England, caused bitter resentment and was represented by nationalist opinion as an example of Scotland's essentially colonial status. Margaret Thatcher, in particular, was perceived as a very English politician pursuing exclusively English political interests. By the early 1990s there were considerable political repercussions: in the 1992 general election the SNP won 21.5 per cent of the popular vote and Conservative representation in Scotland remained weak with only eleven MPs out of the seventy-two.

By 1996 Labour's internal divisions on the devolution issue, which had hampered the 1979 campaign, had mostly faded. The SNP had become more sympathetic to devolution, if only as a first step to outright independence. A national convention held in that year, which included all the main parties together with business, trade union, church and academic representatives, reached a wide measure of agreement on the kind of devolved assembly the Scots might like. Only the Conservatives remained adamantly opposed. Labour's landslide victory the following year (in which the Tories won no seats at all in Scotland) ensured the speedy presentation of a Bill to Parliament.

## Recent events

The 1997 proposals for Scotland went a lot further than those of 1978. Scotland would have a substantial annual block grant (the first budget was £14.8 billion) with some income tax-varying powers (up to 3 per cent). It would have its own 'Parliament' (a term implying higher status than 'Assembly', proposed in 1978) which would have responsibility for those matters, among others, dealt with by the Scottish Office: health, education, local government, law and order, economic development, roads, the environment and the arts. A First Minister would, in effect, be 'Prime Minister', though Scotland would retain a Secretary of State in the UK Cabinet.

This Parliament would have 129 members (the MSPs, 'Members of the Scottish Parliament'), 73 elected for the existing 72 Westminster constituencies (an extra seat was created by dividing Orkney and Shetland). The other 56 would be elected from party lists in the eight Scottish European Parliamentary constituencies by a PR system. Scotland would continue to have representation at Westminster, to be reduced by 2005 from 72 to 59 seats. There was no intention to modify the role of Scottish MPs at Westminster.

The proposals were put to the Scottish people in a referendum in September 1998. There were two questions, one on the Parliament itself, the other on its tax-raising powers; those saying 'Yes' to the Parliament were 74.3 per cent, and those saying 'Yes' to the tax proposals were 63.5 per cent. Turnout was 60 per cent.

Appropriate legislation followed and the Conservatives who, under John Major, had strongly opposed devolution, decided in 1998 that it was a *fait accompli* and they would contest seats for the new Parliament.

### The Scottish Parliament and its powers

The powers of the Scottish Parliament are more extensive than is generally realised. Although overall economic policy, the currency, foreign affairs and defence remain under the control of Westminster, all domestic affairs, except for highly sensitive matters such as abortion, broadcasting and immigration, are the Scottish Parliament's responsibility and it has primary law-making powers over them. The SNP was quick to capitalise on the limits to the range of competence of the Scottish Parliament in its 1999 Scottish parliamentary election campaign, which did not emphasise separatist demands. Instead it urged full use of the Parliament's taxation powers to raise money for education and health (under the slogan 'a penny for Scotland') and sought to reverse the UK 1 per cent income tax rate cut announced in that year's Budget. Immediately after the May 1999 elections, where no party gained an absolute majority, negotiations for a coalition government began between the Liberal Democrats and Labour. Issues such as university student tuition fees emerged as a major bone of contention.

Student fees in themselves affected a relatively small number of people, but they raised an interesting constitutional conundrum, one that is likely to appear in many other issues in the future: to what extent can a devolved legislature, containing parties which have put to an electorate proposals contrary to those of the UK government, implement these proposals against the wishes of the government in London? Can a devolved parliamentary party, such as Labour in Scotland, for example, form a compromise at the devolved level with another party with different policies? Labour in Scotland remained committed to the British Labour party's policy of imposing some contribution towards university tuition on students, but its coalition partner in Scotland, the Liberal Democrats, opposed the policy; the compromise between the two parties seems to have satisfied no one and presages future arguments in Scottish politics. The tuition fees controversy indicated that from the outset Scotland would follow its own distinctive path. Devolution would be a real, not just a paper, exercise.

The degree to which the Scottish Parliament has ploughed its own furrow and to what extent the devolution project has justified itself remains debatable. Certainly there have been some important changes, such as free long-term personal care for the elderly, abolition of tuition fees at Scottish universities and a more open Freedom of Information Act as far as the workings of the Scottish executive is concerned. Critics, such as the Scottish Nationalists, regard these changes as insufficient. Moreover, the critics argue, substantial change is impossible given the constitutional and financial restraints imposed by the current devolution arrangements.

The remarkably smooth formal transfer of power in July 1999 suggests that the new institutions will form a stable settlement, but the situation would be transformed if the Scottish National Party (SNP) should command a Scottish parliamentary majority and thus claim a mandate for a further dramatic change, a referendum leading to withdrawal from the UK. Even if this is regarded as an unlikely scenario, there is nonetheless a nationalist political dynamic inherent in the situation. All political parties will be inclined to stress their Scottish credentials and it would be easy to attribute any shortcomings of the Scottish Parliament to its remaining degree of subordination to Westminster. Moreover, the ceremonies surrounding the opening of the Scottish Parliament in themselves display a renaissance of Scottish cultural identity, an identity that may find further political expression.

There have been some practical problems; for instance, the construction of a new Parliament building, opened in Edinburgh in September 2004, was a source of considerable controversy in Scotland. It provoked strong opposition within the country, especially as its enormous budget overran – to ten times the original estimate of £43 million.

### The 'West Lothian Question'

There are unresolved difficulties in the relationship of the Scottish Parliament to Westminster. One of these is the 'West Lothian Question' (so called because it was repeatedly posed by the MP for West Lothian, Tam Dalyell): the issue concerns whether Scottish MPs should legislate in the Westminster Parliament on matters relating to England, while English MPs would have no such authority on legislation concerning Scotland. Until the general election of 2005 Scotland continued to have some twelve or thirteen MPs more than its population would warrant (seventy-two instead of fifty-nine, as proportionality with the average size of English constituencies suggested). This was very much due to the Labour government's reliance on Scotland to provide it with a substantial proportion of its parliamentary majority. The dependence of the Labour government on Scottish MPs in Westminster to deliver its legislative programme will remain, especially after the loss of so many of its English seats in the 2005 general election. Indeed, Scottish MPs are noticeable by their high-profile role in the Labour government, including powerful Cabinet posts such as Defence and the Chancellor of the Exchequer; even Prime Minister Tony Blair was born in Scotland and educated there.

The West Lothian Question may be resolved by the Westminster Parliament's adoption of appropriate Standing Orders or by the emergence of a convention in which Scottish MPs voluntarily refrain from intervention in specifically English matters. Much has been made of the 'sleeping giant' of English nationalism if this situation is not somehow resolved, though there is little evidence of an 'English backlash'. Nevertheless, the Conservative party was sufficiently moved by fears of English nationalism – or the desire to seek electoral advantage by pandering to it – for William Hague in July 1999 to reveal proposals to remove the right of Scottish MPs to vote on specifically English issues. In any case, Northern Ireland MPs, in a part of the UK where the major British political parties do not put up candidates, have for decades been able to intervene in English issues without any great difficulty arising. Scottish and Welsh politicians point out that English MPs have also been able to vote on Scottish issues in the past, a right only recently removed in the wake of devolution.

Issues raised by the West Lothian Question have not entirely evaporated. It was only with the aid of Scottish MPs in 2004 that the Labour government in Westminster was able to obtain a majority in the Commons for its controversial proposals on NHS Trust hospitals, which applied only in England and Wales. The Health Secretary, Scottish Labour MP John Reid, was suitably relieved at the rescue of a crucial element in the government's health proposals for England and Wales, one that did not apply north of the border.

**An assessment**

As compared with the tribulations of the Northern Ireland Assembly, the Scottish arrangements have had some success. The voting system, which gives 'top up' seats to party lists of candidates within the regions, has produced a more proportional outcome to the Parliament than that of Westminster and so avoids outright Labour domination. The results of the 2003 election gave Labour only fifty seats in the 129-member Parliament, leading to a coalition with the Lib-Dems and their seventeen MSPs. This has produced a more 'consensual' form of politics than that of Westminster, as has the fact that the Scottish Parliament's role is strictly limited, the more divisive issues of economic and foreign policy being outside its remit. Moreover, the chamber is more involved with the executive in the promotion of policy than is the case in Westminster, partly because the executive of eleven ministers is shadowed by parliamentary committees. Within the governing coalition, the Liberal Democrats have asserted themselves to some degree over issues they feel passionate about; for example, in

2003 they pushed hard for the passage of a Land Reform Bill (land ownership is a major issue in Scotland where most of the country is still owned by a tiny elite).

It would be wrong to exaggerate the degree of multi-party co-operation. There is still a Secretary of State for Scotland in Whitehall whose role is to represent Scotland within the Cabinet (albeit he now also has responsibility for transport throughout the UK), but who might also be seen as acting as a conduit of the Labour government's policies north of the border.

## Devolution and Wales

### Historical background to Welsh devolution

The relationship of Wales to England differs markedly from that of Scotland. Wales was conquered by the Anglo-Norman kings and absorbed politically into England in the Middle Ages; formal unification took place in the 1530s. Thus Wales does not have its own legal or educational system and the Church of Wales, unlike the Church of Scotland, was disestablished in the late nineteenth century. From the 1960s there has been a measure of administrative devolution, with a 'Welsh Office' headed by a Cabinet-level Secretary of State for Wales. Politically, there has been a much milder impetus for devolution, still less independence, than in Scotland. The Welsh nationalist party (Plaid Cymru) drew its support almost entirely from the Welsh speaking areas of North Wales (Welsh speakers making up some 25 per cent of the Welsh population). There are sharp cultural, social and economic differences between North and South Wales, and, generally speaking, little desire for devolution in the industrial cities of the South.

Devolution proposals in 1978 were, not surprisingly, far more modest than those for Scotland, involving a transfer of administrative rather than legislative authority. In the event the referendum of 1979 was something of a fiasco: the turnout was only 20.3 per cent and only 11.9 per cent of the electorate voted for devolution. While Wales was, like Scotland, adversely affected by economic and social changes in the 1980s and 1990s, especially the dramatic run-down of the coal and steel industries, this did not translate into a forceful demand for devolution.

## The Welsh Assembly and its powers

Nevertheless, in 1997 Wales was offered a considerable degree of devolution, more substantial than that of 1978. Wales would have an elected Assembly (though without tax-varying powers) which would take responsibility for the functions of the Welsh Office, including education, health, roads and planning, but not home affairs and the judiciary. The Assembly would have sixty members, forty elected on the first-past-the-post system for existing Westminster constituencies and the rest on a PR system on party lists. The Secretary of State for Wales would continue to sit in the Cabinet, although after the 2005 general election he also acquired responsibility for the far more thorny problems of Ulster as Secretary of State for Northern Ireland as well as Wales.

Although the Welsh Assembly would be unable to enact primary legislation, the Assembly elected in May 1999 has rather more power than might at first sight appear (see Table 5.1 comparing the powers of the Scottish Parliament and Welsh Assembly). It could, for example, abolish 'A'-Levels or scrap the beef production controls introduced in the wake of BSE, and its first annual budget was £7 billion. The outcome of the May 1999 Assembly elections proved something of a disappointment to advocates of devolution; the turnout was only

### Table 5.1 The powers of the Scottish Parliament and Welsh National Assembly compared

| Powers | Scottish Parliament | Welsh National Assembly |
|---|---|---|
| Run services | Yes | Yes |
| Allocate funds | Yes | Yes |
| Organise administration | Yes | Yes |
| Vary tax levels | Yes | No |
| Make, repeal or amend laws | Yes | No |

46 per cent, suggesting widespread public indifference; no party achieved a majority, though Labour was, as expected, the largest party in the Principality and subsequently formed a minority administration. Plaid Cymru, which had played down its secessionist objectives, did better than polls had suggested. These results have produced a situation where the powers of the Welsh Assembly might in future be presented as inadequate and thus increase demands from the Labour and Liberal Democrat parties for a more powerful body, if only to outflank Plaid Cymru.

**An assessment**

The record of devolution in Wales since 1999 has been, at best, patchy. Support for devolution among the Welsh electorate has always been lukewarm (in 1979 devolution had been decisively rejected in a referendum). The Assembly has fewer powers than the Scottish Parliament, and those powers are administrative rather than executive. In some ways this has been of positive advantage, since power has been consolidated in the all-party Assembly committees rather than in the executive, and their influence has been enhanced by the fact that no party has had an overall majority (Labour was the largest single party in 1999 with twenty-eight seats out of eighty). Although Labour decided to 'go it alone' in forming the executive in Wales, it failed to persuade other parties in the Assembly to grant the executive further substantial powers outside the Assembly's detailed supervision.

Labour's potential for domination has been further weakened by internal party conflicts between **Old Labour** and **New Labour** as well as personality clashes. The resignation of Ron Davies (Secretary of State for Wales and Welsh Labour party leader) for reasons which remain unclear, as well as blatant interference in the Welsh party by Downing Street to secure the leadership for Alun Michael (generally regarded as a Blairite) instead of the more popular Rhodri Morgan, further weakened Labour in Wales. Matters came to a head in February 2000 when Michael lost a vote of confidence and was succeeded by Morgan. This led to a major shift by Labour to a more distinctively 'Welsh' policy, the formation of a coalition with the Lib-Dems, and a series of political collisions with London, notably in May 2002 when the Assembly voted for free personal care for the elderly.

Few commentators regard the present state of Welsh devolution as final. There are institutional points of conflict with central government; the Secretary of State for Wales can sit in the Assembly, and was, at least initially, assumed to have a 'guiding' role – that is guiding Wales from London. In addition, on many issues salient in Welsh politics, central government is deeply involved, such as agriculture, the NHS, regional aid from the EU; and it is precisely on these issues that London has been most at odds with the Assembly (it was the failure of Alun Michael to win sufficient central government support for EU regional aid to Wales that led to his downfall). Pressure for further reform to give the Assembly powers of **primary legislation** is likely to gather momentum, pressure which will not be confined to Plaid Cymru or the Liberal Democrats.

## Devolution and England

### The English regions

While devolved government in Northern Ireland, Scotland and Wales has received much attention, another aspect of devolution, that of the English regions, has proceeded almost invisibly, yet it is potentially a very significant development, so significant that the Labour party manifesto in 1997 made an explicit commitment to English regional devolution:

> We will introduce legislation to allow the people, region by region, to decide in a referendum whether they want directly elected regional government.

While there is no strong sense of regional identity in England comparable to the nationalist sentiments in Wales and Scotland, there is a certain degree of grievance in some English regions, a resentment especially evident in the North and the South West at the actual, or supposed, domination of London and the South East in English national life. The Northern English regions, for example, have relatively high levels of unemployment; they have suffered the same decline and disappearance of traditional industries as Scotland and Wales, but have failed to receive levels of central government development aid similar to that which stimulated new industries, especially electronics and information technology, in Scotland and Wales in the 1980s and 1990s.

The Regional Development Agencies Act 1998 provided the legislative framework, and in April 1999 'Regional Agencies' came into effect for eight English regions: Northern, North West, Yorkshire and Humberside, West Midlands, East Midlands, East Anglia, the South West and the South East. Each Agency has a 'chamber', 70 per cent of which consists of representatives of local authorities, the rest being nominated representatives of business, unions and other 'stake holders' (it is envisaged that representatives will eventually be elected).

While these bodies have received little media attention, it would be a mistake simply to discount them: though they meet only four times a year, and have budgets of under £2 million each, their decisions may have considerable importance. In November 2004 the unelected East Anglia Regional Assembly, that manages the East Anglia Agency, approved very controversial government plans to build nearly half a million new homes in the area, with significant environmental and transport implications.

These Agencies are essentially planning institutions and at first sight do not appear seriously to alter the basic structure of centralised power in Britain. However, the European dimension is important here. Each region has a permanent office in Brussels which will bid for funding under the European 'regional programme'. In fact, much of the drive for the new regional administrative structure comes from the EU; parallel developments are occurring in continental European countries, some of which, like Germany, have a federal tradition, while others, like Spain, are moving in the same direction. This 'Europe of the Regions' has developed into a major theme of EU policy and will to some degree lead to the bypassing of national governments. The European dimension is underlined by the fact that the new UK constituencies, which came into operation in the June 1999 European Parliament elections, correspond exactly to the new regions. Thus one might argue that some sort of 'federal' UK is emerging, which together with devolved arrangements for Northern Ireland, Scotland and Wales, might replace the unitary state which has characterised Britain for several centuries.

Regional devolution received a notable boost after 2001 when it was enthusiastically promoted by Deputy Prime Minister John Prescott. In 2002 a White Paper, *Your Region, Your Choice: Revitalising the*

*English Regions*, proposed elected regional assemblies with considerable administrative (as opposed to legislative) powers, managing economic development, European funding, local housing and strategic planning. They would be funded by a block grant from the government and have the power to tax local authorities and borrow. There would be twenty-five to thirty-five elected members, some of whom would be elected by party list system, using the whole region as one constituency, in addition to those elected for existing parliamentary constituencies. Each region would have a six-member executive. Crucially, each region was to be consulted on whether it wanted such devolution via regional referendums.

By November 2004 referendums were scheduled to take place in three regions of the UK: Humberside and Yorkshire, the North East and the North West. There was initially little public or media interest, though in July 2004 an ICM poll suggested that 39 per cent of those polled were in favour. There was, however, considerable opposition, not least from Labour MPs who believed the party would 'get a good kicking' in the referendum. Conservatives argued that another expensive and pointless layer of bureaucracy would be created. Graham Stringer, a Labour MP from the North West and the leader of the 'No' campaign, claimed that there was little public support, that there was no natural identity of interests between, say, Cumbria and Manchester, and that the role of existing local government structures would be overshadowed. Only in the North East was there much popular support for an elected regional assembly.

In the event, the referendums in Yorkshire and Humberside and the North West were postponed (presumably until after the General Election in 2005) on the stated grounds that experiments in postal balloting in the European and local elections in June 2004 had, in these regions, produced complaints and irregularities.

This delay did not augur well for the planned assemblies. Even if they were to go ahead, their powers would be very limited; learning and skills, and also transport were omitted from the Bill published in July 2004. Such powers as the assemblies had might lead to tensions between them and central government, as has been the experience with the Welsh Assembly. Besides, referendums might well produce a situation where some parts of England had devolved government while others did not.

> ## Box 5.2  The outcome of the referendum on regional government in the North East
>
> Hopes for regional devolution appeared to be utterly dashed by the referendum which did take place on 4 November 2004: on an all-postal turnout of 48.3 per cent, only 197,310 (22.1 per cent) supported a regional assembly, while 696,519 (77.9 per cent) opposed it. Every one of the twenty-three council areas of the North East recorded a majority against a regional assembly.

In actual fact, there was a lack of voter support even in the North East. In the 2004 referendum nearly 80 per cent opposed the proposed innovation (see Box 5.2).

A defeat on this scale strongly indicates that elected regional government is dead as a political issue for the foreseeable future. It may be the cause is not lost for ever, though; devolution for Wales and Scotland were decisively rejected in referendums in 1979, only to re-emerge two decades later. Moreover, the EU is strongly committed to regional government: it may be that pressure from this quarter ultimately produces positive results. Some defenders of the regional concept have argued that it is not regionalism as such that was rejected but what Liberal Democrat Leader Charles Kennedy called a 'half-baked' scheme which promised a £50 million a year bureaucracy with minimal powers.

The demise of proposed elected regional assemblies raises awkward questions concerning the existing eight unelected regional assemblies. As the Conservative local government spokesperson, Caroline Spelman, observed, 'The transfer of powers to regional government by the Labour administration was predicated on the ultimate establishment of elected regional assemblies. There is a clear democratic deficit. The existing regional chambers have no accountability, no mandate and no legitimacy.'

### An English parliament

Until recently it was assumed that specifically English affairs would continue to be dealt with much as before by the Westminster Parliament: while Wales and Scotland would have their own legislatures there would be no parallel body for England. During the 1997 election campaign the Conservatives pointed out this 'democratic deficit', but mainly as part of their root-and-branch opposition to any form of devolution.

Throughout 1999 the Labour government gave the matter some attention and various schemes were considered; one example was an English Regional Affairs Committee to oversee the emerging Regional Development Agencies; another suggestion was an English Grand Committee of MPs, much like the old Scottish Grand Committee, to consider legislation relating specifically to England. Clearly, Departmental Select Committees will require modification since the remit of some of them covers matters that have been devolved to the new Scottish and Welsh legislatures. Already the responsibility of ministers to MPs is changing: from May 1999 Westminster MPs could no longer question the Secretary of State for Scotland on matters which have been transferred to the Scottish Parliament. If English regional assemblies acquired similar devolved powers the question would arise as to whether ministers would be answerable to them, rather than to the Westminster Parliament. Given the large populations of the English regions, if their assemblies were to acquire significant devolved powers one would begin to wonder whether the Westminster Parliament had any real functions left. Ultimately, even the role of the Prime Minister and Cabinet within the United Kingdom might be open to question.

## A federal Britain?

One might argue that what is really happening is the emergence of a federal Britain, replacing the old unitary structure. But of what exactly would this federation consist? Would it be England, Wales, Scotland and Northern Ireland? Or would it include, besides these, the English regions? The first suggestion presents difficulties, since England has by far the largest population and economy of the UK (well over 80 per cent of both the people and national wealth). The nearest historical parallel might be pre-1919 Germany, which was in a sense a federation of states but in reality wholly dominated by Prussia. The second suggestion would produce an even more curious arrangement: here, all the constituent parts of the federation would be governed by different institutions, with different powers, and elected by different procedures (though such a wealth of anomalies might fit well into the general British tradition of pragmatic adaptation of the constitution to changing political circumstances).

One might even speculate whether the Republic of Ireland might have some part in such a federation, given its constitutional role in the government of Northern Ireland under the Good Friday Agreement, and the possible development of the Council of the Isles which that Agreement envisaged.

## Devolution and the break-up of the UK

During the 1992 and 1997 general election campaigns the Conservative Leader, John Major, predicted that the end result of the devolution process would be the break-up of the UK. His successor, William Hague, considerably modified Conservative policy; he urged Conservatives to participate fully in the 1999 devolved assembly and parliamentary elections; he even publicly acknowledged that the Scottish parliamentary Conservative party might have some different policy positions from those of the English party.

While it might appear that the Blair government had embarked on devolution without fully realising its potentially seismic consequences for the politics and constitution of Britain, during 1999 steps were taken to lock Wales and, more particularly, Scotland more fully into the United Kingdom, steps that were political, administrative and constitutional:

- *Political*: In Scotland every effort was made to secure outright victory in the Scottish parliamentary elections; and in Wales the party ensured by a complex selection procedure that a Blairite loyalist, Alun Michael, was chosen to be Labour's candidate as First Minister in the Welsh Assembly. Thus the Labour party became in itself the linchpin of unity among the constituent nations and regions of the UK.
- *Administrative*: Prime Minister Blair has made it very clear that civil servants in the Welsh and Scottish Offices will remain employees of the United Kingdom civil service, and that they can expect their career advancement to be within the UK civil service, even if

transferred to Wales or Scotland. Even more significantly, a joint ministerial committee is to work to establish a consensus between the devolved governments and Whitehall. This committee would be under the Prime Minister's personal direction, and would consider such matters as relationships with Europe (already, by early 1999, Scotland and Wales had established their own offices in Brussels and Strasbourg in 'co-operation' with UK offices). It has also been indicated that Whitehall departments and their Welsh and Scottish counterparts would co-operate through a system of 'concordats'. Thus a civil service consensus would be established throughout the UK to discourage too much divergence by the devolved legislatures.

- *Constitutional*: Proposals here have been less precise, but may ultimately prove more enduring. For example, it has been suggested that Princess Anne should play an almost vice-regal role in Scotland, being more or less permanently resident there, opening Parliament's sessions and generally playing an active part in the nation's life. The White Paper which presented the terms of reference for the Royal Commission on reform of the Lords specifically recommended that at least some of the Second Chamber's members be representatives of the Welsh, Scottish and Northern Ireland assemblies. ('The Second Chamber could provide a forum where diversity could find expression and dialogue, and where such expression could work towards a strengthening of the Union.')

These measures may cumulatively add up to an even closer Union of the constituent nations of the UK – or they may not. Critics have argued that they bear all the marks of inadequate ad hoc responses to a barely understood problem, responses which might actually exacerbate tensions if, for example, nationalist parties come to dominate the Welsh and Scottish legislatures. Furthermore, there seems little grasp of the possible consequences of Northern Ireland devolution. The United Kingdom currently consists of 'Great Britain and Northern Ireland'. It is with 'Great Britain' that the Unionist Party in Northern Ireland identifies, not with England and Wales. There are strong historical, geographical, cultural, religious and family connections between Northern Ireland and Scotland (over 85 per cent of Northern Irish Protestants are said to be of Scottish descent). The secession of Scotland, or even its drift away from the rest of Great Britain, must surely impact on the delicate and fragile settlement emerging from the 1998 Good Friday Agreement.

• • • • • • • • • • • • • • • • • • • • • • • • • • • • • • • • • • • • • • • • • • • • • • • • • • • • • • • • • • •

## ✓ What you should have learnt from reading this chapter

- Three of the constituent nations of the UK now have devolved authorities with substantial powers, which will become the focus of their own national political life with their own elections, parties, issues, pressure groups, media, political culture and, no doubt, constitutional principles. A similar process may conceivably occur in the English regions in the future.

- These developments raise profound questions concerning Britain's future constitutional development. How will the relationships of these bodies with each other, with central government, and with Europe be articulated? Will there be conflict? How will any conflict be resolved and will such conflict be a positive or negative feature of political life? Should these developments be left to some sort of natural evolutionary process or should they be formalised in a written constitution? If Scotland and Wales developed their own constitutional principles, assumptions, practices and conventions, how far would these feed through to the wider UK polity?

- One might foresee the evolution of a federal UK based on equality between its constituent elements, with firmly entrenched institutions replacing the unitary state of the past three centuries. Alternatively, one might predict the ultimate break-up of the multi-national British state if a federal state were created; no state exists that has a federal constitution in which one of its constituent members is as overwhelmingly more powerful than its neighbours as England would be within a federal UK.

- Even if such apocalyptic visions are discounted, it is clear that a number of unresolved issues remain. One issue concerns the nature of citizenship in the UK. Can we speak of 'equal citizenship' if the standards of state provision in, for example, health vary considerably between England, Scotland and Wales? Will a sense of 'British' identity begin to fade and the relations between the various nations that comprise the United Kingdom become a major fault-line in the body politic? Another factor is the distribution of the tax burden within the United Kingdom. The supposedly 'special needs' of Scotland, in such areas as health, education, regional aid and care for the elderly, require higher levels of government spending; in practice, paying for these needs means that English voters will face higher taxes: a prospect which will become increasingly unpalatable to voters south of the border. Finally, there seems to have been little thought as to how the devolved administrations are to be co-ordinated on a United Kingdom, rather than a bilateral, basis. The main co-ordinating body, the Joint Ministerial Committee, seems to have been rarely used.

- More optimistically, one might envisage a fairly smooth transition with devolution being yet another constitutional modification quietly absorbed like so many others. Britain's constitution has comfortably survived more dramatic changes in the past, such as the secession of southern Ireland and the creation of a wholly independent Irish Republic. In any case, the collapse of the UK as a unitary state does not seem imminent. The SNP vote in the 2005 general election fell to 17.7 per cent from 19.9 per cent in 2001. In Wales, contrary to widespread expectations, Plaid Cymru did not with its three seats improve on its parliamentary representation of 2001. The most unionist of all the parties, the Conservatives, raised their number of seats in Wales from none to three; while in Scotland the Tories (at 15.7 per cent, almost identical to that of 2001, when they had no MPs in the country) won just one seat at Westminster. However, if devolution is placed in the context of the many constitutional upheavals currently under way, it is hard to avoid the conclusion that a revolutionary process is occurring and that the British constitution will be totally transformed.

## Glossary of key terms

**Legitimacy**  The right a government has to rule a state. In a democracy, a government's legitimacy is established by the sovereign people taking part in an electoral process.

**Old Labour/New Labour**  After its defeat in the 1979 election, the Labour party underwent a radical change of policy, ideology, constitution, political culture and membership, especially after Tony Blair's accession to the leadership in 1994. These developments were crystalised in the semi-journalistic phrase 'New Labour'. New Labour emphasised the free market, the consumer, civil society, reform of public services, and general 'modernisation'. 'Old Labour' was presented as preoccupied with state ownership, producer interests, inflexibility and a general irrelevance to the twenty-first century.

**Paramilitaries**  Non-state military organisations (usually in Northern Ireland) which use force to pursue a political goal.

**Primary legislation**  Legislation which grants legal authority for any subsequent 'delegated legislation' and the creation of regulations (which have the force of law) which a minister, departmental officials or other public bodies may issue in the implementation of that legislation.

**Sectarianism**  A term used to describe political and social conflict based on religious identity (usually in relation to Northern Ireland).

## ? Likely examination questions

'A unique constitutional experiment.' Comment on this view of the Good Friday Agreement in Northern Ireland.

'The New Federalism.' Does this term accurately describe the devolution process in Great Britain?

'A pragmatic and intelligent response to changing needs and circumstances.' Comment on this view of the creation of devolved authorities in the UK.

Discuss the case for and against the creation of elected regional assemblies for England.

It was necessary to establish regional assemblies for Scotland and Wales 'in order to provide greater democratic control over the already established administrative institutions in those countries'. How important a consideration was this in the creation of those devolved legislatures? What other factors were taken into account in making the case for devolution?

## Suggested websites

www.ni-assembly.gov.uk    Northern Ireland Assembly

www.cfer.org.gov.uk    Campaign for the English Regions

www.plaid.cymru.org.uk    Plaid Cymru

www.snp.org.uk    Scottish National Party

www.scottish.parliament.uk    Scottish Parliamentary

www.wales.gov.uk    Welsh Assembly

www.reu.gov.uk    Regional Coordination Unit

##  Suggestions for further reading

Bogdanor, V. (1999), 'Devolution: Decentralisation or Disintegration?' *Political Quarterly*, 70, 184–94.

Denver, D. (2001), 'The Devolution Project', *Politics Review*, 11: 1, 20–3.

Dixon, P. (2001), *Northern Ireland*, London: Palgrave.

Dorey, P. (2002), 'The West Lothian Question in British Politics', *Talking Politics*, 15: 1, 19–21.

Elcock, H. and Keating, M. (eds) (1998), *Remaking the Union: Devolution and British Politics in the 1990s*, London: Fontana.

Hopkins, S. (1999), 'The Good Friday Agreement in Northern Ireland', *Politics Review*, 8: 5, 2–6.

Jeffrey, C. (2005), 'Devolution: A Fractured Project', *Politics Review*, 14: 4, 17–19.

Lomas, B. (2000), 'The Good Friday Agreement', *Talking Politics*, 14: 1, 28–31.

Loughlin, J. (1998), *The Ulster Question Since 1945*, London: St Martin's Press.

Lynch, P. (2004), 'Towards an England of the Regions', *Talking Politics*, 16: 3, 126–8.

Nairn, T. (2000), *After Britain*, London: Granta.

Norris, P. (2004), 'The 2003 Northern Ireland Assembly Elections', *Talking Politics*, 16: 3, 129–31.

Rathbone, M. (2003), 'The National Assembly for Wales', *Talking Politics*, 15: 3, 188–91.

Rathbone, M. (2005), 'The November 2004 Referendum in the North East', *Talking Politics*, 17: 2, 61–5.

Tongue, J. (2002), *Northern Ireland: Conflict and Change*, London: Pearson.

# Electoral Reform and Referendums

## Contents

## Overview

Electoral systems and referendums are two perennial issues associated with the British constitution. We will discuss in this chapter the role of electoral systems on the British constitution and discuss some of the issues arising from the increasing use of referendums in British politics.

While electoral systems and referendums can be approached as either a political issue or a constitutional issue, we wish to emphasise that politics and the constitution are intimately intertwined and cannot be discussed as separate topics. This is true of all constitutional elements, but is especially so when one considers political expression in the form of elections and referendums.

## Key issues to be covered in this chapter

- What is meant by the terms 'representation' and 'indirect democracy'? How does representative democracy compare with the idea of 'direct democracy'?
- What is meant by the terms 'first-past-the-post' and 'proportional representation' with regard to electoral systems?
- What new voting systems are emerging for elected bodies in the UK?
- What might be the constitutional implications if some form of proportional representation system were adopted for the Westminster Parliament?
- What are referendums and how do they pose a challenge to the doctrine of parliamentary supremacy?

# Electoral reform: background

Electoral systems have an important role in democratic constitutions. Many written constitutions make clear who is entitled to vote, when elections must be called, who is eligible to become a candidate and what type of voting system should be used. In Britain's unwritten constitution these issues are decided by ordinary legislation and constitutional convention.

Voting systems affect political processes and outcomes. Had Britain used a different system for elections to Westminster than the so-called 'first-past-the-post' one, general election results would have created a different composition of MPs in the Commons and, as a consequence, different governments and different policies. No political party since 1935 has won an election on a majority of the voter turnout; in fact, in 1951 and February 1974 the party that won most House of Commons seats received fewer votes than the party that 'lost' the election.

It is worth bearing in mind that the Conservative party election victories of 1983, 1987 and 1992 all had a share of the vote similar to the Labour victories of 1997 and 2001 – around 43 per cent – yet parliamentary majorities were assured, though they ranged from only twenty-one to a massive 179.

The different voting systems now in use for the Northern Irish and Welsh Assemblies, the Scottish Parliament, the European Parliament, and local council and Westminster elections will create either a politically sophisticated electorate or voter apathy and mass confusion. Whatever happens, they will certainly change British politics.

The procedures by which the citizen is represented are often assumed to be one of the immutables of the British system, though who was to be represented was a source of vigorous controversy throughout the nineteenth century. This debate led to substantial extensions of the franchise in 1832, 1867, 1884, 1918 and 1928, which eventually included all eligible men and women over twenty-one. The Representation of the People Act 1948 abolished the university seats in the House of Commons and the associated multiple voting for graduates. Only in 1948, therefore, was the principle of one person, one vote finally established. The age of majority, and with it the voting age, was reduced to eighteen in 1969. There are proposals abroad for the voting age to be further reduced to sixteen at some point in the future.

The procedure for local, national and European assembly elections has until very recently been the 'simple majority in single member constituencies', or 'first-past-the-post', system in which each parliamentary constituency returns one MP – the candidate who gets the most votes.

Although this system has often been presented as the generally accepted norm, it was in fact criticised from many quarters throughout the twentieth century. As early as 1918 Labour committed itself to electoral reform on more proportional lines, as did the Liberals (later Liberal Democrats) from 1945. Pressure groups such as the Electoral Reform Society and Charter 88, a campaign group for wholesale constitutional change, agitated for electoral reform. The Labour party, while in opposition, set up the Plant Commission which reported in 1993. In October 1998 the Jenkins Report was published. The essence of the Plant and Jenkins recommendations was that the electoral system should be modified so as to achieve a more accurate link between the votes cast nation-wide for a party and the seats it received in the legislature.

Voting arrangements, as recommended by Plant and Jenkins in their reports, that produce a close correlation between the votes cast and the number of seats in a legislature are usually referred to as 'proportional representation' (PR). There is no shortage of systems, in operation or proposed, to achieve this goal, numbering at least twenty-seven varieties of electoral systems operational in the democratic world. It should be noted that few of them give exactly proportional results, but most, although not all, are more proportional than the existing British arrangements.

As we are concerned here with the constitutional dimensions of electoral reform, we will not examine the pros and cons of even the main systems but briefly state what are the main features of those with immediate relevance in the British context.

## Recent developments

The Northern Ireland Assembly is elected by a PR system, as are the Welsh Assembly and Scottish Parliament. Moreover, the June 1999 elections to the European Parliament used a PR system for the first time. If the Jenkins Report was eventually adopted as a basis for government policy in this area, and is approved by a national referendum, the next general election could be the last to be fought on a 'first-past-the post' basis. All this has occurred with little public debate, though the public is generally in favour of proportional representation in some form, if the opinion polls are to be believed.

What is very surprising is that all the above institutions are elected on different PR systems. No body of voters in any democracy faces as many – and potentially very confusing – different systems of voting for different elements in the political system: Westminster; the Welsh, Scottish and Northern Irish devolved legislative chambers; the European Parliament; and city mayor and local council elections. If there is any coherent plan behind the changes it is very well hidden. One danger is that elections will become less a representative demonstration of voters' views than an erratic throw of the electoral 'dice' depending on which part of the democratic system is being voted for at the time, and on which PR system is in use. Another danger is that of 'voter fatigue' at the number of elections, chambers and systems of voting, a consequence that could result in very low voter turnouts, undermining the democratic authority of the chamber or office being elected.

We will now look at these elected bodies in turn.

### Northern Ireland Assembly
The Northern Ireland Assembly was first elected in 1998 on the Single Transferable Vote system (STV), as were the post-1972 assemblies in the Province and the Irish Republic's Parliament since 1921. Large constituencies exist, with four or five members; each voter numbers the candidates in order of preference; a quota is calculated from the minimum number of votes required to win. Surplus votes, after a candidate has achieved a quota, and has thus been elected, are transferred to other candidates according to the voters' second and lower preferences. Candidates who now achieve the quota are also elected, and the process continues with third preferences and so on until the required number of candidates have achieved the quota. The result is quite accurately proportional.

### The Scottish Parliament and the Welsh Assembly
The mechanism for the Scottish and Welsh devolved representative bodies is the Additional Member System (AMS). Most members are

elected on a 'first-past-the-post' or plurality basis, where the candidate who achieves the greatest single number of votes is elected, but other 'additional' members are elected as 'top ups' selected from party lists in multi-member constituencies; so each voter has two votes, one for a candidate in a single-member constituency, as in the present Westminster elections, the other for a party list in the multi-member constituency. A similar arrangement applies to elections to the Greater London Assembly.

### The European Parliament

European parliamentary elections from the election of 1999 onwards were based on a closed party regional list system in large constituencies; the more votes a party receives, the more of its candidates are elected. This voting system certainly changed the composition of Britain's delegation to the European Parliament. In the 1999 and 2004 elections more Liberals were elected than previously and, in the latter election, a number of candidates for the United Kingdom Independence Party (UKIP), committed to bringing about Britain's withdrawal from the European Union, were able as MEPs to express their dislike of the EU (see Table 6.1).

### The London Mayor

The London Mayor is elected on a 'Supplementary Vote' (SV), a variant of the 'Alternative Vote' (AV) system. Here the voter records only first or second preferences, so that if no candidate wins an outright majority of first preferences, all but the two top candidates are eliminated. The second preferences for the remaining candidates are then added to their first preference votes, the candidate getting the most votes winning.

### Westminster

As for future Westminster elections, the Jenkins proposals, produced by Labour's 'Independent Commission on Voting Systems', are a curious hybrid. If adopted (as is now highly unlikely), some 80 per cent to 85 per cent of the 530 to 560 MPs would be elected for single-member constituencies on the Alternative Vote system. There would also be a second vote to 'top up' these with other MPs who would represent areas

## Table 6.1  The outcome of the 2004 European elections

| Party | % votes | % seats | No. of seats |
|-------|---------|---------|--------------|
| Conservatives | 26.7 | 36.0 | 27 |
| Labour | 22.6 | 25.3 | 19 |
| UKIP | 16.1 | 16.0 | 12 |
| Liberal Democrats | 14.9 | 16.0 | 12 |
| Green | 6.3 | 2.7 | 2 |
| BNP | 4.9 | 0.0 | 0 |
| Respect | 1.5 | 0.0 | 0 |

**NB** In addition to the above parties, the Scottish Nationalists won two seats, and Plaid Cymru, the Democratic Unionists, the Ulster Unionists and Sinn Fein won one each.

based on counties or cities (not constituencies) to correct 'the disproportionality left by constituency outcomes'.

How politically realistic these proposals are is debatable. Proponents of reform can certainly claim substantial intellectual, if not political, support. As early as 1990 Labour set up a Commission of Inquiry (the 'Plant Commission') to examine the case for PR and propose appropriate systems. The Commission has clearly been influential. Its 1993 report recommended the Additional Member System for a Scottish Parliament; the Plant Report also recommended a regional list system for the British elections to the European Parliament. Both these proposals have been acted upon, though the third recommendation, a Supplementary Vote System for Westminster elections, officially awaits a national referendum on the subject. The experience of Wales and Scotland may make PR for Westminster elections 'thinkable' at last, but over ten years after the Plant Report published its recommendations there is no firm evidence that changing the voting system for Westminster elections is likely to happen in the foreseeable future.

There can be little doubt that the Jenkins proposals were framed so as to make them as acceptable to mainstream opinion in the Labour party as possible. The Cabinet appeared split on the issue and seemed disinclined to submit proposals to the electorate in a referendum in the near future. By 2001 the whole idea of reforming the parliamentary electoral arrangement seemed to have been quietly shelved, Labour's huge majorities in 1997 and 2001 showing there was no political advantage in any reform that would jeopardise its dominant position in Westminster. By 2004, however, there were indications that the Labour leadership was reconsidering the position. The rise of the Liberal Democrats and widespread disillusion among traditional Labour voters implied that the 2005 election would be much less likely to produce a massive Labour majority (as indeed proved to be the case) and offered hope to the Liberal Democrats that the price of their parliamentary support would be a commitment to electoral reform (as was not the case). By the end of 2004 informal talks had taken place between the two parties to determine if the Liberal Democrats would accept the Alternative Vote (AV) System. Press reports suggested that Peter Hain, Leader of the House, was a keen supporter. Such change remains highly unlikely.

The general election of 2005 provided powerful ammunition for advocates of PR, as a brief review of election statistics illustrates. Labour won 36.1 per cent of the vote and gained 355 MPs, while the Conservatives on only 3 per cent less gained only 197 seats. However, although the Conservative share of the popular vote barely changed over 2001 (32.7 per cent), they increased their seats by 35. The Liberal Democrats got 22.6 per cent of the vote but just over 10 per cent of the Commons seats (62). In the case of England (as opposed to the UK), the Conservatives actually got 60,000 more votes than Labour but 92 fewer seats.

The election produced the startling result that Labour, with just over one-third of the votes cast, gained a healthy parliamentary majority (of 66) but with the votes of only 22 per cent of the registered electorate.

## Consequences of electoral reform

Although the aim, and indeed effect, of all the new electoral systems now in use in the UK is to make seats won more proportional to votes cast, it is impossible to predict how voters will actually behave within this new electoral climate. It does not follow that the share of the vote for political parties in previous general elections, based on the 'first-past-the-post' system, will be repeated if some sort of PR system were to be put in place for future general elections. The present voting system, for example, squeezes out extremist parties by encouraging 'extremist' voters to vote for Labour or Conservative candidates as they are more likely to win elections than, say, communist or fascist parties respectively. If a PR system were in place, such voters might be more likely to vote for extremist parties and thereby give them a voice in any assembly.

The growth of extremist parties does not appear to have happened in elections to the Scottish and Welsh legislatures through the systems of PR in place there. In Northern Ireland the introduction of PR under Direct Rule after 1972 was designed to encourage 'moderate' political parties, marginalise extremist parties and encourage involvement in peaceful, democratic politics by those who were attracted to paramilitary violence. What happened in practice was the growth of Sinn Fein and the Democratic Unionist Party, generally regarded as at the extremes of the political spectrum, and the reduction of political representation in the Northern Irish political system of the moderate SDLP and the Ulster Unionists. This tendency was underlined in the 2003 Assembly elections, where Sinn Fein (with twenty-four Assembly members and 24 per cent share of the vote) and the DUP (thirty-three members and 26 per cent share) overtook the SDLP (eighteen and 17 per cent) and UUP (twenty-seven and 23 per cent) as the largest parties representing the Catholic and Protestant communities.

Proportional representation, a low turnout and a general apathy, if not antipathy, towards the European parliamentary elections are some of the reasons that minority parties like the United Kingdom Independence Party (UKIP) were elected in 2004. Another factor might be at play here: voters might be more willing to support UKIP, the British National Party (BNP), Veritas and other marginal parties if the result is not seen to be important, as compared to elections to Westminster. Such voting may be warning the major parties not to take their support for granted. However, a protest vote in elections to the European Parliament (a body that is perceived by many voters to be an ineffectual institution) is likely to be followed by a return to traditional allegiances in a general election when the outcome is the creation of a British government.

It seems probable that the outcome of elections under a PR system will less often be one of a single party's outright victory: **coalition governments** are more likely (as has been the case in the Scottish and Welsh legislative elections) or **minority governments** become the norm. Of course, there are implications for that dominance of the legislature by the executive that has characterised the twentieth century and today. Parliament may re-emerge as the focus of political life in Britain and the real political sovereign, as it was in the supposedly 'Golden Age' of the mid-nineteenth century. Governments could not take their control of the House of Commons for granted, as they can to a great extent at present; the executive would have to negotiate, bargain and seek compromise in order to get legislation approved. MPs would also have to change their behaviour under the new dispensation. More power would flow into the hands of elected politicians and thereby enhance their ability to make the executive accountable. Party discipline may weaken in a PR-elected legislature. The Welsh, Scottish and Northern Ireland bodies are worthy of study to discern whether political behaviour is changing along the lines suggested above.

If coalition (or minority) government does become the political norm, the 'balance' of the existing constitution will alter, with consequences throughout the system; for example, anxieties about an overmighty executive might evaporate, but be replaced by concern about the 'ungovernability' of Britain.

Although New Labour has proved lukewarm about reforming the voting system for local and Westminster elections, it has been concerned about the dismal turnout in recent elections. Local election turnout, for example, rarely exceeds 30 per cent of the electorate, while general election turnouts have steadily fallen from almost 84 per cent in 1950 to 59.4 per cent in 2001 (one of the lowest turnouts for a century). Turnout in 2005 was only slightly up at 61.3 per cent.

As a result, a number of changes have been implemented, notably the widespread use of postal ballots in the June 2004 local government elections. In four English regions postal ballots were decreed as the only means of voting. The experiment was not an unqualified success. Many complaints were made about fraud, undue pressure and the sheer complexity of the ballot papers and the procedure for voting. A report by the Electoral Commission in August 2004 highlighted many problems, including the 'timescale imposed', the complexity of the voting method, logistical issues and reports of abuse, all of which had resulted in a 'lessening of public confidence'. The Commission therefore recommended that 'based on the evidence of the pilots, all-postal voting should no longer be pursued for use at UK general elections'. These doubts were subsequently cited by John Prescott when he withdrew referendums on regional assemblies in Yorkshire and Humberside, and the North West; the humiliating rejection of a proposed elected regional assembly for the North East was not cited by Mr Prescott as affecting his decision to abandon the other regional referendums.

Given that there were ten ongoing enquiries into specific cases of electoral fraud only weeks before the 2005 general election and that the government had said that there was no possibility of changing the rules beforehand, and that a record 15 per cent of the electorate, many in marginal seats, were forecast to use a postal ballot, public concern would seem justified.

Controversy over postal ballots increased after the 2005 election. In the immediate aftermath of the election, there were no fewer than eighteen police enquiries into alleged fraud; in Birmingham 20,000 ballot papers, out of 60,000 applied for, mysteriously disappeared. The

---

### Box 6.1  Fraud in Birmingham: the council elections, June 2004

Senior judge Richard Maavrey QC, sitting as an elections commissioner, produced a report in April 2005 on allegations of fraud in council elections in Birmingham that was even more scathing than the above-mentioned one by the Electoral Commission: he said that he found evidence of electoral fraud 'that would disgrace a banana republic'. In wider comments he accused the government of 'complacency, even denial', stating, 'The systems to deal with fraud are not working well. They are not working badly. The fact is that there are no systems to deal realistically with fraud and there never have been. Until there are, fraud will continue unabated.'

turnout over the UK as a whole grew marginally (up 2.2 per cent on 2001), but in some constituencies it remained below 50 per cent, the lowest being Liverpool Riverside (41.49 per cent). There was little evidence that postal voting had significantly increased turnout, but as Sam Younger, Electoral Commission Chair, observed, 'What is absolutely clear is that postal voting has knocked the public's confidence in the system.'

## Referendums: background

A recent, and to some disturbing, innovation that appears to be becoming a major feature of the constitution is the 'referendum', a device by which the electorate are invited to vote on a single question presented in a simple 'yes/no' format. It is a form of direct democracy; in other words, referendums involve the participation of citizens in a democracy by means of their voting on an important political issue. Referendums have been used so far in the UK only on constitutional issues, but there is no reason in principle why they should be so restricted.

The 1909–11 constitutional crises over the Budget and House of Lords reform stimulated proposals for the use of referendums to resolve them, but were never implemented. The great constitutional writer A. V. Dicey fruitlessly proposed a referendum on Irish Home Rule (which he opposed) as a way out of the crisis of 1912–14. For most of the twentieth century British political leaders resisted the use of referendums. Referendums did, however, become a feature of British politics from the mid-1970s onwards.

**Referendums** have been held in Britain on continued membership of the EEC (1975), on Welsh and Scottish devolution (1979), on the Good Friday Agreement in Northern Ireland (1998), on the proposed London Mayor (1998), and on Welsh and Scottish devolution (1998) – though the last six applied only in parts of the United Kingdom. In 1993 the Labour party promised a referendum on electoral reform, a promise reiterated after Labour won the 1997 election. Both the Labour and the Conservative parties have mooted a referendum on Britain's membership of the European currency – the Euro – at some point in the future, 'when economic conditions are right', and on Britain's adherence to the proposed European constitution.

Referendums are well-established in continental Europe and in many countries whose constitutions historically derive largely from the Westminster model, for example the Irish Republic and New Zealand. Only six democracies in the world have never held a national referendum. In most of these countries constitutional law determines that referendums are to 'guide' government and the legislature, not to compel them. Constitutionally, therefore, Parliament could reject the 'people's will' as manifested in a referendum but it would be most unlikely to do so in practice on political grounds.

## Some constitutional and political advantages with referendums

In Britain and elsewhere, referendums have been considered by their supporters as a natural development to extend the democratic nature of modern democracies, with their well-educated, informed and politically concerned electorates. While not replacing representative democracy, referendums are seen as important ways of strengthening democracy and extending support for democratic institutions in society by greater voter involvement in key political and constitutional decisions of the day. Referendums, supporters suggest, may even enhance British democracy by narrowing the present wide and growing gulf between electors and politicians.

A referendum offers a clear guide to public opinion on a particular issue; although one might point out that this approval questions the traditional view of the role of a mandate at general elections in giving political legitimacy to a party's programme. If a party has already won a general election, having put a clear programme before the voters, why, one might ask, should parts of that programme be put before the same voters in a referendum? An answer might be that voters can broadly agree with a party's overall programme, but profoundly disagree about some important elements that ought to be put separately to the electorate in a referendum.

Referendums do produce a final decision on a controversial issue: the referendum on continued British membership of the EEC in 1975, for example, demonstrated this for most people for two decades. Some politicians and citizens still argued for withdrawal, but from a very weak position after the referendum. Only during the 1990s, when the implications of further European integration began to dawn on the British public, did membership of the EU begin to reappear as a controversial issue, involving promised referendums on membership of the Euro and on the European constitution.

Governments may return to the electorate if a referendum does not give the result they desire. The Danish electorate rejected the Maastricht Treaty (also known as the Single European Act) in a referendum in 1992, only to accept it in a further referendum in 1993. Jacques Delors, former President of the EU, intervened in the French EU constitution referendum in April 2005 to declare his belief that there might be a further referendum if the constitution was rejected (as in fact it was in June 2005).

One view in support of referendums is that they can safeguard democracy against an all-powerful dominant party in the House of Commons, especially when one remembers how weak the House of Lords is as a constitutional check on the government. This claim for referendums has to be weighed against the fact that no government dominating the House of Commons with party discipline is likely to call a referendum to check its own power.

## Some constitutional and political problems with referendums

Britain lacks an established constitutional mechanism, other than the government's introduction of appropriate legislation, to trigger a referendum. In many American and European states there are well-established legal procedures for calling a referendum. In the Irish Republic, for instance, the President may decline to sign a bill on the grounds that it 'contains a proposal of such national importance that the will of the people thereon ought to be ascertained', if so requested by a majority of the **Seanad** and a third of the **Dail**, and he/she may opt to hold a referendum.

In Britain, it is political elites, not voters, who decide whether, when and on what issue a referendum should be held. There has recently been some movement towards putting referendums on a firmer legal footing. The Committee on Standards in Public Life in 1998 made a number of suggestions about how referendums might be conducted, many of which were incorporated in the Parties, Elections and

Referendum Act 2000. The Act created an independent Electoral Commission to oversee both elections and referendums. Organisations that want to campaign in referendums have to register as 'permitted participants' and then apply to be 'designated' as an official, campaign group. The Commission then selects whichever group in its opinion 'appears to them to represent to the greatest extent those campaigning for that outcome'. Such designated organisations receive a grant of not more than £600,000 as well as free delivery of leaflets and an equal number of broadcasts. The government is not allowed to campaign, only to provide factual information; this last rule has proved problematic. In the referendum in the North East on an elected Regional Assembly in November 2004 the government was accused of covertly campaigning for a 'Yes' vote under the guise of providing information about the advantages of such an Assembly. The 'No' campaign won and the proposed Assembly was dropped. Proposed referendums for other regional assemblies in Northern England were also promptly withdrawn.

There remain in Britain no legally defined circumstances in which referendums should take place other than the convenience of the ruling party. For example, the 1975 referendum on Europe was used to manage Labour's deep divisions on continued membership. Collective government responsibility was suspended on this issue, so deep were the divisions over membership of the EEC in the Cabinet and the Labour party. The referendum result (an overwhelming 'Yes' vote) did help to overcome the divisive nature of this particular issue. In 1993 demands for a referendum on further integration within Europe (after the Maastricht Treaty) were rejected by the Conservative government, partly to conceal that party's serious divisions on the matter. By contrast, the Labour government has shown no enthusiasm for a referendum on such a far-reaching constitutional reform as the House of Lords.

There is evidently no consistency in the application of referendums to constitutional change – or any other issue for that matter. This was sharply illustrated in 2004 when the government, having consistently ruled out a referendum on the proposed European constitution, abruptly reversed its position, announcing that one would take place. The inception of the United Kingdom Independence Party (UKIP) and its surprising success in the 2004 European elections appeared to have played a part in this decision. The referendum was to have taken place in 2006, but the French and Dutch rejections of the European constitution in the spring of 2005 were immediately followed by an announcement from Jack Straw that Britain's referendum on the same issue was to be suspended. A referendum on the Euro, promised in 2001, has not yet taken place. Perhaps most startling was the decision in June 2004 not to hold referendums scheduled for November 2004 on regional assemblies in Yorkshire and Humberside and North West England, even though the official campaign groups had been designated and had already spent a good deal of money. Sceptics attributed this action to political motivation. Graham Stringer MP, a leading 'No' campaigner, said, 'They have realised the strength of feeling in the North West means they have very little support for a regional assembly.'

There is some disquiet that, whatever the precise legal position, referendums in effect undermine the political legitimacy and constitutional sovereignty of Parliament. Referendums were held in Northern Ireland precisely because a substantial section of the population did not accept the authority and legitimacy of existing institutions to legislate for the Province. Moreover, regular submission of crucial constitutional issues to the electorate implies that, contrary to British constitutional theory, there is sovereignty above that of Parliament, a 'sovereignty of the people'. If the principle of the sovereignty of the people is established, a fundamental change will have occurred at the heart of Britain's constitution.

Practical difficulties also surround the type of referendum; chief among these is the wording of the question presented to the voters. In 1997 the Referendum party campaigned for a referendum on the value of EU membership for Britain. Two questions were proposed: 'Do you want the United Kingdom to be part of a Federal Europe?' and 'Do you want the United Kingdom to return to an association of sovereign states that are part of a common trading market?' Opponents argued that the questions were loaded: did the 'Federal Europe' referred to mean the EU as then constituted, or some possible future 'super-state'? It should not be assumed, however, that all referendum questions are so problematic: the referendum planned, and later abandoned, for the North West of England in November 2004 would have asked simply, 'Should there be an elected assembly for the North West region?'

Besides these constitutional anxieties, there are political concerns that are likely to have consequences for the constitution:

- Historically, referendums have tended to reinforce conservative political standpoints – objectionable if one is not a conservative! For example, in Switzerland repeated referendums rejected voting rights for women long after they had been accepted throughout the rest of Europe. In the USA referendums have supported the reintroduction of capital punishment, as well as cuts in welfare provision for the 'undeserving poor'.
- Issues may be hopelessly oversimplified and the full implications of a decision not thoroughly thought out by the voters; for example, a Swedish referendum in 1980 rejected nuclear power (to be phased out by 2010) without any provision for alternative means of electricity generation. A referendum in Britain on the reintroduction of capital punishment would, if it ever took place, probably be approved; but it might create more violent crime, rather than deter it, as criminals who risk execution are likely to kill witnesses or police in their desire to avoid arrest.
- Holding a referendum can be a means by which politicians dodge their responsibilities: they try to govern, and to overcome political divisions within their own party, by passing the responsibility for a decision on to the public. Even then, the decision by voters in a referendum, while being sought to reduce party in-fighting within a government, may still not be considered binding on the politicians. The 1975 referendum on continued membership of the EEC was considered to be consultative, rather than binding on the Labour government of the day. Only a brave or arrogant government will treat a referendum that produces a clear result as merely consultative.
- Referendums are expensive and open to manipulation by the ruling party. The 2004 referendum which proposed a regional assembly in the North East is illustrative of the situation in the UK. Having earlier simply announced that there would be referendums on the issue in Yorkshire and Humberside, and the North West, as well as in the North East, the government simply cancelled the first two on the stated grounds that there had been complaints of electoral malpractice in that year's local and European elections in

those areas. Sceptics pointed to an **opinion poll** in Yorkshire and Humberside showing that 95 per cent would vote 'No'. The official 'Yes' and 'No' campaigns had already each received £100,000 of state funding and a further £3.2 million of public money was spent on an information campaign allegedly highlighting the benefits of regional assemblies. Deputy Prime Minister John Prescott and Local Government Minister Nick Rainsford spent another £184,000 on their own campaigning. The total cost to the public has been estimated at £10 million. Substantial sums had already been spent in the other two regions, where the promised referendums seem to have been postponed indefinitely.

- Referendums may become a vote on the popularity or otherwise of the government of the day rather than a vote on the issue in hand. This could, so it is argued, weaken the message of the referendum result; voters use referendums to express opinions on other issues: for example, in the Irish Republic a referendum on joining the Euro became the focus for campaigning on extraneous issues, such as abortion law.

- Dictators have at times consolidated their position through referendums, as Hitler did following the 1934 'Enabling Law' which provided the legal and constitutional basis for his dictatorship. Clement Attlee (Prime Minister 1945–51), taking fascist regimes as a warning, dismissed referendums as a 'device of dictators'. While true, this argument is often used as a last-ditch argument against referendums.

Nevertheless, referendums are increasingly seen as a valid means of assessing popular opinion on subjects of vital constitutional and political concern in modern Western liberal democracies. Western electorates are becoming better educated and informed, with a much more sophisticated view of politics and society than previous generations. The spread of telephone and computer technology, especially the internet, may make electronic referendums a frequent feature of modern democracies.

It is, however, political expediency rather than constitutional principle that has driven the introduction of referendums as a feature, however tentative, of the British constitution. The EEC referendum in 1975 and the Scottish and Welsh devolution referendums in 1979 arose out of the political divisions and weakness of a Labour government with a small and, after mid-1976, non-existent parliamentary majority; devolution was forced on the Labour party by the nationalists in return for their support.

Twenty years later the position is different. The Labour government since 1997 is in a position of great strength in the Commons, with large parliamentary majorities and a deep commitment to constitutional reform, such as Welsh and Scottish devolution. Referendums in Scotland and Wales preceded legislation, unlike in 1978–9; devolution was part of government policy, not forced on it by nationalists. Labour's commitment to a referendum on membership of the Euro ('when conditions are right') is, nevertheless, a reaction to the high levels of 'Euro-scepticism' among the electorate and the need to assure them that Labour was not too pro-European on this issue.

............................................................................

## ✓ What you should have learnt from reading this chapter

- It may well be that reform of the electoral system, together with the growing acceptance of referendums as part of the political process, will have major, perhaps unintended, consequences for the constitution, both in theory and in practice.

- A PR electoral system for the Commons would, in practice, almost certainly end outright majorities by one party; in these circumstances minority governments or, more likely, coalitions would be formed and power would shift dramatically from the executive to the legislature. Optimists might see this as the beginning of a new age of parliamentary government analogous to the mid-nineteenth century: pessimists might fear the onset of weak and ineffective government lacking clear direction, authority and public respect, as was the situation in the French Third and Fourth Republics.

- The possibility of a reformed House of Lords based on a substantial elected component, especially if elected by some form of PR, injects a new and highly speculative factor into the constitutional equation. Such a chamber might, quite rightly, claim equal legitimacy with the Commons, thus causing conflict between the two Houses to revive as a serious constitutional problem at the beginning of the twenty-first century as was the case at the beginning of the twentieth.

- The principle of parliamentary sovereignty, once regarded as the bedrock of the whole constitutional structure, is already much weakened by the process of European integration. The extensive use of referendums, especially on matters of major constitutional reform, would seem further to undermine the principle of parliamentary sovereignty by supplanting it with the concept of 'popular sovereignty'. On the other hand, the constitutional standing of a Parliament comprising a Commons elected on a more proportionate system than at present might well be enhanced.

- All things considered, both the spreading of PR within the electoral and representative framework of the British constitution and the tentative, but growing, use of referendums on important political and constitutional issues could be regarded as necessary elements in the process of modernising and democratising the British constitution.

## Glossary of key terms

**Coalition government** A situation when two or more parties combine to form a government, as in 1916–22, 1931–5 and 1940–5, as opposed to the more usual situation in Britain where one party has a majority in the House of Commons and thus forms the government.

**Dail** The Parliament of the Republic of Ireland.

**Minority government** The situation when a single party forms a government while not commanding a majority in the House of Commons, as did Labour in 1924, 1929–31 and 1976–9.

**Opinion poll** A mechanism for ascertaining public opinion on a matter by interviewing a representative sample rather than the whole population.

**Referendums/Referenda** A vote in which a single question (or a very few questions) are put to the electorate. Although the plural of 'referendum' is 'referenda', it is generally acceptable today to use the term 'referendums'.

**Senead** The Senate or upper house of the Parliament of the Republic of Ireland.

## Likely examination questions

'Representation in Britain is undergoing a profound transformation.' Do you agree? What are likely to be the constitutional consequences of such a development?

'The extensive use of referendums in recent years in itself represents a constitutional revolution – the replacement of the sovereign Parliament by the sovereign people.' Examine the truth and further implications of this claim.

It is said that the British electoral system does not reflect the principle of 'one person, one vote, one value'. How true is this now, following the introduction of proportional representation into some parts of the British political system?

'The many electoral systems that exist for the many legislative bodies in the UK ensure that they are neither representative of, not responsible to, the people.' Discuss.

'Referendums should have no place in the British constitution.' To what extent would you agree with this statement?

## Suggested websites

www.electoralcommission.gov.uk    The Electoral Commission

www.electoral-reform.org.uk    Electoral Reform Society

www.referendum.org.uk    On Referendums

## Suggestions for further reading

Agnew, D. (1999), 'Electoral Reform in the United Kingdom', *Politics Review,* 8: 4, 15–19.

Baimbridge, M. and Darcy, D. (2000), 'Putting the "proportional" into PR', *Politics Review*, 9: 4, 16–18.

Boal, L. (2000), 'Electoral Reform in the UK', *Talking Politics*, 12: 2, 303–7.

Davenport, I. (2004), 'Electoral Reform', *Talking Politics*, 17: 1, 30–3.

Davenport, I. (2005), 'Electoral Reform', *Talking Politics*, 17: 2, 66–9.

Denver, D. (2003), 'Whatever Happened to Electoral Reform?', *Politics Review*, 13: 1, 8–10.

McCartney, M. (2003), 'Oh Referendum, Where Art Thou?', *Talking Politics*, 16: 1, 19–22.

Outhwaite, B. (2001), 'UK Electoral Systems', *Politics Review*, 11: 2, 32–3.

# CHAPTER 7

# The European Union and the United Kingdom Constitution

## Contents

### Overview

Since the early 1970s Britain has become ever-more enmeshed in the European Union (EU). Although the EU is a unique political entity without historical parallel (it is not a 'super-state', but not just an alliance or confederation), it has a clear written constitution in the Treaty of Rome (1957), with its own principles, and its own constitutional culture expressed by its institutions. In many ways the historical development, the evolving traditions and underlying assumptions of the EU are markedly different from those of the UK. Yet the EU is having (and will continue to have) a profound impact on the development of the British constitution. Much of this development is indirect, much incremental, but no branch of the constitution, from civil rights, the electoral system and devolved government to the mutual relationships of judiciary, executive and legislature, as well as the concept of parliamentary sovereignty, will remain unaffected. It is to the European Union and its implications for the British constitution that we now turn.

### Key issues to be covered in this chapter

- How far is British government now integrated into the European Union?
- In what ways is the European Union alien to the British constitutional tradition?
- In what ways and to what extent does European integration raise issues of national and parliamentary sovereignty?
- How does the evolving nature of Britain's relationship with Europe affect the question of a written constitution?
- How will the development of the European Union's own constitutional arrangements affect the British constitution?

## A brief historical outline

After having successfully experimented with the European Coal and Steel Community (ECSC) from 1951 onwards, France, Italy, the Federal Republic of Germany, Belgium, the Netherlands and Luxembourg signed the Treaty of Rome in 1957. This created the European Economic Community (EEC), often but misleadingly referred to in Britain as the 'Common Market'. British attempts to join in 1961, under the Conservatives, and in 1967, under Labour, failed because of French objections. However, in 1972 the Conservative government's application was successful and in the same year Britain signed a Treaty of Accession. The necessary legislation having been enacted, Britain officially joined the EEC on 1 January 1973.

While consolidation proceeded, though fairly slowly, in the 1970s, serious doubts about membership remained, especially within the Labour party and Labour government (1974–9), doubts which culminated in a referendum on continuing membership in 1975. A two-to-one majority of the turnout voted to remain in Europe.

Margaret Thatcher's governments in the 1980s were not at ease with Europe. They energetically pursued 'British interests', notably achieving a 66 per cent rebate on Britain's financial contribution to the EC at the Fontainebleau Summit (1984): a rebate which the present Labour government finds is still a bone of much contention within the EU: in mid-2005 many member states, led by France, began a determined effort to end or to phase it out.

The 1975 referendum did not remove Labour unease about membership of the EC; its 1983 manifesto even called for British withdrawal. By the end of the 1980s, however, Labour hostility had begun to moderate, partly as a result of the party's internal evolution and partly as a result of the EC becoming a more 'worker friendly' institution under the energetic leadership of Commission President Jacques Delors (1985–95) and a predominantly socialist-dominated European Parliament. (Socialist domination of the European Parliament ended with the 1999 election; the 2004 election confirmed the centre-right domination of the European Parliament.)

The Single European Act 1986 aimed to create a free internal market by 1992 and the introduction of a system of 'qualified majority voting' (QMV) in which each state would have a vote roughly proportionate to its size in the Council of Ministers. Here, crucially, matters on twelve policy areas would be decided, not solely by a unanimous vote (as had previously been the case), but also by a majority; and no state would have the right to cast a veto on every issue brought before the Council of Ministers. QMV, little debated at the time, was much criticised in retrospect by Mrs Thatcher (after she had left office) as a fundamental threat to British sovereignty. She claimed her approval at the time was secured by her having been 'misled'.

Further moves towards integration came with the 'Delors Plan' (1989), which proposed moves towards a common European currency in which national currencies would be linked in an **'exchange rate mechanism' (ERM)**. This was intended to act as a prelude to full monetary union. Although Britain joined the ERM in October 1990, Mrs Thatcher became increasingly suspicious of what she anticipated as a remorseless drive towards a 'federal' Europe underpinned by, in her opinion, a 'socialist' ideology. Tensions within her government over Europe were a major factor in her overthrow in November 1990. Her successor, John Major, talked of putting Britain at the 'heart of Europe', but his Cabinet was even more bedevilled by conflict between 'Europhiles' and 'Eurosceptics', supporters and opponents respectively of greater British integration within the EU.

Matters came to a head with a summit conference at Maastricht in December 1991 that transformed the European Community into the European Union. The Maastricht Treaty (also known as the Treaty of European Union) involved a huge expansion of the Union's role (see Box 7.1).

Linked to the Treaty in a separate protocol was a 'Social Chapter' to extend the EU's role into such areas as employment rights and social protection. For Mr Major, who was deeply concerned about the reaction of the Eurosceptic wing of his party after the 1992 general election had reduced his majority to below twenty, this was a step too far. After a bitter debate the necessary legislation passed through Parliament without the Social Chapter (Britain having negotiated a special opt-out at the Maastricht Summit) and the Treaty came into effect on 1 November 1993.

Unhappiness within Conservative ranks over relations with Europe continued. In September 1992 speculative pressure created a financial crisis culminating in 'Black Wednesday' when sterling was forced to

---

**Box 7.1 Features of the expanded role of the European Union following the Maastricht Treaty, 1991**

- Two more **'pillars of activity'** were added: firstly, a common foreign and security policy; secondly, a common home affairs and justice policy
- Within the Union all citizens of member states would share a common European citizenship
- A timetable for the creation of a full economic and monetary union was established
- The principle of 'subsidiarity' under which decisions would be made at the lowest appropriate level was established
- Amplified amending and scrutiny powers were accorded to the European Parliament
- Extension of QMV into thirty new policy areas.

---

withdraw from the ERM. Thereafter the Eurosceptic wing, encouraged by Margaret Thatcher (now Baroness Thatcher in the House of Lords), became ever-more powerful. A complicated conflict over the **BSE** issue, which involved cattle disease and resulting slaughter, with its implications for human health and farmers' income, developed into a bitter struggle with the EU, a period of British 'non-co-operation' and a general alienation of Britain from other EU members.

Divisions among the Conservatives over Europe undoubtedly played a part in their disastrous defeat in the 1997 general election, and have clearly troubled the party under the leadership of Major's successors, William Hague, Iain Duncan Smith and Michael Howard. Hague's position on the central question of monetary union was officially little different from that of Labour, that is, not to rule it out at some future date and to have a referendum on Britain's joining the single European currency (the 'Euro'). Conservative attitudes towards all things European hardened under Duncan Smith and Howard. The Conservatives expressed deep anxiety over the constitutional implications for Britain of both membership of the Euro and ratification of the European constitution.

Labour, meanwhile, had become more favourable to Europe, first under Neil Kinnock (1983–92) and then John Smith (1992–4). Under Tony Blair the Labour government is, in principle, in favour of joining the Euro, is preparing public opinion for this step and has put into place appropriate institutional measures to do so; the government has also announced the date for the referendum on the European constitution (although the British referendum was put on hold after the French and Dutch referendums on the European constitution voted 'No' to ratification in 2005). Political controversy was stirred up by the government's pro-EU policies, both within the party and beyond.

The Conservatives fought European parliamentary elections in 1999 and 2004 strongly opposed to further integration and membership of the Euro. This strategy appeared to pay political dividends; the Conservatives became the biggest British party in the European Parliament in both votes and seats as Labour lost much ground. However, the Conservative share of the vote fell from 35.8 per cent in 1999 to 26.7 per cent, and their share of the seventy-eight British MEPs fell from thirty-six to twenty-seven. Turnout in Britain for the European parliamentary elections increased sharply, from 23 per cent in 1999 to 38 per cent in 2004, probably because European elections were arranged to coincide with local government elections and because postal voting was more widely used.

The Liberal Democrats maintained their reputation as the most Europhile party in British politics, being pro-Euro, pro-European constitution and strongly in favour of a greater role for the EU in international affairs. Forthright in its opposition to the EU and its commitment to 'an ever closer union' is the UK Independence Party (UKIP), which campaigns for British withdrawal from the European Union.

The push for further EU integration advanced with the Treaty of Amsterdam (1997) and the Treaty of Nice (2001).

---

### Box 7.2  The Amsterdam Treaty, 1997

This included:

- provisions on employment and social policy
- the European Parliament's procedures for decision-making were extended, including its acquisition of some veto powers
- QMV extension to sixteen policy areas.

### Box 7.3 The Nice Treaty, 2001

This was part of the preparations for the enlargement of the EU in 2004 and included:

- changes to the number of MEPs per state in the European Parliament
- the redistribution of votes between states in the Council of Ministers
- changes to the structure of the Commission
- QMV extension to thirty-one more policy areas.

The ratification of these treaties caused problems in some member states, but the ratification process finally went ahead. However, widespread disquiet at the pace of European expansion and integration was to become clear during the ratification of the Treaty Establishing a Constitution for Europe (2003). Of this, more later.

### Table 7.1 Landmarks in the Relationship of Britain and the European Community /Union

| Year | Event | British approach |
|------|-------|------------------|
| 1951 | Treaty of Paris, establishing the ECSC | On sidelines, reluctant to commit to developments on the Continent |
| 1955 | Messina talks on further integration | Remained aloof from discussions, sent an 'observer' |
| 1957 | Treaty of Rome, setting up EEC | Unwilling to join any new organisation with supranational implications; remained on sidelines |
| 1961–3 | First (abortive) British application to join EEC | Macmillan (Conservative) government came to see advantages in joining; thwarted by de Gaulle |

## Table 7.1 (continued)

| Year | Event | British approach |
| --- | --- | --- |
| 1967 | Second (abortive) British application to join EEC | Wilson (Labour) government also attracted by prospects of large tariff-free market; attempt again vetoed by de Gaulle |
| 1973 | Third (successful) British application to join EEC, as part of First Enlargement | Heath (Conservative) government entered negotiations in a positive mood; new French president sympathetic to British entry; signing of Treaty of Accession, January 1972 |
| 1979 | First direct elections to the European Parliament | Britain elected MEPs for the first time, instead of sending some MPs and peers to Strasbourg |
| 1986 | Passage of Single European Act | Thatcher (Conservative) government keen on free trade implications of single market; did not recognise the scale of this step towards integration, brought about by the introduction of qualified majority voting in the Council of Ministers |
| 1991 | Signing of Maastricht Treaty | Major (Conservative) government had an opt-out of the proposed single currency and of the Social Chapter |
| 1995 | Accession of Austria, Finland and Sweden, as part of Fourth Enlargement | Supported enlargement, not least in the hope that widening the Union might be a means of slowing down the momentum towards integration |

| | | |
|---|---|---|
| 1997 | Amsterdam Treaty | Blair (Labour) government agreed to Social Chapter on entering into office; summit then cleared up some outstanding issues, paving way for future enlargement and introducing more majority voting |
| 2000 | Nice Treaty | Treaty seen as a victory for large EU states; Britain strongly defended its national interests on issues such as harmonisation of taxation arrangements. Progress towards enlargement, but no clear agreement on streamlining the Union and improving its decision-making procedures |
| 2004 | Accession of ten new (mainly Central/Eastern European) countries, as part of Fifth Enlargement | Strongly supported by Blair government; 'new democracies' in several cases sympathetic to British view of how the EU should develop |
| 2005 | Referendum votes on proposed EU constitution lost in France and Holland, creating confusion over future direction of EU | Initially did not see need for constitution, but came to portray it as a useful tidying-up exercise of several outstanding issues, one that would make an enlarged EU function more effectively. Promise of referendum in 2006, but the rejections make it unlikely that this will go ahead |

# The impact of Europe on the British constitution

British membership of the EU and the ever-deepening process of European integration has had a more profound impact on the British constitution than any other process. Moreover, the changes which have resulted, both direct and indirect, have been the outcome not of the intentions of the British government or Parliament, still less of the British people, but are the result of processes in which Britain, as just one state among many, has had limited input.

There is a fundamental difference in attitude between Britain and the states of continental Europe. This is chiefly due to Britain's very different historical experience as a nation state. For Britain, liberal democracy has evolved within the context of a nation state based on parliamentary sovereignty, and has been underpinned by the historically successful defence of its independence over many centuries.

For continental Europeans their experience of the nation state in the twentieth century has been different. It has often been associated with tyranny rather than liberty, as in the experience of fascism in Germany, Italy, Spain and Portugal, and communism in the states of Central and Eastern Europe. Consequently, moving away from the nation state towards an integrated Europe is an acceptable policy to many continentals, who see freedom and democracy as most likely to be preserved by such integration.

The British viewpoint perceives increased European integration in terms of economic goals only, such as higher levels of trade and improving living standards; assessing European developments from the standpoint of Britain's economic advantage, while at the same time resisting calls for closer political integration in Europe. Pro-European politicians in Britain have tended to play down the implications for British national sovereignty arising from membership of pan-European institutions. Continental Europeans, particularly the drivers of the European project, such as Germany, France and the Benelux countries, have believed economic integration to be an essential precursor of some form of European political union.

Two further points need to be grasped in order to understand this persistent mismatch. Firstly, Britain joined the EC when European legal and institutional frameworks were already well-developed. As a result, French and German administrative practices, political assumptions and constitutional arrangements were already deeply embedded, for example the French tradition of *etatisme* (a powerful proactive state bureaucracy) and the Germany tradition of powerful regional authorities. Secondly, European integration has proceeded vigorously, with the reluctant and tardy acquiescence of Britain. British politicians and voters have been so critical of the EU that Britain is often regarded in the rest of the EU as 'the reluctant member' or 'awkward partner'.

## Issues arising from Europeanisation

Creeping Europeanisation clearly raises questions about the principle of 'ministerial responsibility'. Well over half of UK legislation now derives from the European Union. In what sense can a minister now be held responsible for decisions which are really those of Brussels, and which the minister does little more than implement?

Even the position of the Prime Minister vis-à-vis the rest of government has clearly been affected by Europe. Tony Blair has set up a European Secretariat in the heart of his government with direct access to himself and a vigorous stance in relation to other ministries. As Europe now affects virtually the whole range of government activity the Prime Minister's position is greatly strengthened. The British political elite's preference for strong governments at home and inter-governmental-level relations within the EU has been reinforced by recent institutional developments within the EU. For example, the developing role of the Council of Ministers and the continuing relative weakness of the European Parliament have together bolstered the constitutional and political position of Cabinet Ministers in relation to the British Parliament.

The extent of integration, little realised by the electorate, makes some of the debate on the sovereignty issue rather remote from reality. Nevertheless, the matter has surfaced in various forms over the past three decades and appears to be an important factor in current hesitations by both Conservative and Labour parties over joining the Euro and also over signing up to the European constitution.

## The sovereignty issue

Sovereignty is the most important constitutional issue as far as the British are concerned. British domestic politics conflicting with the logic of EU institutional politics produces the potential for trouble.

## Box 7.4 The extent of British integration

It is not generally realised just how far **integration** has developed to date, both in terms of the range of governmental activities concerned and of the transfer of authority, and therefore of sovereignty, to European institutions.

Initially the EU concentrated on specifically economic matters (although the Treaty of Rome vaguely referred to 'an ever-closer union'). Nowadays the EU deals with virtually the whole range of government activity. Admittedly, some matters such as taxation, welfare benefits and employment rights belong among economic issues, but others go far beyond, to include policy areas such as drugs, immigration, combating organised crime, and even attempts to create a common foreign and security policy. Britain has fought a rearguard action against some of these developments, but the process seems inexorable.

Much of the impact on Britain of membership of the EU has proceeded quietly, with little publicity; cumulatively, however, the effects have been profound. Within central government senior departmental civil servants are regularly seconded to Brussels; they are in regular touch with their continental counterparts in agriculture, health, regional policy, and law and order. All Whitehall departments have EU sections within them to manage their relations with Brussels. Interdepartmental committees also exist to co-ordinate policy with the EU.

The **'Europeanisation'** of government has taken effect very rapidly in many departments of state such as the Department of Trade and Industry and Customs and Excise. The Department for Environment, Food and Rural Affairs (DEFRA), for example, is virtually an outpost of Brussels in the heart of Whitehall. The central executive is well-integrated into the EU: ministers take part in the deliberations of the Council of Ministers; the Prime Minister, along with other heads of government, attends meetings of the European Council and every few years acts as President of the Council.

Paradoxically, the process of gradual integration has been furthered by what might seem to be its minimal impact on Cabinet government: there is no 'Ministry for Europe' or 'Secretary of State for Europe'. In practice, this has meant that Europe is regarded as a sphere of domestic policy and so is expected to affect all departments. The ending of the distinction between 'European' and 'foreign' policy may have made the once-mighty Foreign and Commonwealth Office almost redundant. From another perspective, however, the FCO role in Europe has enhanced its role within

Whitehall as the fount of foreign policy expertise, expertise which is now required by other government departments.

Thus major areas of government, such as trade and agriculture, have been thoroughly Europeanised, while others, such as the environment, equal opportunities, regional policy, consumer protection, transportation and energy now have a major European dimension. Only health, education, and law and order remain relatively outside the European sphere of influence.

Local authorities now deal directly with Brussels in applying for European Regional Development grants and help from the European Social Fund. This is a process which is likely to accelerate with regional assemblies in Wales and Northern Ireland, a Parliament for Scotland, and the new Regional Development Agencies in England. Local government might actually be strengthened by the EU. Under the Maastricht Treaty the principle of 'subsidiarity' was enshrined: functions should pass to higher levels in government only when they are likely to be better performed at that level. The British government pressed for the inclusion of subsidiarity in the Treaty, but it is clear that the British move was one designed to protect the powers of the nation-state and not to strengthen local government: county council and urban local government continue to lose powers to central government under both Conservative and Labour governments.

Although regional identities tend to be stronger in many EU states than in the UK, the Welsh and Scottish devolved legislatures and the English Regional Development Agencies do all have offices in Brussels.

Pressure groups of all kinds have direct representation in Brussels and Strasbourg; this is true of both trade unions and employer organisations such as the Confederation of British Industry (CBI), as well as of cause groups, such as environmental campaigners. Political parties contest European elections and may even present a joint platform with continental parties, as did Labour with the German Social Democrats in June 1999. One might argue that many key issues in the domestic political agenda are increasingly shared by Europe, for example the long-running BSE saga and the panic in 1999 at the talk of 'tax harmonisation'.

In domestic politics British governments find transfers of sovereignty to the EU costing them political capital rather than boosting it; at the same time other EU member states often perceive British opposition to plans for further European integration as marginalising British influence over policy formation. Sovereignty is often the issue over which the British make most noise within the EU.

Two types of sovereignty can be discerned:

**National sovereignty:** the right of the British people to govern themselves by means of British political institutions free from external interference.

**Parliamentary sovereignty:** the right of the British Parliament, as the supreme institutional expression of the national political sovereignty of the British people, to pass whatever legislation it desires in governing the territory of the United Kingdom.

**1. National sovereignty:** Some critics predict that Britain will simply be incorporated in a 'United States of Europe', marking an end, as Hugh Gaitskell (Labour Leader 1955–63) once put it, to 'a thousand years of history'. Conservatives often express horror at the 'f'-word – federalism – in relation to the European Union and remain opposed to European monetary union and its concomitant Central European Bank as two things that together would destroy national political sovereignty. As Eurosceptic academic and electoral candidate Alan Sked, in his *A Proposal for European Union* (1990), observed:

> National sovereignty is to nations in international society what civil rights are to individuals in civil society; their defence against superior power. To ask a nation to surrender its sovereignty is like asking an individual to surrender his civil rights. In Europe, historically the enemies of national sovereignty have always been the enemies of freedom.

This view has been rejected from two different standpoints: the view of those who argue, as did John Major, that the essence of national identity would remain undisturbed – England would still be a land of cricket, warm beer, and spinster ladies cycling through the mist to early morning church service. A less romantic but more pragmatic view is that whatever national sovereignty signified in the past it has no validity nowadays; modern Britain is part of a global economy, in which any British Chancellor of the Exchequer can make only a marginal impact on the nation's economic policy. One might also point to the role of **multi-national corporations** and **international currency movements** in order to question the degree of practical sovereignty any government now has over the running of its economy.

The Treaty of Rome (1957) is only one of many international treaties Britain has signed and the EU (in 1972) only one of many international organisations which Britain has joined that curb British sovereignty, in both legal and practical matters. It could even be argued that Britain joined the EU as an expression of its sovereignty in order to pool sovereignty with other states and to extend its real degree of control and influence on those processes which affect its citizens. Foreign and defence policy, for example, is firmly integrated within NATO and, arguably, directed or strongly influenced by the USA, while trade policy is mostly in the hands of the EU.

It can also be argued that Europe now dominates key elements of social policy. For example, a ruling by the European Court of Justice in 1995 pronounced free medical prescriptions for pensioners to be discriminatory and therefore illegal, as men were eligible for pensions at 65, women at 60. The government promptly allowed men free prescriptions at 60. Health and safety legislation is mainly EU in origin, as are aspects of immigration policy, proliferating areas of food safety regulations, and many of the standards for consumer protection.

In short, according to these views, in the modern world national sovereignty is largely a myth and the European Union is only one factor in undermining autonomy.

Supporters of the European Union and greater European integration believe that national sovereignty can be – and is – enhanced by membership of the EU. States of the size and power of those in the EU, so it is argued, are too small and weak effectively to defend national sovereignty from the threats posed by financial markets, multi-national corporations and economically powerful states such as the USA, Japan and China. Only by 'pooling' sovereignty within the EU and acting together to co-ordinate policies can national sovereignty be protected. The European Union, so it is argued, strengthens members' states and their influence in world economic and political affairs, thus collectively enhancing the national sovereignty of each constituent state.

**2. Parliamentary sovereignty:** The perspective just presented generates the impression that, although parliamentary sovereignty is still a fundamentally operative part of the British constitution, it is threatened by recent developments. Already seriously impaired by the present level of European integration, it will be destroyed along with the British constitution if the process goes much further. That would, the Eurosceptics contend, be the future prospect if sterling were to be superseded by the Euro.

Those who maintain this opinion point out that the devolved legislatures of Wales and Scotland are subordinate creations of the Westminster Parliament and can, in principle, be abolished by it. The referendums that preceded devolution were technically advisory, rather than legally binding. Even the recent incorporation into British law of the European Convention on Human Rights was not entrenched: it could, theoretically, be abrogated by a later Parliament. Similarly, the UK could, as an act of sovereignty, withdraw from the EU and its composite treaties.

It is the basic principle of parliamentary sovereignty that, sceptics believe, is fundamentally challenged by Europe. Legislation produced by European institutions, in particular the Commission, has direct applicability to the UK. If it conflicts with existing British legislation, then the European law takes precedence. Rulings by the European Court of Justice (the 'supreme court' of the EU) override the British Parliament and British courts. The Single European Act (1986) further strengthened the role of the EU, as have the Maastricht (1991), Amsterdam (1997) and Nice (2001) treaties; a process of undermining parliamentary sovereignty that, its critics claim, will be exacerbated by the proposed European constitution.

As a consequence of the Amsterdam Treaty the role of the European Court of Justice has been further developed by enabling it to incorporate 'human rights' considerations into its rulings, thus considerably expanding its remit into many areas of domestic policy. The Nice Treaty, as we have seen, opened the way for extension of the EU into Eastern Europe. As part of the institutional reforms required to ensure that expansion was manageable, the voting weight of member states in the Council of Ministers was reformed. The Nice Treaty also committed member states to reforming the composition of the Commission.

Under the system of Qualified Majority Voting (QMV) embodied in the Single European Act, major decisions relating to the Single

Market in the Council of Ministers are made by a 'weighted major-ity' in which states have their approximate population size taken into account in calculating their voting significance. A majority counts as 71 per cent of the votes cast by member states. This means that as there is no veto arrangement, Britain could be outvoted by other member states in Council meetings and might therefore have to accept decisions and the resulting legislation that it did not want. The problem was vividly illustrated in the controversy over new European regulations for the art market proposed in early 1999: although Britain controls 60 per cent of the European art market, those regu-lations were devised in the interest of all member states – especially France – while Britain was unable to muster sufficient votes to prevent the regulations being passed.

The range of topics covered by QMV arrangements might well in the near future affect the entire spectrum of governmental activ-ity, much to the alarm of many British politicians and voters. The Single European Act and the Maastricht, Amsterdam and Nice treaties extended the QMV to eighty-nine new policy areas. One wonders what is left for national governments to decide on their own. Admittedly, the Maastricht Treaty influenced many policy areas in inter-governmental discussions outside the existing EU institutional framework, but it was clear by 1999 that such matters as immigration control, tax harmonisation and anti-terrorist mea-sures would eventually have to be resolved within that institutional framework.

It is difficult to insist that parliamentary sovereignty remains unchanged by these developments. The usual counter-argument is that sovereignty has been 'pooled' with that of other states in Europe to allow all of them greater practical sovereignty. There is, after all, full British participation and representation in every branch of the EU: the European Parliament (seventy-eight British MEPs out of 732), the Commission (two British Commissioners out of twenty-five), the Council of Ministers (one minister) and the European Court of Justice (one judge out of the twenty-five).

It is still actually possible that Parliament could pass an Act that expressly overrules an EU law, or part of it, and British courts would be expected to support such a position under the doctrine of parliamentary sovereignty. Indeed, the British Parliament could always vote to withdraw from the EU, which would constitute a major act of sovereignty (both national and parliamentary)!

It could be conceded that parliamentary sovereignty has been a constitutional fiction for many years. Parliament is, in practice, politically controlled by the executive. Party discipline along with the dominance of the Prime Minister and Cabinet is, one could argue, more damaging to parliamentary sovereignty than is the EU. The concept is simply ceasing to be meaningful in the wake of devolution to Scotland, Wales and Northern Ireland which will create alternative centres of political legitimacy and even sovereignty that may challenge Westminster. The changing nature of traditional notions of sovereignty should not arouse undue alarm. The real purpose of parliamentary sovereignty, the protection of liberty and democracy, will in future be maintained by such developments as the incorporation of citizens' rights, the implementation of the Maastricht principle of 'subsidiarity' (by which decisions are taken at the lowest level compatible with democracy and efficiency) and the general improvement of the European Parliament in the wake of its revolt against alleged corruption in the Commission with the consequent dismissal of all its commissioners in January 1999.

Whatever validity there is in claims of a decline in British sovereignty, there is a striking reluctance among both the British government and Opposition at the present time to debate the constitutional consequences of European integration. The official position of both Labour and Conservative leaders, for instance, is that Britain should join the Euro if and when it is in her economic interests to do so: neither party makes reference to the constitutional impact of such a decision.

## Europe and a written constitution

Quite apart from the sovereignty issue, Europe has affected the British constitution in other ways, even if the impact has been indirect and little discussed. When Britain joined the EEC on 1 January 1973 it acquired in the Treaty of Rome the first written constitution since the Instruments of Government of the Commonwealth in the 1650s.

In practical terms, moreover, it is difficult to imagine how the new political arrangements for Northern Ireland, with their implications of virtually joint sovereignty for the Province shared between Britain and the Irish Republic, could have evolved without common membership of the EU by the two states. Again, the intellectual climate of public debate has surely been influenced by the European experience of written constitutions, entrenched civil rights, proportional representation and devolved authority. The formerly 'unthinkable' has become open to rational discussion and even political implementation.

There is a major gap, almost a 'black hole', in public discourse. Although the constitution is the subject of unprecedented political debate and radical change, little has been said about the European context. Yet Europe impinges, and will impinge more, on every aspect of the nation's life. European developments clearly have profound constitutional consequences; the principle of subsidiarity and the 'Committee of the Regions' created by Maastricht, for example, might well enhance the powers of the devolved regions so much that the nation state with its particular institutions becomes a political and constitutional irrelevance.

With the transfer of defence, foreign affairs and the currency to Europe, which might well occur early in the twenty-first century, together with emerging devolved authorities, Scotland, and even Wales, may become de facto if not de jure independent of England altogether in domestic matters. The current situation is, as far as the British constitution is concerned, one where British MEPs in the European Parliament exist in a 'parallel universe' to that of Westminster. This situation can hardly continue, especially if the European Parliament enlarges its powers and if MEPs sit, as may be the case under one proposal, in a reformed House of Lords.

One might remark, in passing, that a form of constitution for the European Union has itself evolved through a succession of treaties rather than any sort of Europe-wide 'constitutional convention'. It is a constitution characterised by 'checks and balances', a three part decision-making system (Commission, Council of Ministers, Parliament) with an emphasis on being a **participatory democracy** rather than an **accountable democracy**.

The accession of ten new member states to the EU in May 2004, and proposals for a Draft Constitutional Treaty for Europe in June 2003, as well as controversy over a common European asylum system in late 2004 (which its opponents claim will end Britain's ability to control immigration), have reawakened fears that the UK's national sovereignty is being fatally undermined. European elections in 2004 delivered the new United Kingdom Independence Party (UKIP), which campaigns for Britain's withdrawal from the EU, as a potentially influential political force with twelve MEPs – as many as the Liberal Democrats. Opponents of a 'federal' Europe maintain that the general tendency of the EU is a remorseless drive towards further integration, with national political institutions becoming ever-more peripheral. The Conservative party began to talk in terms of 're-negotiating' the EU treaties so as to 'repatriate' important powers that have been transferred to Brussels. In a pointed attack on this trend the Shadow Home Secretary, David Davis in October 2004, warned: 'Once we give up the veto [on asylum policy] we will see the development of a whole body of European law which will put inexorable pressure on us to give up any opt-out clauses. They chip away piece by piece at our national sovereignty until what we have left is meaningless.'

Other developments have fuelled criticisms that key areas of national independence are being abandoned. Of these, the most important is the constitution constructed from a series of proposals drawn up by former French President Valéry Giscard d'Estaing during 2002–3, and entitled *A Draft Treaty Establishing a Constitution for Europe*. Giscard d'Estaing was clear in wanting the European constitution to turn Europe into 'a political power which will talk on equal terms to the greatest powers on our planet.' Jack Straw, the British Foreign Secretary, and Prime Minister Blair have both described the proposed European constitution in more modest terms: as a 'tidying-up exercise', simply putting existing treaty obligations into a coherent form and making the EU, with its membership now standing at twenty-five states, more efficient. The Labour government has emphasised that it has set a series of 'red lines' that it will not cross, dealing mainly with tax, defence and foreign policy. Opponents are not convinced of either the limited nature of the proposed constitution or the commitment of the Labour government to defending its series of 'red lines' from being breached. *The Daily Mail*, 'Europhobic' to the last, condemned the constitution as a 'blueprint for tyranny'. Conservative Leader Michael Howard observed that 'states make treaties, countries make constitutions'. Mr Howard was quite correct.

The hybrid nature of the 'constitutional treaty' reflects the political realities of the EU: a body made up of states but not itself a state, although having acquired some features of statehood.

A great deal of the proposed European constitution can be described as a 'tidying-up exercise': three-quarters of its clauses are adapted from previous treaties, and the supremacy of European law over domestic law has been confirmed by treaty and judgements of the Court of Justice since the early 1960s.

Specific provisions of the constitution also have important implications. Citizens' rights will be expanded, since a new 'Charter of Fundamental Rights' will go beyond the rights already incorporated in the Human Rights Act, including social security provision, housing assistance, health care and environmental protection; they would be interpreted and enforced by the European Court of Justice.

The EU has also been accorded powers usually associated with sovereign states; for example, the right of a state on its own behalf to sign

---

**Box 7.5  The proposed European constitution's major innovations**

- The enshrining of the principle of subsidiarity and prime role for the state in policy areas associated with territorial integrity and law and order
- The reduction of the size of the Commission: not all states will have a commissioner
- A common EU asylum policy
- The reduction of national vetoes in the Council of Ministers
- A new post of EU President, elected by EU leaders, to be created
- Greater use of QMV to overcome the problems of decision-making in a twenty-five-member organisation
- A more powerful EU Parliament
- The creation of an EU Foreign Minister to replace the EU Commissioner for External Affairs and the EU High Representative
- A strengthening of the EU's defence role
- Greater tax harmonisation in line with the requirements of the single market and single currency
- The right of a member state to withdraw from the EU after having given two years' notice.

treaties with other states. At a more trivial level, though symbolically important, the European constitution specifies an EU flag, a motto ('United in Diversity'), an anthem and even a 'national' day (9 May). More significantly, there will be a permanent President and a Foreign Minister, heading an 'External Action Service', together with a common defence policy. These elements, together with an increase in the EU's authority over immigration, energy and health, would appear to diminish still further any vestige of the principles of national or parliamentary sovereignty.

The European constitution was signed in Rome by the heads of government of all the member states on 29 October 2004. A process of ratification began. Referendums were to be held in ten member states; the UK referendum was scheduled for spring 2006, but indefinitely postponed after the French and Dutch rejections in their referendums in 2005. If the constitution were to be ultimately approved in some manner by all twenty-five states (which seems unlikely in the summer of 2005) it would have important implications for the UK.

Several states, including Germany, had ratified the European constitution by late May 2005. Spain ratified it by a referendum earlier in the year. Soon after this successful start to the ratification process the draft constitution ran into trouble. On 29 May the French referendum returned a 58 per cent 'No' to the constitution, followed by a Dutch rejection on 1 June (with 62 per cent voting 'No'). A British vote on the constitution in spring 2006 became overnight unlikely and Foreign Secretary Jack Straw promptly announced that the proposed referendum was to be suspended.

Eurosceptics have asserted that a federal European super-state is being created by stealth, in particular by extending the system of qualified majority voting (QMV) into areas previously regarded as the business of the member states. UKIP MEP Nigel Farrage declared in October 2004 that, 'The plan in Brussels is to implement as much of the constitution as they can before it has been ratified.' This is a view supported by Neil O'Brien of the 'Vote No Campaign': 'There is a general trend to try to bring in the European constitution by the back door. By the time we get to having a constitutional referendum they will say, "All these things have already happened – there is nothing to worry about." '

In the unlikely event of the proposed European constitution coming into force (or some such agreement corresponding to a European constitution at some future date) it would become increasingly difficult to justify Britain's partially unwritten constitution within the context of an overarching, written EU constitution; a fully written UK constitution would seem to be an inevitable consequence.

···········································································

## ✓ What you should have learnt from reading this chapter

- Britain is now more deeply integrated into the European Union than is commonly realised. This integration has had, and will have, a marked impact, both direct and indirect, on the British constitution.

- The relationship of executive to legislature, the regions and devolution, civil rights, the electoral system, all have a European dimension, and that dimension will become ever-more significant. From one perspective Britain could be regarded as simply a part of a well-developed constitutional body – the EU – with its own written constitution, its underlying principles and emerging conventions.

- In this context it is important to realise that the EU is itself evolving rapidly. Not only is the EU 'broadening' by acquiring new members and 'deepening' by extending its functions, but it is changing constitutionally as well. The driving force here is mainly the will of Members of the European Parliament (MEPs). For example, in 1999 demands for the abolition of Qualified Majority Voting (QMV) in all areas of the EU's activity came from the European Parliament: they wanted a simple majority.

- The European Parliament now has important powers over EU legislation and the EU budget; for instance, power to amend legislation through two readings and to amend spending priorities in most policy areas. Most dramatic of all is the power to censure the Commission and force its resignation. This was widely thought to be only a notional power of the Parliament until it occurred in reality early in 1999, much to the surprise of all, including the Commission and MEPs!

- Within this context vigorous political debate is occurring, with the general theme of greater openness and greater participation. In May 1999, for example, the election manifesto of the party of the European Socialists (broadly speaking, the Left-Wing parties in Europe) called for human rights reforms, while the basically conservative European People's Party called for shared responsibilities between member states and the EU, with a strong emphasis on regional authorities.

- There can be little doubt that the modern European Union will be marked by substantial constitutional change in the future. Constitutional debate in Britain has proceeded with little reference to this probability, though there are, perhaps, a few indications of change here: one of the proposals to reform the Lords has been to include MEPs as members, which would constitute a modest institutional recognition of the European dimension to the British constitution.

## Glossary of key terms

**Accountable democracy**  An accountable democracy is one that stresses the ability of its citizens to remove a government which they find unsatisfactory.

**BSE**  In 1984 a cow in a herd in Sussex developed a disease, BSE, previously only encountered in sheep. It was dubbed 'mad cow disease' by the media. Despite initial official denials that the disease could be passed on to humans, the Health Minister eventually admitted it could do so in the form of vCJD. The eventual outcome was an enormous consumer scare, the loss of billions of pounds, a collapse of public confidence in government and ultimately major restructuring of the Ministry of Agriculture, Fisheries and Food (MAFF) into the Department of the Environment, Farming and Rural Affairs (DEFRA) and the creation of the independent Food Standards Agency.

**ERM**  The exchange rate mechanism was an element of the European Monetary System (EMS) set up in 1979, which Britain joined in 1990. The ERM involved fixing the currency exchange rates of EU member states so that they could move only marginally. In the event market forces undermined Britain's ability to maintain parity with other European currencies: on 16 September 1992 (known as 'Black Wednesday') Britain withdrew from the ERM. This event destroyed the Conservative party's reputation for competent economic management and also the political career of the Chancellor of the Exchequer, Norman Lamont.

**EU 'Pillars of Activity'**  The institutional structure of the EU established by the Maastricht Treaty (1992). The Treaty declared the EU to consist of three 'pillars', or areas of institutional and policy concern: pillar one concerns the EU's supranational functions; pillar two deals with common foreign affairs and security policy; and pillar three concentrates on common home affairs and justice policy.

**'Europeanisation'**  The process whereby EU rules increasingly constrain national political debate and law-making. It also involves the creation of an ever-stronger sense of political, economic, social and cultural identity with 'Europe' by the people of the member states of the EU.

**Integration**  In this context the term means the 'ever-closer union' of the member states of the European Union in economic, political and social terms. Both market forces and political institutions contribute to this process of encouraging greater integration within Europe.

**International currency movements** Billions of dollars' worth of currency transfers occur each hour in the global currency markets: they are on such an enormous scale that they are often believed to be undermining traditional forms of state sovereignty and the ability of governments to respond to the democratic wishes of the citizenry.

**Multi-national corporations** These are businesses whose activities (production, management, finance, distribution) span more than one country.

**Participatory democracy** A participatory democracy is one that stresses the involvement of all citizens in the political process.

## Likely examination questions

'Whether we like it or not, Europe is inexorably reshaping the British constitution.' Discuss.

'European integration has destroyed for ever such supposedly established features of the British constitution as parliamentary sovereignty, a unitary state and even an unwritten constitution.' How far do you agree with this statement?

To what degree might British membership of the European Union have actually strengthened national sovereignty while reducing the importance of parliamentary sovereignty?

'It is small wonder that the British are the "awkward partner" in the European Union. Their constitutional traditions, a thousand years in the making, are threatened by moves towards greater European integration in a way that is not likely to be the case in other EU member nations.' Discuss.

Outline and assess the ways in which the British constitution has been altered by membership of the European Union.

## Suggested websites

www.fco.gov.uk    Foreign and Commonwealth Office

www.europarl.eu.int    The European Parliament

www.europa.eu.int/cj/en/index.htm    European Court of Justice

www.europa.eu.int/comm    The European Commission

## Suggestions for further reading

Blair, A. (2004), 'A Constitutional Treaty for the European Union', *Talking Politics*, 16: 2, 71–2.

Falla, S. (2002), *New Labour and the European Union*, London: Ashgate.

Henig, S. (1997), *The Uniting of Europe*, London: Routledge.

Newman, M. (1996), *Democracy, Sovereignty and the European Union*, London: Hurst.

Stephens, P. (2001),'The Blair Government and Europe', *Political Quarterly*, 71: 3, 67–75.

# The 'Hollowing-Out of the State'

## Contents

## Overview

A new, interesting and potentially very fruitful approach to the understanding of government in Britain has appeared in recent years which has been variously described as 'the new governance', 'the new magistracy' and, as is the case here, 'the hollowed-out state'. The essence of the concept is that government has changed radically over the last two decades or so in a number of areas. The cumulative effect of the changes is such that the traditional understanding of the role of government and the nature of the state is now obsolete, and that constitutional principles derived from government practice over the last couple of centuries are also defunct. The outward form of government remains much the same and has been the focus of energetic constitutional reform; the inner reality, however, has changed utterly, so that constitutional reforms are not so much 'good' or 'bad', 'desirable' or 'undesirable' as simply irrelevant. The state is 'hollowed-out' in that the appearance of state power and importance has little substance behind it. It is this that we will investigate here.

## Key issues to be covered in this chapter

- What is the nature of the hollowed-out state?
- How is globalisation linked to the hollowing-out of the state?
- The rise and decline of the 'big state' and the creation of the hollowed-out state.
- Some features of the reorganised state in the post-big state era.
- The regulatory nature of the new state.

## The concept of the hollowing-out of the state

The concept of the 'hollowed-out state' was formulated during the last twenty years or so and is associated with the phenomenon of **'globalisation'** and its impact on state sovereignty.

Globalisation can be said to have begun over five centuries ago with the early European voyages of discovery to Africa, Asia and the Americas. By the end of the nineteenth century a small number of Western European states had developed with enough power to dominate the political and economic levers of global power: chief of these was Britain and its vast empire, sustaining a political, financial and trading system worldwide.

The term 'globalisation' is a relatively new one, appearing in the early 1990s and describing the present state of world society as having a number of unique characteristics.

Globalisation, it is said, undermines the sovereign capacity of states to take policy decisions and implement them because there is no correlation between the national authority of the state and the global and trans-national forces in the world economy. State power is weakened by globalisation which places many constraints on governments; so many constraints that state authority is being undermined, as promises made by politicians are frequently frustrated by the realities of global economic and political forces. Inevitably, the constitutional arrangements by which states are governed are also

---

### Box 8.1  Unique characteristics of a 'globalised' world society

- 'Stretched social relations': cultural, political and economic networks now connect people across the world
- 'Interpenetration': cultures and societies progressively face each other at local levels and extend diversity
- 'Intensification': the impact of events in other parts of the world is felt with increasing force
- 'Global infrastructure': the creation of informal and formal global institutions to manage these changes

undermined by globalisation. David Held, in his *Models of Democracy*, observed that:

> the operation of states in an ever more complex international system both limits their autonomy . . . and impinges increasingly upon their sovereignty.

When one considers the British constitution, little of the traditional description of it appears to have changed in the era of accelerating globalisation. The United Kingdom is a unified state with a highly centralised government. Legislation is passed by a democratically elected Parliament and is implemented by government departments staffed by non-partisan career civil servants. Policy is formulated and carried forward by ministers with the advice of their senior civil servants. Ministers are individually and collectively responsible to Parliament. Overall direction of government is in the hands of the Cabinet, headed by the Prime Minister whose position is 'first among equals'. The constitution is sustained by a structure of legislation, convention and political practice, which can be described as the 'constitution'.

It is this traditional understanding which, according to critics, is no longer relevant because globalisation has forced the state itself to alter its functions. On the surface the traditional institutions of Parliament, Cabinet government and government departments survive pretty well intact; but below the surface all has changed and the accepted separation of 'government' and 'governed' has dissolved. 'New governance' (in the forms of rules and regulations governing state service provision, economic management and the relationship of the citizen to the state) has gradually replaced 'old government' (the formal political and constitutional structures of state power).

The discrepancy between the outward show of traditional state power and its established constitutional arrangements, and the weakness of actual state power and the consequential irrelevance of constitutional arrangements, is summed up by the term 'the hollowed-out state'.

## The post-war 'big state'

World wars and welfare created 'big state' structures in the UK. State intervention into almost every aspect of wartime life helped Britain defeat its foreign enemies; Labour and most Conservative supporters alike believed that a similar application of state power could eliminate poverty, ignorance, homelessness, want, sickness, unemployment and a whole host of other social evils: the social democratic consensus was born, and with it the pursuit of 'big state' solutions to Britain's problems.

During the immediate post-1945 years great steps were taken to put this left-of-centre ideology into effect in a variety of areas:

*welfare*: the creation of the National Health service, a wide range of benefit payments, expansion of educational provision and a major role for the state in housing;

*state industries*: coal, steel, gas, electricity, water, railways and the canal network came under state ownership by means of nationalisation; and

*economic management*: the state intervened in order to maintain high levels of employment, encourage economic growth and a favourable balance of payments in foreign trade.

Large bureaucracies were created, Conservative and Labour governments competed with each other to expand state services, state employment rose to unheard-of levels, taxes increased, the standard of living rose and the constitutional arrangements that underpinned the UK state appeared to work excellently – until, that is, the 1970s.

During the Conservative and Labour governments of the 1970s economic decline, rising inflation and unemployment, and the apparent failure of the social democratic consensus to deal effectively with those crises resulted in demands for change in the role of the state. The rather smug assumptions about the efficacy of Britain's constitutional arrangements also came under challenge from nationalists, trade unionists, terrorists and the public at large.

## The challenge to the 'big state'

Institutional change is certainly an element shaping the British constitution; political power, the life-blood of political institutions, has steadily leached from central government in the UK to the European Union, to devolved government bodies in Scotland and Wales, and to international organisations such as the United Nations and, in military matters, NATO. Non-political and institutional factors seem to be more important. The global economy has shifted economic power, once the prerogative of national businesses and national governments, to multi-national and trans-national corporations that dominate global manufacturing, trade and finance. Work in a growing number of areas is 'outsourced' from Britain to, say, India and China, where labour and other production costs are significantly lower than in the UK. Cultural changes, stimulated by the globalisation of television, immigration and emigration, and the homogenisation of popular culture, have all eroded allegiances and identities that supported the state and its institutions. Governments no longer have the grip on their societies that they once had and are less able to create and deliver policies free of non-domestic influence and interference.

Specific policies have given concrete expression to these developments over the last quarter of a century. The 'roll-back' of the state began under Margaret Thatcher during the 1980s, reversing the tendency of the previous eight decades for the state to acquire ever more functions. Under Mrs Thatcher's governments the operation of dismantling state-owned industries and utilities initiated a process known as **'privatisation'** which continued, if at a gentler pace, under her successors, the Conservative John Major and Labour's Tony Blair. Railways, the coal and steel industries, telecommunications, water supplies, gas, electricity production and supply, and many other state enterprises were all transferred to the private sector. Council housing was sold off to tenants or passed into the control of private businesses or housing associations. Many bus services became the responsibility of private, rather than local authority, enterprise. 'Big' government was seen as 'bad' government by a wide spectrum of political opinion – and not only within the Conservative party. The reduction of the role of the state was believed by many on both Left and Right to be necessary if Britain was to adapt successfully to the increasingly competitive demands of the global economy.

Most significantly, the distinction between the 'state' and 'civil society', so important to the liberal political ideology that underpins much of the traditional model of the British constitution, has disappeared: the public sector is now often merged with the private and voluntary sectors. The formal institutions of government are less important than the process of governing (or 'governance'); the state no longer acts as a monopoly provider of a range of public services, as was the case during most of the post-1945 era, but enables others to do so either from within the public sector or from private sector suppliers. Governments no longer automatically assume that the state is the most effective provider of, say, education, health, pensions, water, gas, electricity and, in some situations, personal security and policing.

A more horizontal structure of bargaining, contracting, facilitating and partnering is said by supporters of the 'new' state to exist today in the government's delivery of services, replacing the top-down system of command and authority that was a feature of most service provision within the traditional welfare state. Passive citizens, grateful but subservient recipients of shoddy state services, are to be encouraged to act as consumers of state products and demand higher quality and more efficient spending of their hard-earned taxes. Citizens are supposed to have an increased role in determining the nature of service provision: grants, increased choice, access to league and performance tables, and tax incentives were intended to 'empower' the citizen.

During the 1980s and 1990s efforts were made to promote competition and a generally commercial approach towards those organisations still in public hands, like schools and hospitals. 'Internal markets' and 'market testing' were introduced into the NHS and into some areas of education as an integral part of the process of getting greater value for money and more efficient use of taxpayers' monies than had previously been the case. Government strongly believed in introducing competition within public services to promote efficiency and a greater responsiveness to the public, who were increasingly described by government spokesmen as 'consumers' of health, education, housing, water, gas and electricity. Both Conservative and Labour governments believed in the reduction of the role of the state as a provider of services and the new role for the state as a 'facilitator' of service provision by state, private or voluntary organisations (or a combination of all three). The state would continue to be the most important provider of funds for these services but it would have a less direct role in their delivery.

Attempts were also made to involve private capital in public services via the private finance initiative (or PFI, as it was known): instead of the government borrowing to fund a large project such as a hospital, the private sector would build and manage it, leasing it back to the public sector.

Although Labour was vigorously opposed to such developments during the long years when out of government, once returned to power in 1997 it adopted them wholesale and even extended the process. **Re-nationalisation** of the privatised sector was abandoned. Compulsory competitive tendering (by which public bodies like hospitals outsource services like meals and laundry to businesses which have won the right to provide them by offering the most financially efficient deal) continued, if slightly modified. Public–private partnerships and PFI were enthusiastically taken up, for example for the long-overdue modernisation of the London Underground. By 2004 publicly owned bodies such as hospitals, schools and colleges were allowed a great deal of financial and operational autonomy. Everywhere, from health care to social services, from education to help and advice over employment, a commercial ethos and a market economy bias in policy choice prevailed.

While public sector services were becoming subject to the disciplines of the private enterprise economy and its values, a trend developed by which traditionally private sector organisations were moving in the opposite direction. To an ever-greater extent the voluntary sector was brought under the umbrella of government during the 1990s. Charities like Age Concern or the NSPCC, concerned with providing help for disadvantaged groups in society, were contracted by government to deliver services in exchange for the receipt of amplified government funding. It became an article of faith on the part of ministers that charitable organisations could deliver many key services to the public more effectively and less expensively than state agencies with their complex, extensive (and expensive) bureaucratic structures.

## The reorganisation of the state

At the same time the state itself was being reconstructed. The civil service had been extensively reformed under Margaret Thatcher. In 1988 an 'Efficiency Unit', headed by Robin Ibbs, produced a report usually referred to as 'The Next Steps', which emphasised managerial autonomy within government departments and the replacement of state bureaucracies, as far as possible, by 'agencies' which would be given a particular task to do by government, though how they went about it would be largely their own concern. Major and, later, Blair adopted these ideas so that by the end of the 1990s there were 133 agencies employing three-quarters of the civil service and carrying out a huge range of government functions, including licensing cars, paying teachers' pensions and supplying passports.

Under Labour the monopoly role of the civil service in advising government, first challenged by their predecessors, the Conservatives, remained under attack. Many special advisors, usually from the private business sector, were imported into government at great expense and some of them were highly influential on the development of government: civil service culture was to be 'modernised'.

Modernisation was the keynote of other reforms after 1997. A White Paper, *Modernising Government* (1999), led to a host of initiatives. A Modernising Public Services Group was set up within the Cabinet Office to drive the market-style approach forward. Themes proclaimed by the Labour government were 'responsiveness', 'efficiency', 'effectiveness', 'quality' and, above all, **'joined-up government'** (the last meaning the co-ordination of local and central government with other bodies to produce specific goals that were presumed to be desirable). Business-style approaches, such as 'value for money', were embodied in the 'Better Quality Services' initiative, which implied that services were to be provided by who ever could do so best.

At the same time the near monopoly of advice to government, once the preserve of the senior civil service, was definitively eroded. The process that had begun under Margaret Thatcher and continued under John Major was greatly accelerated under Tony Blair. Much reliance was placed on external **'think tanks'** such as Demos and the Institute for Public Policy Research. Special advisors of various kinds poured into Whitehall, unrestrained as they were by traditional civil service **'mores'**. Contracts of employment proliferated. Besides these 'policy' advisors there were 'political' advisors mainly concerned with political tactics and strategy; some of these, for example Alastair Campbell, were responsible for media relations (cynics would say media manipulation); others, such as Jonathan Powell in his role as Chief of Staff, exerted much influence across Whitehall. Since 1997 the number of special advisors has more than doubled from thirty-five to seventy-six (including twenty-six at Downing Street, where the number has trebled). Most departments now have two or more such advisors. In spite of the fact that they were Labour party appointed, not elected, Campbell and Powell were allotted extraordinary powers to give orders to civil servants.

These developments have not taken place without criticism. Both the Public Administration Select Committee and the Committee on Standards in Public Life have called for restraints on the number and power of advisors. An example of the problems special advisors can create for government ministers is illustrated by the extraordinary case of Jo Moore. Moore, a special advisor to the Secretary of State for Transport, suggested in a leaked e-mail to her minister that 11 September 2001 was a 'good day to bury bad news'; rather tasteless advice on the day of the al-Qaeda attacks on the USA. She was ultimately forced to resign; the resignation of Stephen Byers, her departmental minister the Transport Secretary, followed in 2002. The Hutton and Butler enquiries in the wake of the Iraq War highlighted the role of advisors in government as a point of concern.

However, Tony Blair's government has been reluctant to tackle the anomalies created by a profusion of advisors: it did publish a draft Civil Service Bill in late 2004, but without proposing, as the Public Accounts Select Committee demanded, any cap on the number of advisors.

If the term 'advisor' is broadened to include consultants hired by government departments and agencies, the figures become astronomical. The cost of consultancies for the Home Office alone rose from £4.5 million during 1998–9 to £21 million in 2001–2. The Department for Work and Pensions spent £291.5 million on external advisors during 2002–3, while the Ministry of Defence spent £262.8 million on private advisors during the same year. Much of the advice is related not to controversial administrative matters but to politically sensitive issues: for example, the Home Office hired PA Consulting to advise on how to implement the 1997 election pledge to speed up the youth justice system. According to The *Daily Telegraph* (23 October 2003) the total of consultancy costs across Whitehall per year was in the region of £1.75 billion.

While advisors and consultants of various types have proliferated, the civil service has declined in numbers, role and importance. Civil servants are not much loved by the British public and announcing cuts in their numbers has often been a means by which government ministers can curry favour with voters in the run-up to a general election.

However, many consultants are doing the work of civil servants, while the Chancellor of the Exchequer promised in his 2004 budget a drastic cull of civil servants over the next few years. One wonders how much this announcement was driven by the need to give the impression that the government was tackling rising public debt, rather than any serious reduction in the size of the civil service.

What remains of the civil service has itself been considerably altered. Many of the staff were unhappy in their dealings with advisors and resigned; within a year of Labour coming to power in 1997 twenty-five Heads or Deputy Heads of Information had been replaced and a year later only two of the Directors of Communications from before 1997 still held office. Particularly striking was the departure of Sir Terry Burns, Permanent Secretary at the Treasury in 1998, who apparently felt special advisors to the Chancellor, such as Ed Balls (who in 2005 became a Labour MP), were eclipsing him.

Another development that has probably transformed the traditional civil service is its alleged 'politicisation'. This process is often thought to have begun under Margaret Thatcher who famously asked 'Are they one of us?' when considering senior civil service appointments. In the 1980s the Cabinet Secretary, Sir Robert Armstrong, acted as the UK government's witness in the Australian courts to support the attempts of his political masters to ban the *Spycatcher* book, with its lurid revelations of security service misbehaviour. In 1983 Armstrong, in his role as Head of the Civil Service, while reaffirming the traditional doctrine of ministerial responsibility in an important memorandum of guidance to civil servants, pronounced that the civil servant's first duty was to the minister – which in practice meant the government of the day, which of course is a political party. This assertion of the proper relationship of civil servants to their ministers was maintained by a Civil Service Code (1996) and a Code of Conduct for Ministers (1997). Perhaps the most remarkable blurring of the distinction between official neutrality and partisanship was disclosed by the Butler and Hutton reports of 2004. These revealed an astonishing number of discussions that took place between security chiefs, special advisors and senior ministers in the preparations of dossiers on intelligence on Iraq.

It would seem, therefore, that the traditional characteristics of the civil service – impartiality, anonymity, permanence and confidentiality – have been substantially eroded, especially that of impartiality.

Official enquiries have expressed unease. Lord Neill's Committee on Standards in Public Life did so in its report in 2000 and recommended a code of conduct to limit the role of advisors, but so far there has been little action.

The role of the civil service has also been affected by institutional changes, notably the installing of 'task forces' as an agent of government, especially since 1997. These bodies include not only civil servants but also professionals in a particular field, plus various advisors: by 2001 there were about 300. They bypass the existing Whitehall structures and by so doing endeavour to produce both 'joined-up government' and original solutions to problems facing government.

At the same time as attempting to reduce the role of the state to enable Britain to cope successfully with the stresses and strains of an increasingly globalised economy, Conservative and Labour governments extended the coercive and surveillance powers of the state. The police and intelligence services were given greater powers to watch for and deal with mounting domestic and international threats to the security of the state (threats which were often global in origin, but with elements of support among Britain's domestic population).

The concept of 'joined-up government' has also found expression in local government. Not only has the range of services once provided by local authorities been reduced, but new government mechanisms for delivering the remaining public services have been devised. The Local Government Act 2000 allows local authorities to adopt a new structure: transferring power from a committee-based system to one with a leader or mayor with a 'cabinet', while leaving committees with a mere scrutinising role; other structures are permitted, but the majority of councils have adopted this one.

## The regulatory state

Conservative and Labour governments pursuing the goal of a reduced role for the state in service provision in British society did not entirely relinquish the functions of the state: regulation was to be the answer. No government would consider the re-nationalisation of industries now in the private sector; but regulation remains strong in the areas of gas, water, electricity, railways, telecommunications and other services that are supposedly free from the dead hand of the state and subject only to the rigours of the market. Not only does the state seek to regulate services that were once nationalised, but there has been a growing temptation to introduce regulation into areas of the economy where self-regulation was the norm: law, medicine, universities, the City of London financial services.

More significant from a constitutional perspective has been the move from the provision of services solely by the state to facilitation by the state of assorted 'partnerships' between local authorities, businesses, central government organisations and voluntary bodies. Examples include Education Action Zones, Employment Zones, Health Action Zones, New Deal and Sure Start. Sure Start is a particularly good example of this policy: the idea was to improve the pre-school experience of deprived children and their families by the co-operation of education, health and social service agencies, with substantial financial input from central government, combined with central government inspection.

While the Blair governments have been inclined to present these developments as self-evidently sensible and modern, pragmatic solutions to difficult problems, it is important to grasp that a fundamental shift has taken place. Under the previous, 'traditional' model of local government, services were provided by departments staffed by officials and directly accountable to democratically elected councils. It is this element of democracy based on accountability and representation that has been replaced by a system based on participation. The term 'the new magistracy' has been applied to this process: new officials appointed by central government are expected to check on and in some cases control services at the local level.

To ensure that public money is being well spent and that central government policies are being carried out by schools, hospitals, colleges, universities and other such publicly funded bodies, there has been the growth of audit systems and a range of sanctions that auditors can apply to bodies that fail to comply with government policies. 'Paper trails' have become an audit requirement to 'prove' that the institution in receipt of state funding is carrying out its duties. One doubts whether audit on the scale now infesting the public sector contributes to better service provision or merely adds costs and work to those attempting to provide the service.

Perhaps the most important element in the evolution of the 'regulatory state' has been the emergence of 'quangos' ('quasi-autonomous non-governmental organisations'), a term that covers bodies which perform functions of government but are not directly under the control of elected representatives.

The diversity of these bodies is vast in terms of size, budget, political importance and accountability. As to numbers, no precise figure can be given (as definitions of quangos vary), but 7,000 would seem a reasonable figure. The Thatcher government said in 1979 it would reduce them but in fact they multiplied, with further spurts occurring under the Major and Blair administrations. It is fair to say that no area of government is without its constellation of quangos; compared with agencies, they are even more autonomous and unaccountable, being in part the product of the Thatcher government's desire to hive off activities from traditional state institutions and in part that of Mr Blair's 'regulatory' or 'enabling' state.

It is only in recent years that quangos have been properly charted. It seems clear that a further expansion of quangos is fundamental to the New Labour 'project'. Proposals for a Commission for Equality and Human Rights announced in November 2004 illustrate this well. Formed from an amalgamation of the Commission for Racial Equality, the Equal Opportunities Commission and the Disability

## Box 8.2  Types of quango

There is some dispute as to exactly which bodies may be so termed; the government tends to favour a very narrow definition, while academic and journalistic understanding is much wider. To add to the complexity, there is a wide variety of different government functions carried out by the various 'species' of quango. A useful classification might be: 'executive' (such as the Commission for Racial Equality, the Arts Council); 'advisory' (Electoral Commission, the Human Genetics Advisory Committee); 'quasi-judicial' (Rent Tribunals, Pension Tribunals); 'regulatory' (Ofsted, Ofgas, National Audit Office); and 'overarching' (the Social Exclusion Unit, for example, is typical of such a body in that its remit covers the work of several government departments).

Rights Commission, and due to come into operation in 2007, the Commission for Equality and Human Rights will have extensive advisory and executive powers: it will be able to call enquiries into alleged discrimination and compel witnesses to give evidence; bring legal action without reference to the Secretary of State against people or businesses accused of 'unlawful discrimination'; produce a regular 'state of the nation' report on equality and human rights; enforce new laws against discrimination on grounds of religion or belief; combat prejudice and strive to reduce 'hate crime' against minorities; promote human rights and raise awareness of responsibilities under the Human Rights Act; and set its own priorities as to which equality cases it chooses to support.

## What you should have learnt from reading this chapter

- The developments outlined above may seem individually modest, but their cumulative effect is extraordinary. From a constitutional perspective a strong case can be made that an almost invisible revolution in the constitution is occurring. Take the concepts of accountable and responsible government. In what sense can a government minister be 'responsible' for policies and decisions decreed from Brussels? How far is a minister responsible for the actions of an agency? This was a question raised in 1995 when the chief executive of the Prison Service, Derek Lewis, was made to resign after a number of prison escapes, while the then Home Secretary, Michael Howard, survived on the rather dubious grounds that this was not a 'policy' matter but an 'organisational' matter. A rather similar situation occurred in November 2004 when the head of the Child Support Agency, Doug Smith, resigned after investigation by the Work and Pensions Select Committee revealed a catalogue of failures in the Agency; the Secretary of State, Alan Johnson, remained in office.

- One might wonder if the more appropriate term for the 'dispersal' of power to which the present government claims to be wedded should be 'diffusion'. Power is often now located not in identifiable and therefore accountable elected assemblies, but less visibly in a plethora of unrepresentative bodies. Not only is the idea of Britain as having a 'responsible' government questionable but also the notion of that government being a representative one; recommendations involving decision-making and adjudication policies are largely in the hands of non-elected bodies. Indeed, it seems a growing 'democratic deficit' has opened up, leading to such criticisms as: 'Never have there been so many opportunities for the citizen to vote and never was there less point in doing so.'

- A more positive view may yet be taken. If representative democracy is being eclipsed it is being supplemented, perhaps even replaced, by a new style of 'participatory' democracy, with unprecedented opportunities for the citizen to become involved directly or through pressure groups in the democratic process.

- The processes of globalisation are unlikely to wither in the foreseeable future. Whether the state and the constitution that defines the political arrangements within it can continue to act as the prime focus of political loyalty for the citizen in the face of its increasing ineffectiveness under the pressure of global economic and political forces is an open question.

## Glossary of key terms

**Globalisation** A general term for the growing connections and interdependence of all countries of the world in many fields of human activity: commerce, travel, trade, finance, production, labour and culture. It is believed by many that this process is binding humanity into a sense of global identity and community.

**'Joined-up government'** The attempts by governments, especially New Labour, to confront problems across all relevant government departments so as to produce integrated and co-ordinated policies. The process has been institutionalised through bodies created outside the traditional departmental boundaries, such as the Social Exclusion Unit (set up by the Labour government to design policies that would bring the poor, deprived, neglected and other such 'excluded' sections of the population into mainstream economic and social life).

**'Mores'** The customs and values of a specific time and place.

**Privatisation** A policy which involves the transfer of previously publicly owned industries and services to the private sector. This policy is particularly associated with the Thatcher governments of 1979–90, but the Major and Blair governments that followed also believed that the private sector is generally more efficient in the delivery of services and production than the public sector and should be encouraged.

**Re-nationalisation** The taking back into public ownership of previously privatised industries, as has been suggested, for example, for the railways.

**'Think tanks'** These are usually private sector bodies set up to devise and develop public policy proposals and to promote their implementation by government, such as the Centre for Policy studies (associated with the Conservative party) and Demos (associated with New Labour).

## ? Likely examination questions

In what ways is the UK state changing as an entity?

How accurate is the description of the modern state as having been 'hollowed-out'?

'The idea of the "hollowed-out state" is a mere figment of the imagination of academics and journalists. The modern state is as robust as ever, only its priorities have changed.' Discuss.

'Audited to death.' Does this phrase accurately describe modern public services?

'The state is dead, long live the state.' Is this statement valid? Can one see the debate over the hollowed-out state as being one of the state's role changing, rather than the state becoming obsolete?

## Suggested website

www.ucl.ac.uk/constitution-unit    The Constitution Unit

## Suggestions for further reading

Held, D. (1996), *Models of Democracy*, Cambridge: Polity.

Moran, M. (2001), 'The New Regulatory State in Britain', *Talking Politics*, 13: 3, 109–12.

Newman, J. (2001), *Modernising Governance: New Labour, Policy and Society*, London: Sage.

Power, M. (1999), *The Audit Society: Rituals of Verification*, Oxford: Oxford University Press.

Pyper, R. and Robins, L. (2000), *United Kingdom Governance*, Basingstoke: Palgrave.

Rhodes, R. (1994), 'The Hollowing Out of the State', *Political Quarterly*, 65: 136–51.

Strange, S. (1996), *The Retreat of the State*, Cambridge: Cambridge University Press.

# Conclusion: A Constitutional Agenda?

## Contents

## Overview

Having examined the most important areas of constitutional debate and change in the preceding chapters, we are now in a position to make some final comments on the nature of the constitution and the possible future it faces in the twenty-first century.

It is strange that at a time of unprecedented constitutional change the British public and the British political class appear to be little interested in the implications of these changes: relatively few academics, politicians and citizens appear to be exercised by the present era of constitutional upheaval. Perhaps these changes are so piecemeal and technically difficult to grasp that a point will be reached when a constitutional conference will be needed to resolve the contradictions and conflicts inherent in the new arrangements. One might, though, challenge the assumption of continuing radical change to claim that the constitutional 'revolution', so dramatic during the first few years of the present Labour government, is now at an end: only some tinkering with the powers of the devolved assemblies and minor changes to the composition and powers of the House of Lords is likely to occur in the foreseeable future. The apparent end of the likely ratification of the European constitution during the summer of 2005 has even put on hold the potential impact for the British constitution of further political integration within the EU. It is to these issues that we shall now turn.

## Key issues to be covered in this chapter

- Why, during a period of unprecedented constitutional change, has there been relatively little public interest in the matter?
- Is a written constitution a likely outcome of current developments?
- Have any of the main parties a clear agenda for constitutional reform?
- Would a national constitutional convention be preferable to the present ad hoc process of reform?
- Is the turn of the century witnessing a 'constitutional revolution'?

## Constitutional change

The end of the twentieth century witnessed an intensity of constitutional change unparalleled in Britain for nearly a hundred years (see Box 9.1 for a summary of the main changes outlined in this book). Comparisons with the early twentieth century may be odious but are surely inevitable: it is immediately clear that there are sharp differences between the two periods.

During the early years of the twentieth century the nation was convulsed by ferocious political debate, even to the point of organised **civil disobedience**. There was armed insurrection in Ireland, constitutional crises between Lords and Commons, and civil war over social and economic issues seemed a real possibility. Major parties adopted strongly opposed policies on such fundamental issues as

---

### Box 9.1  Constitutional changes under the Blair government: a summary

- The incorporation of the European Convention into British law, via the Human Rights Act
- The introduction of a new electoral system for European elections
- The near-abolition of the hereditary system in the second chamber (Phase One): the establishment of a Royal Commission, and then discussion of plans for a new body to replace the existing House of Lords (Phase Two)
- The introduction of devolution for Scotland and Wales via the Scotland Act and the Wales Act
- The passage of a Freedom of Information Act
- The creation of a new authority for London, including an elected Mayor – along with provision for the adoption of elected mayors in other parts of the country
- Talks leading to the Good Friday Agreement in Northern Ireland: the creation of an assembly and power-sharing executive (currently suspended)
- The wider use of referendums to establish support for constitutional change
- Other changes are in the process of delivery, notably that relating to reform of the office of Lord Chancellor and the creation of a supreme court, as part of the Constitutional Reform Bill

Ireland, the Lords and the extension of the franchise to women and the lower working classes.

As the twentieth century came to a close the national debate on no less weighty constitutional matters was curiously muted. For example, in August 1999 *The Economist* reported on a survey which showed that only 2 per cent of those polled thought the state of the constitution was 'one of the most important issues facing Britain today'. Even when a major party took a clear stand, as the Conservatives did on the devolution issue in 1997, it failed dismally to ignite public opinion (at least outside Scotland). Nor have constitutional changes been the outcome of vigorous campaigning by mass organisations or energetic debate among the political elite; for instance, nothing today remotely compares to the agitation surrounding Irish Home Rule or women's suffrage before World War One. The **'Irish Question'**, which haunted British politics for decades before 1922, has to a great extent remained firmly **quarantined** in Northern Ireland. Such debate as has taken place, especially as the twenty-first century opened, has concerned such issues as religious intolerance or tactics in combating terrorism rather than strictly constitutional matters. Even the Conservative opposition to Lords reform seems merely the posturings of a party desperate for any stick to beat an apparently near-impregnable Labour government. It is interesting and quite surprising how little major constitutional issues have impinged on public consciousness. Even Europe as a constitutional issue has not really ignited strong feelings; the UKIP surge in the European parliamentary elections in 2004, while impressive at the time, appears to have been little more than a blip.

There does not seem to be any obvious overarching principle or serious ideological agenda underpinning constitutional changes that might stir public interest, which raises the question of whether or not there is any real New Labour 'project' for the constitution comparable to its social and economic agenda.

The creation of a Department of Constitutional Affairs in 2003, headed by Lord Falconer, might suggest some attempt to remedy this deficiency. However, Lord Falconer in his role as Lord Chancellor seemed preoccupied with matters directly associated with the judiciary, for example the scarcity of women, ethnic minorities and disabled persons among senior judges; he launched a major 'consultation exercise' on his proposals for reform in late 2004. There are some indicators that Lord Falconer is broadening his remit: he had the task of overseeing the implementation of the Official Secrets Act (1999) which came into full effect in January 2005. This does not add up to an overnight change in a generally slow and unfocused approach to constitutional reform.

One might plausibly argue that the numerous constitutional changes are quite discrete, merely separate responses to particular circumstances, rather than coherent components of any overall plan. Scottish devolution, for example, though on the face of it part of a general process of power dispersion (as with Northern Ireland, English regionalism and European 'subsidiarity'), in reality owes very little that process. In fact devolution is very much a party device to restore Labour's electoral fortunes in Scotland by outflanking the SNP. This pragmatic approach is equally evident in Lords reform, which illustrates what appears to be the government's general outlook very well. The rights of most hereditary peers to vote in the House were abolished in June 1999 before any real consideration of what the Lords was for, what its major faults were, what should replace it and, strikingly, without any consideration of the fundamental principles which should be the basis of a second parliamentary chamber.

Constitutional change is the result of political struggle. Given that all constitutions develop in a world of political competition rather than in a university seminar room, political considerations are bound to form part of the process of constitutional reform.

The political drive to change the constitution is the product of a number of factors. During the 1980s the Thatcher governments determined a more limited role for the state. By 1997 this perspective had been largely adopted by New Labour. The globalised economy, market forces and the impact of international bodies such as the European Union and the World Trade Organisation confirmed the realism of this assumption. At the same time New Labour recognised a 'democratic deficit' in existing institutions and a general need for modernisation. Reform of the constitution was within the capacity of government, even if fundamental social and economic change was not. Furthermore, such change would reaffirm New Labour as a radical political movement. Not surprisingly therefore, the government elected in 1997 had the most ambitious constitutional reform agenda of any government in the twentieth century.

A particularly trenchant critique of New Labour's constitutional reforms was presented by Professor David Marquand in the Mishcon Lecture (May 1999). He observed that while the reforms were fundamental there was no coherent end in view. There was a theme, 'populism': the assumption being that constitutional reform would lead to greater social and political harmony rather than conflict because the 'sovereign people' are of one mind; but according to Marquand this is simply not the case in the new multi-identity world that is developing. For Marquand the priority is a well thought out constitution, based on the old principles of constitutional 'checks and balances', which does not seem to accord with the government's view. For Marquand only an elected second chamber would provide an effective and legitimate counterweight to the Commons.

Contrary to Marquand, one might argue that the recent changes appear to be fully in line with the tradition of British constitution-building, that is, ad hoc responses to specific circumstances. In sharp contrast to Britain, the continental practice has been to create constitutions from scratch and according to fundamental principles. From one perspective, the British approach has produced a constitution that is organic, evolving and finely adjusted to its environment, a constitution which both works well and is held in universal respect and affection. An alternative view is that the real outcome of this approach is a ramshackle, ineffective, outdated system in urgent need of root-and-branch reform.

The idiosyncratic nature of current restructuring is evident when we examine the actual methodology of reform. Whereas most constitutions, certainly written ones, have specified procedures by which they can be amended, the recent British changes display amazing variety. Lords reform, for example, has proceeded by means of legislation, followed by a Royal Commission, to be followed presumably by further legislation. Welsh and Scottish devolution, on the other hand, involved referendums even before legislation. Perhaps most astonishing has been the Northern Irish 'peace process' which involved negotiation among all contending parties within the Province and the British and Irish governments, along with referendums north and south of the Irish border (but not in the rest of the UK). As we have observed, significant changes in the doctrines of collective and individual ministerial responsibility have occurred without any formal procedure at all, as is always the way with constitutional conventions.

One can perceive an ad hoc approach to constitutional change by the use of referendums over Britain's relationship with the European Union. Continued British membership of the 'Common Market', as the EEC was popularly known, was submitted to a referendum in 1975; crucial developments involving further European integration in 1986 and 1994 were the product of inter-state treaties which in the UK involved no repetition of popular participation. Until April 2004 the government ruled out a referendum on the proposed European constitution, only to change its collective mind abruptly and announce that one would take place after all. This appeared to be purely a party political move: European elections were due in June 2004 and a 'no referendum' campaign by Labour would have been politically damaging to their chances. British membership of the Euro is, as the Labour and Conservative parties have declared, to be decided by a referendum at some distant and unspecified date 'when the conditions are right' to join.

Lord Chief Justice Lord Woolf observed in 2004 that there had been fifteen 'significant' constitutional reforms since 1997, each affecting the rule of law. Speaking with particular reference to the announcement in June 2003, as part of a Cabinet reshuffle, of major alterations to the role of Lord Chancellor and the creation of a supreme court, he said, 'The flexibility of our constitutional arrangements is undeniably desirable, but they should not be so malleable that they can be changed by Prime Ministerial announcement in the course of a government reshuffle.'

Continuity, rather than change, is also apparent in the jealous guarding of such doctrines as parliamentary sovereignty. For example, the referendums on Welsh and Scottish devolution were technically advisory only. Westminster could quite legally, if not politically, have ignored their outcome. Moreover, the European Convention on Human Rights has been 'incorporated' into British law but not entrenched, so it could lawfully be later amended or even abrogated by a future Parliament through the normal legislative processes. The Conservative party has promised, if it should be returned in a future general election, to reform the Human Rights Act.

Talk of a 'constitutional revolution' may have been exaggerated, but the cumulative effect of so many changes in so short a time suggests that the term 'revolution' is not inappropriate to describe recent constitutional events.

## A constitutional conference?

The foregoing remarks raise some questions about the future. Are we proceeding with reform in the wisest manner, following tried and tested traditions of evolutionary and incremental change? Or are we going to end up with a supposedly reformed constitution which is just as inefficient and ramshackle as the one it has replaced? This in turn poses the question of whether or not an entirely different approach should be adopted: a constitutional conference resulting in a written constitution.

At such a conference the entire constitution would be thoroughly examined and debated and a final document would emerge that would form the constitutional basis for the whole range of government.

Objections can, of course, be made immediately. The procedure would be wholly outside the British national experience. Who would attend such a conference? What would its remit be? Would its proposals have to be further debated in Parliament and be subject to parliamentary approval? Would a referendum on the matter be required? Would not such a conference unnecessarily divide the nation and swamp all other political debate?

Formidable though these objections at first appear, in reality the problem is far less daunting than has been made out. Continental European countries have devised such constitutions; Britain itself has formulated constitutions for former colonies at their independence and there are precedents for constitutional conferences in both Northern Ireland and Scotland in recent years. There have even been 'one-man productions': Tony Benn personally prepared his own republican constitution, submitted to the House in a predictably unsuccessful **private member's bill** in 1991.

The real question is surely: 'Does the political will exist to produce such a constitution?' Opinion within the present government would seem to be divided. Gordon Brown in 1999 was quoted as saying:

> We must move from an old, centralised, uniform state – the Britain of subjects – to a modern, pluralist democracy – the Britain of

citizens. . . . Britain will need not only unifying ideas of citizenship, but the new constitution we propose.

Lord Irvine, then Lord Chancellor, speaking in the same year was much more negative:

> We have embarked on a major programme of constitutional change realigning the most fundamental relationships between the state and the individual . . . we are not, however, hunting the chimera of constitutional master plans, nor ultimate outcomes.

He went on to describe Labour's constitutional changes as 'incremental', being efforts to 'try to manage and respond [to political and social change] by modernising and reforming existing political procedures'.

It is, of course, possible that events may force the hands of politicians. Most constitutions arise from political crisis; it is perhaps not inconceivable that such a crisis might befall the United Kingdom. Paradoxically, the very reforms themselves might precipitate such a crisis: if, for example, a nationalist majority in Scotland demanded outright independence or a reformed House of Lords, buttressed by democratic legitimacy, came into conflict with the House of Commons.

## Constitutional change on hold?

By mid-2005, after May's general election, constitutional change no longer seemed to be on the political agenda. The Conservative party has never shown much interest in constitutional reform, and Labour seems to regard its reforms as being largely completed. In the general election campaign the Liberal Democrats made much of the constitution in their manifesto. The media gave constitutional issues scant attention beyond a brief mention of the vulnerability of postal voting to fraud and the suggestion, supported by Labour, that the voting age be lowered to sixteen.

The constitution as it emerged in the nineteenth century had much to commend it: surviving the expansion of the franchise to full democracy, the rise of Labour, two world wars, a succession of severe economic crises, the loss of empire and the dangers of the Cold War confrontation. Nevertheless, that constitution was the product of a particular social, cultural, political and intellectual environment that has changed almost beyond recognition over the last twenty years or so, let alone the last century and a half.

We will, by way of illustration, briefly explore a number of areas where significant social change has occurred, with implications for the future of the constitution.

The decline of the homogeneous nation state is the first issue to consider. No longer does the state appear as the obvious prime focus of political loyalty, or as an adequate instrument for the tackling of social, economic, security and, especially, environmental problems. Perhaps subconsciously, voters are aware that the state's powers in the modern world are enfeebled: globalisation, large-scale immigration, devolution and the ever-growing European dimension have eroded British national identity. For many people in Britain the sense of shared national culture and shared national values, beliefs and ideals, of an agreed national historical narrative, has faded. One can also discern that the traditional cultural values such as deference towards authority, veneration for the past and confidence in national institutions have receded from British society. How might one agree on the form of constitutional change to be undertaken if a sense of shared national experience is lacking in modern Britain?

Other forms of identity, such as class, religion, neighbourhood, community, workplace and even family, are less significant than they were in binding individuals into larger social communities. People think, feel and act as autonomous individuals seeking their own personal fulfilment untrammelled by deeply held and shared beliefs, values or principles. Participation in churches, trade unions and voluntary organisations is in decline. Can such a fragmentation (or even 'atomisation') of society into a loose collection of individuals, each pursuing their own interests with little regard for each other, really form the basis for a constitutional system that will work?

The political process itself has been affected by the developments outlined above. This is most obviously the case with established political parties: membership has fallen, single-agenda and minority parties have mushroomed. Party, and even government, policy is being developed with little regard for the rank-and-file party members who were once indispensable in such vital party activities as canvassing, propaganda and fundraising. Popular participation in parties frequently takes place less through permanent organisations than through ephemeral coalitions inspired by isolated issues such as foxhunting or the Iraq War.

Voter identification with specific parties also appears to have declined; only two weeks before the 2005 general election nearly 40 per cent of the respondents told opinion pollsters they hadn't yet decided how they would vote. Tactical voting in that election appears to have been widespread; indeed the electors were exhorted to vote not to choose a government but to 'send Blair a message'.

The developments described above surely support the view that the system of representation of the people is in urgent need of revival if government is not to become wholly alienated from those it is supposed to serve.

If there are problems with the representative dimension of the constitution, there are even more problems with the element of responsibility, meaning the accountability of the government to the elected representatives of the people. The focus of concern, one might suggest, is decision-making. Decision-making on the economy, on social policy, even on peace and war has, depending on the issue involved, been exported, either de jure or de facto, to either the European Union, the United Nations, the United States government or the international financial system, multi-national corporations and the global market economy. Moreover, at the domestic level, the delivery of services such as health care and education is becoming the outcome not of concrete government decisions but of market forces, themselves the product of individuals acting as consumers and exercising choice. The current orthodoxy of all major political parties emphasises the centrality of consumer choice; but if this is so, then government is abdicating its responsibility on a dramatic scale. It may be that government controls the global sum of what is spent on public services, but how it is spent and to what effect is now out of its hands.

'Freedom under the law' may be said to be a major principle of the British constitution. Both freedom under the law and its sustaining notion of the 'separation of powers' pre-date parliamentary democracy. Although often taken for granted as eternal and immutable, these principles may not be as secure in the twenty-first century as is commonly assumed. Historically, the rule of law has been underpinned by a general consensus as to what constituted morally acceptable behaviour; this consensus no longer exists. Moreover, Parliament and the judiciary, the institutions that enacted and enforced the law, were generally revered; this reverence is far less evident today.

Society now confronts a range of problems to which draconian executive power may seem to be a reasonable, or even a necessary, option: one may point to terrorism, not only Islamist but also that associated with anti-abortion and animal rights campaigns. Another problem, rarely alluded to in the 2005 general election, is that of environmental protection. Although environmentally orientated parties like the Greens emphasise their liberal democratic credentials, it is by no means obvious that defending the environment can be achieved without drastic curtailment of individual rights and freedoms. At the same time, technical advances are placing powerful weapons in the hands of governments to enable them to curtail individual liberty.

## Conclusion

Can the dramatic changes in the constitution now in progress be regarded as 'revolutionary', or is 'evolutionary' a more appropriate term to describe them? The 'revolutionary' argument is that the sheer scale, rapidity and range of reforms is cumulatively producing such an upheaval that a dramatic break with the past is implicit in the process. All the received wisdom about a unitary state, an unwritten constitution, a sovereign Parliament and so on, will be simply consigned to the dustbin of history with unforeseen and unforeseeable consequences. On this analysis we live in interesting times, paralleled only by those of the seventeenth century.

Sceptics might argue that Britain has undergone profound constitutional change before. The very term 'evolutionary', with its biological resonances of adaptation to changed environment, of organic growth in accordance with a survival imperative and without any pre-ordained blueprint, is a particularly apposite description of both present and past British constitutional history.

The central issue, as yet unresolved, is whether the sheer volume of change will produce not just a quantitative transformation but a qualitative one as well. If the latter, not only will we have a new constitution but a new politics as well. Whatever the ultimate result, a challenging future is assured.

## Glossary of key terms

**Civil disobedience** The deliberate violation of the law, usually in a non-violent manner, to advance a political cause.

**'Irish Question'** This was a term used in the late nineteenth century to describe the problem of Ireland in the context of British politics. The question concerned the matter of reconciling Irish majority aspirations for their own Parliament (Home Rule) with the unity of the United Kingdom and the interests of the Loyalist minority in Ireland.

**Private member's bill** A bill introduced into Parliament by an MP or peer without the support of the government. Such proposed legislation usually fails to be enacted into law, but may be if the government decides that the bill is sufficiently important to warrant government support.

**Quarantined** In this context, the deliberate confining of the Irish Question to the island of Ireland, so as to avoid its disruption of the politics of the rest of the United Kingdom. Between the Partition of the island of Ireland into the Republic and Northern Ireland (1921) and the end of the devolved Parliament in Northern Ireland (1972) this policy was largely successful.

## Suggestions for further reading

Beetham, D., Nean, P. and Weir, S. (2001), 'Democratic Audit: Labour's Road So Far', *Parliamentary Affairs*, 55, 376–90.

Granath, A. (2002), 'Constitutional Reform: A Work in Progress', *Talking Politics*, 14: 3, 103–6.

Hazell, R. (1999), 'Labour's Constitutional Revolution', *Politics Review*, 9: 2, 2–5.

Hazell, R. et al. (2002), 'The Constitution: Coming in from the Cold', *Parliamentary Affairs*, 55, 219–34.

Masterman, R. and Hazell, R. (2002), 'The Constitution: Labour's continuing revolution', *Politics Review*, 12: 2, 14–17.

McNaughton, N. (2004), 'Constitutional Reform in the UK', *Talking Politics*, 16: 3, 121–5.

Smith, N. (2002), 'New Labour and Constitutional Reform', *Talking Politics*, 14: 1, 24–7.

Weir, S. et al. (2002), *Democracy Under Blair: A Democratic Audit of the United Kingdom*, London: Politico's.

# References

Many of the sources suggested below are to be found at the end of relevant chapters. We have added a few other major works for those ambitious students who wish to pursue some of the issues further.

Agnew, D. (1999), 'Electoral Reform in the United Kingdom', *Politics Review*, 8: 4, 15–19.

Bagehot, W. [1867], introduction by R. H. S. Crossman (1963), *The English Constitution*, London: Fontana.

Baimbridge, M. and Darcy, D. (2000), 'Putting the "proportional" into PR', *Politics Review*, 9: 4, 16–18.

Baldwin, M. (2002), 'Reforming the Second Chamber', *Politics Review*, 11: 3, 8–12.

Beetham, D., Nean, P. and Weir, S. (2001), 'Democratic Audit: Labour's Road So Far', *Parliamentary Affairs*, 55, 376–90.

Benn, T. and Hood, A. (1993), *Common Sense: A New Constitution for Britain*, London: Hutchinson.

Blackburn, R. (ed.) (1992), *Constitutional Studies: Contemporary Issues and Conditions*, London: Mansell.

Blackburn, R. and Plant, R. (eds) (1999), *Constitutional Reform: The Labour Government's Constitutional Reform Agenda*, London: Longman.

Blair, A. (2004), 'A Constitutional Treaty for the European Union', *Talking Politics*, 16: 2, 71–2.

Boal, L. (2000), 'Electoral Reform in the UK', *Talking Politics*, 12: 2, 303–7.

Bogdanor, V. (ed.) (1988), *Constitutions in Democratic Politics*, Aldershot: Gower.

Bogdanor, V. (1997), *Power and the People*, London: Gollancz.

Bogdanor, V. (1999), *Devolution in the United Kingdom*, Oxford: Oxford University Press.

Bogdanor, V. (1999), 'Devolution: Decentralisation or Disintegration?' *Political Quarterly*, 70, 184–94.

Buckley, S. (2004), 'A Student Guide to the Hutton Enquiry', *Talking Politics*, 17: 1, 22–6.

Davenport, I. (2004), 'Electoral Reform', *Talking Politics*, 17: 1, 30–3.

Davenport, I. (2005), 'Electoral Reform', *Talking Politics*, 17: 2, 66–9.

Denver, D. (2001), 'The Devolution Project', *Politics Review*, 11: 1, 20–3.

Denver, D. (2003), 'Whatever Happened to Electoral Reform?', *Politics Review*, 13: 1, 8–10.

Dixon, P. (2001), *Northern Ireland*, London: Palgrave.

Dorey, P. (2002), 'The West Lothian Question in British Politics', *Talking Politics*, 15: 1, 19–21.

Elcock, H. and Keating, M. (eds) (1998), *Remaking the Union: Devolution and British Politics in the 1990s*, London: Fontana.

Falla, S. (2002), *New Labour and the European Union*, London: Ashgate.

Flinders, M. (2002), 'Shifting the Balance? Parliament, the Executive and the British Constitution', *Political Studies*, 50: 2, 23–42.

Foley, M. (1993), *The Rise of the British Presidency*, Manchester: Manchester University Press.

Foley, M. (1999), *The Politics of the British Constitution*, Manchester: Manchester University Press.

Forman, N. (2004), 'The State and the People: Britain's Changing Constitution', *Politics Review*, 13: 3, 26–8.

Foster, L. (2000), 'The Encroachment of the Law on Politics', *Parliamentary Affairs*, 53: 2, 328–46.

Freeman, M. (1997), 'Why Rights Matter', *Politics Review*, 7: 1, 31–3.

Granath, A. (2002), 'Constitutional Reform: A Work in Progress', *Talking Politics*, 14: 3, 103–6.

Griffith, J. A. G. (1997), *The Politics of the Judiciary*, London: Fontana.

Hazell, R. (1999), 'Labour's Constitutional Revolution', *Politics Review*, 9: 2, 2–5.

Hazell, R. (ed.) (1999), *Constitutional Futures – A History of the Next Ten Years*, Oxford: Oxford University Press.

Hazell, R. et al. (2002), 'The Constitution: Coming in from the Cold', *Parliamentary Affairs*, 55, 219–34.

Henig, S. (1997), *The Uniting of Europe*, London: Routledge.

Hennessy, P. (1990), *Whitehall*, London: Fontana.

Hennessy, P. (1995), *The Hidden Wiring: Unearthing the British Constitution*, London: Gollancz.

Hennessy, P. (2000), *The Prime Minister: The Office and its Holders since 1945*, Harmondsworth: Allen Lane.

Hopkins, S. (1999), 'The Good Friday Agreement in Northern Ireland', *Politics Review*, 8: 5, 2–6.

James, S. (1998), *British Cabinet Government*, London: Routledge.

Jeffrey, C. (2005), 'Devolution: a fractured project', *Politics Review*, 14: 4, 17–9.

Johnson, N. (1980), *In Search of a Constitution*, London: Methuen.

Johnson, N. (2002), 'The Missing Piece of the Constitutional Jigsaw', *Talking Politics*, 14: 2, 48–51.

Kavanagh, D. (2002), 'Tony Blair as Prime Minister', *Politics Review*, 11: 1, 14–7.

King, A. (2001), *Does the UK Still Have a Constitution?*, London: Sweet and Maxwell.

Lomas, B. (2000), 'The Good Friday Agreement', *Talking Politics*, 14: 1, 28–31.

Loughlin, J. (1998), *The Ulster Question Since 1945*, London: St Martin's Press.

Lynch, P. (2004), 'Towards an England of the Regions', *Talking Politics*, 16: 3, 126–8.

Madgwick, P. and Woodhouse, D. (1995), *Contemporary Political Studies: The Law and Politics of the British Constitution*, Hemel Hempstead: Prentice Hall/Harvester Wheatsheaf.

Marr, A. (1995), *Ruling Britannia: The Failure and Future of British Democracy*, London: Michael Joseph.

Masterman, R. and Hazell, R. (2002), 'The Constitution: Labour's Continuing revolution', *Politics Review*, 12: 2, 14–7.

McCartney, M. (2003), 'Oh Referendum, Where Art Thou?', *Talking Politics*, 16: 1, 19–22.

McNaughton, N. (2002), 'Prime Ministerial Government', *Talking Politics*, 15: 1, 12–4.

McNaughton, N. (2004), 'Constitutional Reform in the UK', *Talking Politics*, 16: 3, 121–5.

Moran, M. (2001), 'The New Regulatory State in Britain', *Talking Politics*, 13: 3, 109–12.

Morgan, T. (1999), 'Teeth for the Commons Watchdog', *Politics Review*, 8: 4, 6–10.

Mount, F. (1992), *The British Constitution Now: Recovery or Decline?*, London: Heineman.

Nairn, T. (2000), *After Britain*, London: Granta.

Newman, J. (2001), *Modernising Governance: New Labour, Policy and Society*, London: Sage.

Newman, M. (1996), *Democracy, Sovereignty and the European Union*, London: Hurst.

Norris, P. (2004), 'The 2003 Northern Ireland Assembly Elections', *Talking Politics*, 16: 3, 129–31.

Norton, P. (1982), *The Constitution in Flux*, Oxford: Blackwell.

Norton, P. (1992), *The Constitution: The Conservative Way Forward*, London: Conservative Political Centre.

Outhwaite, B. (2001), 'UK Electoral Systems', *Politics Review*, 11: 2, 32–3.

Peele, G. (2001), 'The Human Rights Act', *Talking Politics*, 14: 1, 22–3.

Pyper, R. and Robins, L. (2000) *United Kingdom Governance*, Basingstoke: Palgrave.

Rathbone, M. (2001), 'The Freedom of Information Act', *Talking Politics*, 13: 3, 165–70.

Rathbone, M. (2003), 'The National Assembly for Wales', *Talking Politics*, 15: 3, 188–91.

Rathbone, M. (2005), 'The November 2004 Referendum in the North East', *Talking Politics*, 17: 2, 61–5.

Rhodes, R. (1994), 'The Hollowing Out of the State', *Political Quarterly*, 65, 136–51.

Richard, I. and Welfare, D. (1999), *'Unfinished Business': Reforming the House of Lords*, London: Vintage.

Rush, M. (2000), 'Royal Commission on the House of Lords (the Wakeham Report) (Cm.4534, January 2000) A Summary', *Talking Politics*, 13: 1, 35–9.

Ryan, M. (2003), 'The House of Lords: Options for Reform', *Talking Politics*, 16: 1, 29–31.

Ryan, M. (2004), 'A Supreme Court for the United Kingdom', *Talking Politics*, 17: 1, 18–20.

Seldon, A. (ed.) (2001), *The Blair Effect: The Labour Government 1997–2001*, London: Little, Brown.

Shell, D. (2000), 'Labour and the House of Lords: A Case Study in Constitutional Reform', *Parliamentary Affairs*, 53, 290–310.

Smith, M. (1999), *The Core Executive in Britain*, London: Macmillan.

Smith, N. (2002), 'New Labour and Constitutional Reform', *Talking Politics*, 14: 1, 24–7.

Stephens, P. (2001), 'The Blair Government and Europe', *Political Quarterly*, 71: 3, 67–75.

Thomas, G. (1998), *The Prime Minister and Cabinet Today*, Manchester: Manchester University Press.

Thomas, G. (2002), 'Prime Minister and Cabinet', *Politics Review*, 12: 4, 22–5.

Tongue, J. (2002), *Northern Ireland: Conflict and Change*, London: Pearson.

Weir, S. and Beetham, D. (1999), *Political Power and Democratic Control in Britain*, London and New York: Routledge

Weir, S. et al. (2002), *Democracy Under Blair: A Democratic Audit of the United Kingdom*, London: Politico's.

Wheare, K. C. (1966), *Modern Constitutions*, Oxford: Oxford University Press.

Woodhouse, D. (2002), 'The Law and Politics in the Shadow of the Human Rights Act', *Parliamentary Affairs*, 55: 2, 254–70.

Zander, M. (1997), *A Bill of Rights*, London: Sweet and Maxwell.

Zander, M. (1998), 'UK Rights Come Home', *Politics Review*, 7: 4, 18–22.

The following journals are very useful in finding out about the British constitution and enabling you to keep reasonably up to date with this ever-changing subject: *Parliamentary Affairs* (The Hansard Society, St Philip's Building North, Sheffield Street, London, WC2A 2EX); *Politics Review* (Philip Allen Publishers, Market Place, Deddington, Oxfordshire, OX15 0SE); *Talking Politics* (The Politics Association, Old Hall Lane, Manchester, M13 0XT). They produce well-written articles by Politics teachers and academics, as well as the occasional politician.

Most general textbooks on British politics include valuable chapters on the British constitution. Particularly recommended are:

Ian Budge, Ivor Crewe, David McKay and Ken Newton (2004), *The New British Politics*, Harlow: Pearson.

Bill Coxall, Lynton Robins and Robert Leech (2003), *Contemporary British Politics*, Basingstoke: Palgrave/Macmillan.

John Dearlove and Peter Saunders (2000), *Introduction to British Politics*, 3rd edn, Cambridge: Polity.

Justin Fisher, David Denver and John Benyon (2003), *Central Debates in British Politics*, Harlow: Pearson.

Bill Jones et al. (2003), *Politics UK*, Hemel Hempstead: Prentice Hall.

John Kingdom (1999), *Government and Politics in Britain: A Introduction*, 2nd edn, Cambridge: Polity.

# Index

Bold indicates that the term is defined